Racial Emotion at Work

Racial Emotion at Work

DISMANTLING DISCRIMINATION AND BUILDING RACIAL JUSTICE IN THE WORKPLACE

Tristin K. Green

UNIVERSITY OF CALIFORNIA PRESS

University of California Press
Oakland, California

© 2023 by Tristin K. Green

Library of Congress Cataloging-in-Publication Data

Names: Green, Tristin K., author.
Title: Racial emotion at work : dismantling discrimination and building
    racial justice in the workplace / Tristin K. Green.
Description: Oakland, California : University of California Press, [2023] |
    Includes bibliographical references and index.
Identifiers: LCCN 2023001542 (print) | LCCN 2023001543 (ebook) |
    ISBN 9780520385238 (cloth) | ISBN 9780520385245 (paperback) |
    ISBN 9780520385269 (ebook)
Subjects: LCSH: Racism in the workplace—United States—21st century. |
    Racial justice—United States—21st century.
Classification: LCC HF5549.5.R23 G78 2023 (print) | LCC HF5549.5.R23
    (ebook) | DDC 658.3008900973—dc23/eng/20230501
LC record available at https://lccn.loc.gov/2023001542
LC ebook record available at https://lccn.loc.gov/2023001543

Manufactured in the United States of America

32 31 30 29 28 27 26 25 24 23
10 9 8 7 6 5 4 3 2 1

Contents

Acknowledgments

This book is the product of many conversations and even more hours of reading, wondering, and worrying over the course of more than ten years. I started thinking about the idea of racial emotion at work for a scholarly article published in the *Southern California Law Review* in 2013. I wanted to explore the ways that our institutions matter in our daily lives— and to expose how our law and work organizations fall short of their stated goals of nondiscrimination and inclusion. At one point, I thought this book project might be a relatively simple translation of that earlier work for a broader audience. While the book does draw from that article, most extensively in chapter 3, the book as a whole ended up building from a more personal place: my own feelings of guilt, frustration, anxiety, and anger at what is happening in our world and in our law and our workplaces. The George Floyd murder (among others), Black Lives Matter, #MeToo, the Buffalo mass shooting, the law that I research and teach, as well as my own relations and experiences and those of others I know, led to my own sense of an increased urgency for critical thinking about racial emotion in our interpersonal relations and our institutions—and an increased urgency for concrete recommendations for change. As a result, in addition to updating research and deepening and broadening sources,

I pushed further with this book than I had intended, expanding substantially the story that I tell and the recommendations for change that I make. I put the book to press aware that pushing can sometimes make for unsettling interpersonal moments in the form of questions and critique, and I present myself openly (even if with some trepidation) for what I hope are many more meaningful—and, yes, sometimes difficult—conversations ahead.

I want to thank generous readers of drafts along the way, including Michelle Adams, Rachel Arnow-Richman, Angela Harris, Yvette Lindgren, Orly Lobel, Rhonda Magee, Solangel Maldonado, Camille Gear Rich, Leticia Saucedo, Michelle Travis, and Deborah Widiss. My thanks also to the editorial team at UC Press, including editor Maura Roessner and copy editor Paul Tyler, anonymous reviewers for UC Press, my colleagues at the University of San Francisco School of Law and Loyola Law School, and attendees at various workshops along the way, who provided advice, source suggestions, and many important questions, too, and to Alyssa Carbonel Matsuhara for her excellent work as a research assistant.

Thank you also to the many others whose research and scholarship I openly build upon and whose voices resound in these pages, including the litigants in the legal cases that I describe.

And thank you finally and most deeply to those who support me and my work, enrich my life, and inspire me to open my mind, expand my skill set, and just plain try new things: my mom, Jo Green, my son, Avery Fischbach, and my loving and steady partner, Mark Fischbach.

Of course, all omissions, errors, and missteps are my own.

Introduction

After a long day at work, a white woman sits down for a late-afternoon team meeting next to a Black woman, whose binders and other materials are spread out on the table around her. The white woman nudges the Black woman's materials aside as she sits down. "Why are you moving my stuff?" asks the Black woman. The white woman responds, "Why are you being so aggressive? I was just sitting down." The Black woman, now visibly angry, says, "Aggressive? Do you even know you're being racist right now?" The white woman, tears in her eyes, approaches their supervisor and asks to be moved to another team.[1]

The emotion relayed in this simple story of two people interacting at work is tied to race; it is, in other words, racial emotion. The Black woman is offended by what she sees as someone judging her according to a racial stereotype. The white woman is shocked and ashamed at being called racist. That said, if this were all we took from the story—that our emotions can sometimes involve race—we might make note and move on to bigger problems. But it's not just that these people's emotions involve race. It's that their responses to those emotions are likely to lead to less interaction going forward and therefore less opportunity for them to forge a relationship across racial lines, a relationship that can have positive as well as negative emotions in the mix.

1

What's more, the emotions of these coworkers are not solely a matter of their individual histories or attitudes. Their racial emotions are shaped by our present institutions, among them the organization for which they work and also the law that guides our views about which racial emotions and behaviors are acceptable and when, and which are not. Imagine the scenario playing out one step further: At being asked to move the white woman to another team, the supervisor makes a judgment about whose racial emotion or behavior is legitimate and should be valued. Or maybe the Black woman or the white woman, or both, will complain to HR about the incident as involving racial bias; here, too, someone will determine what happened and what should be done, and that determination may involve judgments about what racial emotion should look like and whose racial emotion is more important and why.

Once we see some of the possible implications of racial emotions in this simple scenario—implications such as how often these two people are likely to interact in the future, who is likely to get moved and who is deemed a "troublemaker," even whether this single interaction is understood as a one-off or as part of broader workplace concern—we can begin to see that our racial emotions in our interactions at work have real-world consequences not just for us and our relations at work but for racial equality and justice.[2] And this makes our racial emotions part of a problem that is well worth our time to consider in more depth. To fail to do so would be to enact continued injustice and inequality in our lives.

.   .   .   .   .

It can be difficult to find words for our emotions, which may be one reason some of us don't talk about them much, at least not outside of our most intimate spaces. But that doesn't mean our emotions aren't there. In fact, emotions push our behavior in sometimes surprising ways. They can lead us to act unfriendly, for example, even when we don't mean to, and they can lead us to avoid important interactions and conversations. This book is about emotions when it comes to race, a subject that is itself a touchy one. But that's exactly the point. Emotions rise up during and around interactions with others every day, and some of those emotions have to do with race.

Racial emotion most broadly is the emotion related to race that people experience when they engage with the world.[3] This makes racial emotion part of all of our lives, even as we experience it in sometimes radically different ways. We can feel racial emotion in response to physical objects, like a noose or the confederate flag, or in response to physical spaces, like the feelings that surface when we walk alone into a room full of people of a race different from our own. We can feel racial emotion in response to a movie or a writing or a real-world scene like the brutal murder of George Floyd caught on video in Minneapolis or the anger-fueled mass shooting of Black people in Buffalo last spring. In fact, when we think about racial emotion broadly in this way, it becomes obvious that racial emotion is everywhere. We feel racial emotion in our protests, on our street corners and our campuses, and at our dinner tables across the country. Our racial emotions propel us into action—and sometimes pull us into despair.[4] And yet despite the obviousness of emotion involving race in all of our lives, there has been very little attention paid, especially by whites, to racial emotion as it is experienced in and affects our daily interactions. If anything, one effort has been to bury racial emotion—the movement in many states to pass statutes that prevent the teaching of "divisive concepts" serves as a prominent example—rather than to acknowledge and assess it.

We are in a time of racial reckoning in the United States, a time when calls to recognize our racial emotions are building and spreading. I am a white woman law professor who teaches at a law school with a racially diverse student body. As I saw the daily experience of students of color become ever more hostile under the Trump administration and the press of violence on Black and brown bodies, I also saw those students rise to speak. Students are forming racial coalitions—and calling for change. They tell us that we expect them to be "professional," which they take to mean "neutral, rational, and devoid of feeling," even when the law that we teach is embedded with racialized injustice. We leave no leeway for feelings to be aired or understood. This generation is joining with others to look at things differently (and in many circumstances reinvigorating calls that have long been ignored); they are asking for a disruption of silence, for space for conversation and learning about our racial experiences within institutions and also the relevance of our identities and experiences outside of those institutions for the work that we do within them.[5]

This book is one way of acting on this call. It seeks learning over silence in one slice of racial emotion in our lives: our interpersonal relations at work. Indeed, what we are missing as we debate next steps for racial justice is that racial emotion surfaces not only in moments of heartbreaking violence; it also surfaces in our more mundane day-to-day interactions, both our interactions with members of other races and with members of our own. And, importantly, racial emotion surfaces in our interactions at work. It can lead to disparities in outcomes, who is fired and who is promoted, who is paid more or less, and who gets which assignment or schedule. And it can undermine our efforts to forge connections, even friendships, and to thereby advance racial equality and justice.

This book focuses on racial emotion in our interpersonal interactions at work for two reasons: first, understanding our race-related emotions in interactions—and our behaviors associated with those emotions—helps us see how important those emotions are for reducing discrimination, enhancing social ties, and increasing equality; second, focusing on racial emotions at work allows us to probe the influence of context on those relations and especially context as it is created by work organizations and shaped by the law. We are at a moment when many people are seeing more clearly how structures, systems, and cultures drive racial injustice. As workers and others with influence on work organizations, we can and should have something to say about how those organizations and the laws that govern them structure our relations and affect our emotions, behaviors, and interactions.

HEARTS AND MINDS

Interest has been rising over the past decade or so in the workings of the mind and discrimination. The terms implicit bias and cognitive bias are increasingly mainstream, as evidenced by the numerous recent calls for antibias and diversity training in our courtrooms, our schools, and across public and private work sectors. Bias training, it sometimes seems, is everywhere. We know more today than ever about "blindspots" in our judgments and decisions because attention to these biases in research, education efforts, and especially in mass media has increased. We're not just studying it more; we're talking about it more. Malcolm Gladwell devoted a substantial portion of his bestselling *Blink* to the science of implicit bias, and Oprah Winfrey brought Gladwell and a prominent implicit bias researcher, social psychologist Anthony Greenwald, onto her show back in 2010. Implicit bias even made it into the 2016 presidential debate, where Hillary Clinton mentioned its role in police shootings.

This is an important development, one that can open us to new ways of shifting and countering our biases to reduce discrimination in work, whether we are reading a resume, evaluating someone's job performance, or reviewing a file for a pay raise or promotion. It can also lead to changes in our institutions—in the ways that we structure our job interviews or develop applicant pools and mentoring programs, for example—and not just in our attention to our own biases.[6]

We've heard much less, though, about the ways that our *emotions* can affect our behaviors and lead to discrimination. The focus has been almost exclusively on the operation of what are often seen as "cool" cognitive biases and stereotypes over "hotter" emotional response. This is the case even as emotion takes an increasingly central position in the study of interracial interaction in the social sciences. Our emotions are inextricably intertwined with our perceptions and brain processing, as we will see. And yet they are also worth considering separately as we seek to understand the problem of discrimination and possible solutions to it.

If all we do is implement implicit bias training, as many companies, government offices, courthouses, and universities currently do, we will miss the mark. We will end up knowing more about our individual biases, to be sure, but we will continue to know too little about how our biases and emotions together affect our interactions and relationships and how and why our institutions like workplaces and laws shape our racial emotions and favor some racial emotions over others—and, most importantly, what we need to do differently.

The now-amassing social science research tells us that reducing negative emotion experienced by members of all racial groups in interracial interaction is an important key to reducing prejudice and intergroup inequality, not only in the workplace but beyond in our families, neighborhoods, and schools. For many Americans today, the workplace is the place where people of different races are most likely to interact on a sustained basis, which means that it provides a principal site for the kind of inter-racial interaction that can reduce negative racial emotion, even generate positive racial emotion. Yet this same research suggests that racial emotion in most workplaces today is likely to be negative—we are likely to experience emotions like fear, disgust, anger, shame, envy, frustration, and anxiety—and that the brunt of this negative emotion and its consequences are likely to be borne by people of color. Negative racial emotions in inter-actions tend to lead to behaviors that are detrimental to our relationships, behaviors like avoidance and antagonism. Responding to our emotions, we pull away—and sometimes even lash out. But positive racial emotions, emotions like affection, respect, admiration, joy, pride, sympathy, and compassion, are possible. And perhaps most promising, even in the face of discomfort, there is another way toward stronger relationships over time: engagement.

INDIVIDUALS, INSTITUTIONS, AND RACIAL JUSTICE

Although we will learn about our racial emotions and take lessons from the research for our own interracial interactions in this book, the book is less about how we as individuals can *feel* better about race, and more about how we as citizens, workers, and leaders can structure our institutions—especially our law and our work organizations—to be more equitable so that our interracial interactions at work will involve positive emotions rather than negative ones over the long term. Indeed, restruc-turing our law and work organizations to see racial emotion and opening ourselves to understand our own emotions, and especially our behaviors around race, will likely lead in the short term to more uncomfortable con-versations, not fewer.

Hewing too closely to our minds and hearts or even our individual rela-tionships can blind us to the ways that our institutions influence our day-to-day interactions and, yes, our emotions. By choosing what to recognize as racial emotion and by judging racial emotion once it is recognized, our law and our work organizations alike play a substantial role in construct-ing our relations and our racial emotions within them. Legislators, judges, lawyers, and leaders in work organizations, in addition to the individuals who do the interacting on a day-to-day basis, are active participants in the construction of racial emotion, just as they are participants in the construction of race.

When our work organizations and law tell us that some white racial emotions are more valuable—by protecting whites from emotions associated with being perceived as biased or racist, for example—and that some racial emotions of people of color are overplayed or out of line—by punishing those who raise racial concerns, for example, or by siphoning racial emotions associated with racial insults and assaults against people of color into the solely "personal"—our institutions are actively setting up people of color for less success in work than their white counterparts. And they are actively (even if unintentionally) sabotaging our efforts to build stronger racial relationships at work.

This book tells a story of our institutions and their treatment of racial emotion at the same time that it teaches us about our own emotions. As we will see, both our law and our work organizations largely close racial emotion out of antidiscrimination concern. At the same time, they construct racial emotion repertoires—stories and expectations around racial emotion—that favor the racial emotions experienced by whites and that place the brunt of negative consequences of racial emotions on people of color. If we've learned anything during these times of renewed action following the murder of George Floyd, it is that racial progress requires us to attend to discrimination within and by our institutions, not just in our hearts and minds. That is the project of this book.

The book is organized in three parts. In the first, we explore what racial emotion is and what it means for our behaviors and our interactions at work. Through attention to key social science research, we see racial emotion in interracial interactions in action and we learn why racial emotion in most workplaces today is likely to be negative rather than positive, leading to weak and ruptured interracial ties. We also see glimmers of hope in this research, ways that interactions can be structured to open space for developing more positive racial emotion at work.

In part II, we turn to our institutions: law and work organizations. Racial emotion is misunderstood and skewed in especially troubling ways in law, which sends signals to employees about what amounts to discrimination and their rights with respect to it and also to employers about what can and should be done. Discrimination has long been understood to involve a substantial emotional component. Prejudice, after all, has animus—a hate- or disgust-related emotion—as its taproot. Despite this history (or perhaps because of it), courts and commentators today tend to conceptualize emotion in discrimination as a one-directional personal state revolving around antipathy or group-based animus by whites rather than as potentially involving multiple emotions that can emerge and change in the process of social interaction. The result is a static notion of prejudice as residing in individual mindsets rather than a contextual idea of racial emotions as they play out in day-to-day relations.

Courts have developed and applied the law of employment discrimination to reflect this narrow view, placing racial emotion outside of antidiscrimination concern. They do so in at least three often interrelated and overlapping ways: (1) by refusing to see emotion in interracial interaction when it occurs; (2) by categorizing emotion in interracial interaction when they see it as "personal" and thereby not racial; and (3) by judging the racial emotion that they do acknowledge as unreasonable. We can see judges doing this with a close look at some judicial opinions involving race and discrimination under the federal Civil Rights Act of 1964, our preeminent federal law prohibiting discrimination in employment. By closing racial emotion out of antidiscrimination concern in these cases in both the design and application of the law, judges signal that addressing racial emotion is not important to reducing discrimination. What's more, they place the burden of bearing the negative consequences of racial emotion on people of color.

There is one prominent exception to this general closing out of racial emotion from antidiscrimination concern by law and work organizations: whites who are called or perceive themselves as being called racist. Here, we see that judges are not just undersensitive to some racial emotions of people of color. They are also oversensitive to some racial emotions of whites, seeking to frame whites as innocent and to protect them from emotional discomfort and shame.

Our work organizations could create space for positive racial emotion apart from law, but there is little reason to believe that they currently do. Work organizations have a long history of regulating and shaping emotion generally, including a move toward seeing individuals as exclusively "responsible" for their own emotions, and also racial emotion specifically, even as they seek to capitalize on diversity in racialized ways. Indeed, we see in part II that work organizations place emotional labor on racial minorities disproportionately and regulate their emotions differently than they regulate the emotions of whites. We have known for some time that work "feeling rules" can reinforce gender boundaries by specifying which emotional displays are acceptable for men and for women. It turns out that feeling rules are also racialized: Whites are allowed to show anger in some circumstances, for example, when people of color are not. And organizations today go further. They ask people of color to do "diversity" work, to be the face of diversity for the organization, while building narratives of diversity that celebrate static identity states without attention to relations. These are just some of the ways that our work organizations currently cue race without attending to racial emotion, thereby setting people of color up as complainers and "bad" workers when they experience and express racial emotions around bias and discrimination at work.

In part III, we revisit the social science research on racial emotion in interaction to consider what is wrong with the prevailing approach of law and work organizations—and we identify solutions. In short, the prevailing approach to racial emotion misses discrimination and disadvantage at work, leaving racial minorities to bear the brunt of negative emotions and their relational consequences. This makes racial emotion at work something we should be concerned about if we seek equality in employment, as our civil rights laws do. But importantly the current approach is also likely to leave society worse off by fostering negative rather than positive interracial interactions at work, thereby cutting off and preventing the kind of interracial relationships that can break down prejudice and inequality.

To open space for developing positive interracial interactions at work, the law needs both to recognize racial emotion fairly as a source of discrimination and to trigger structural and cultural changes within organizations that will create conditions for conversation and learning across difference. Law and organizations alike need to shift their repertoires for racial emotion to more fairly allocate the burdens of racial emotion and to create the space needed to build positive interracial relations in the long term.

The book then digs into how to do this—offering suggestions for citizens, workers, and leaders seeking to make racial justice progress a reality at work. I present three broad measures for shifting our institutions' approach to racial emotion. The first, *Seeing Discrimination*, involves bringing racial emotion into antidiscrimination concern by acknowledging individual behaviors of racial assault, behaviors that are most likely to be disastrous for our interracial relations, while otherwise widening our lens to focus on systems and structures over individuals. The second, *Shifting Repertoires*, seeks to redefine the "good" worker and to expand our language for racial emotion at work. The third, *Sharing Discomfort*, involves undertaking a vision of integration that asks for sharing the burden of discomfort in difference. Together, these proposals shift our institutional approach to racial emotion, drawing it consistently into antidiscrimination concern, and can open space for learning and engagement in our interracial interactions at work. With action at the forefront, I also delineate a set of concrete recommendations that flow from these broad proposals, recommendations that span law, work organizations, and our individual lives.

These measures meet our moment with more than mere words to disrupt the silence around racial emotion. To make a difference, we will have to act, not just listen, talk, and learn. And yet, while changing our institutions is key, it is individuals who are the heroes in all of this. We are the ones who will make the shifts not just in how we understand and navigate our own racial emotions but also in how our institutions structure and shape those emotions for ourselves and others.

PART I Racial Emotion at Work

We start by considering what we mean when we talk about race, and especially how we might best understand our lived experiences around race and racial identity. This is a complicated subject, but even just a brief review of some of the research and thinking on race is important groundwork for our understanding of racial emotion. How we move through a world where race and racial identity are part of our lived realities, after all, affects the emotions we experience along the way. Moreover, understanding the socially constructed and contextual nature of race and our experiences of race reinforces our goal: We seek here not to identify specific emotions of certain racial groups but rather to understand how racial emotion operates in all of us in our daily lives.

1 What Is Racial Emotion?

Most of us have an almost intuitive sense of what racial emotion might look like. Pictures may come to mind of a mob of white men storming the U.S. Capitol in support of outgoing president Trump or of a Black mother grieving the death of her son after a police shooting. Even just hearing of these events can be enough to trigger our racial emotions. On a more individual, interpersonal scale we may recall an incident where we thought someone was calling us a racist, or a time when we thought someone underestimated us—presumed us incompetent—because of our membership in a racial group.

Our intuitions, though, can only take us so far. Indeed, we'll see that when it comes to race and emotion, our lay understandings and intuitions can sometimes be at odds with science. By science I am referring not only to laboratory science, neuroscience and psychology, but also to science in the fields that engage with people outside of the laboratory, such as sociology, anthropology, and history. In all of these areas, scholars and researchers have studied what we mean (and should mean) by race and emotion and especially how race and emotion are experienced by all of us in our daily lives. Bringing this research together, we can build an initial groundwork for our exploration of racial emotion in interpersonal interactions at work.

We will see in this chapter that while we often resort to simplistic, biological frames for thinking about both race and emotion, those frames can obscure a larger truth: Race, emotion, and racial emotion are socially situated historically and also in any present moment. By "socially situated" I mean that they have almost no meaning without reference to how we see ourselves among others, whether in our past, our present, or our future. A quick look into some of the research and thinking about race and emotion will help illustrate this fundamental point.

RACE

The language we use to talk about race can suggest that it is based on biology. Color, after all, is tied genetically to the pigmentation of our skins, so that when we talk about black, white, red, yellow, or brown, we can easily start imagining that it's all about color. This has gotten us into a lot of trouble over the years. Not the specific language, which has changed over time, but the underlying idea that it reflects: that somehow race (and racial advantage and disadvantage) can be identified by specific genetic makeup. I say that it has gotten us into trouble because this idea of "biological race," what is sometimes called an "essentialist" view, traces back at least as far as the sixteenth century, and was regularly used by Europeans to delineate a hierarchy. Black people would not commonly be made slaves in America for another century, and yet the English first arriving on the African continent were already portraying Africans not just as "black" but as inferior, oversexed, and violent.[1]

Of course, we know that this essentialist view of race dominated in the United States during the years of slavery, especially during the years leading up to and during the Civil War, when a biological view was used to justify keeping African Americans enslaved, and also during the bloody removal of Indigenous people from the land on which they had lived for generations.[2] It is also tied closely to the eugenics movement, which was designed to give "the more suitable races or strains of blood a better chance of prevailing speedily over the less suitable than they otherwise would have had," with nonwhites regularly on the receiving end of eugenic policies, including antimiscegenation laws and forced sterilizations (as well as policies aimed at boosting the fertility rates of the white, Protestant, Anglo-Saxon middle and upper classes).[3] Eugenics, it turns out, was not just a favorite "science" of Hitler's Third Reich; it was also a favorite of American policy-makers fearing a "denordicization" of American society.

By the 1940s, however, and especially in the wake of World War II, the biological, essentialist view of race lost ground as scholars began to explore more fully the social construction of race.[4] Race increasingly came to be understood not as a matter of genetics but of social construction. To say that race is socially constructed is to acknowledge that race has meaning only as a social phenomenon. It's not that biology doesn't determine our skin colors or other physical features, but rather that those features matter to us because of invented racial categories, categories used for subordination and domination in our histories. Sociologists Michael Omi and Howard Winant were instrumental in developing this understanding of race in *Racial Formation in the United States: From the 1960s to the 1980s*, published in 1986. They define race very simply as "a concept which signifies and symbolizes social conflicts and interests by referring to different types of human bodies."[5] A concept is a mental representation of a category, and the concept of race is created because our society says that it matters.

Race, in short, is not something that we carry within us at birth, even as it develops immediately from birth. It is a characteristic of a relationship—the creation of a social setting. Race was and continues to be constructed in various ways in society, including through law. Racial identity trials determining free or slave status in the pre- and post-antebellum era and racially restrictive immigration laws, including laws that barred Asians from entry or excluded them from citizenship, are two examples of ways in which race has been constructed through and by law.

This is not to say that the essentialist view has disappeared altogether. The increasing popularity of racial claims upon receiving results of a DNA ancestry test is one indication that we have had a hard time letting go of an essential notion of race.[6] Another is seen in the assisted reproductive technology (ART) industry, where gamete banks are known to attach color-coded labels to vials: a black label for Black donors, yellow for Asian donors, and white for Caucasian donors.[7]

Recent research also suggests that belief in genetic causes of racial inequality remains widespread in American society. Sociologist Ann Morning finds, for example, that scientists tend to describe and teach race (includ-ing in mainstream university science textbooks) in biological terms, much more than in social constructivist ones.[8] Another recent study suggests that one in five non-Black Americans in the United States attributes income inequality between Black and white people to unspecified genetic differences between the two groups.[9] This is the case, moreover, even though there exists no empirical support for a biological race position.

Despite these and other troubling accounts of the stickiness of essen-tialism, race is generally understood to be socially rather than biologically driven (as the science, including the Human Genome Project, fully sup-ports), and this is the view that I take in this book.[10]

Once we understand the social nature of race, we can more easily see that identity and racial experience is often not a matter of one, isolated category but of multiple categories that can intersect and overlap. A gay Black man may experience race differently, for example, than a lesbian Black woman or a Black person who identifies with neither of those sexual categories, and they are all likely to experience race differently from their white, heterosexual counterparts. Many of us are mixed race, which also affects our experiences. Even members of the same racial group can have different racial experiences, with some whites being more "marginal" than others, less certain of their status in the dominant group, and intragroup anxieties can bubble up around color and other features.[11]

Moreover, race is fluid; it can shift both in context and in relation to viewpoint. A Black woman might be considered Black in her hometown neighborhood of Harlem but white in her international school downtown. And she might also think of herself as of a race that is different from that which others consider her. Someone might identify as one race on docu-ments ("documentary race") and as another in public social situations ("public race") and yet another in private ("private race").[12] And this same person may not be consistent in their identification over time.[13] These can each be authentic representations of race by an individual. There is no reason to believe, in other words, that shifts in race claiming are inher-ently suspect or otherwise suggestive of any sort of racial fraud.

Indeed, race can shift not just from social context to social context but from social interaction to social interaction. Legal scholars Devon Carbado and Mitu Gulati use the term "performative identity" to capture this idea that people actively work their identities to shape how others experience them and, in turn, how they experience their own race.[14] Even when we don't actively work our identities, our racial identity as experienced by others is likely to be affected by our performance of that identity. Carbado gives the example of two Black women, one of whom has dreaded hair while the other's hair is relaxed. He points out that neither woman may intend to employ her hair to make a racial statement about herself, yet both will be "racially interpreted" at least partly on the basis of their hair. "As between the two women, people are more likely to 'read' the woman with dreads as racially counter-cultural."[15]

We "do" race, in other words, not just experience it. And while we might be quick to acknowledge that race is something done by people of color, we are mistaken if we miss that whites also do race. Their social spaces and frames for doing race may differ—hair, for example, is not as socially laden with race for whites as it is for people of color, especially Black women—but they nonetheless do race in their day-to-day choices about what to wear, whom to connect with, what spaces to frequent, how to manage conversations about race, and more.

There is a risk that a commitment to race as a social construction will result in a conclusion that race is only a concept and somehow then not "real." Yet to say that race is socially constructed and not fixed is not the same thing as saying that race does not exist as a reality in our lives. Indeed, quite to the contrary. Legal scholar Gary Peller puts it this way:

> The African-American community exists as a group and can be followed through time and space even if the group can never be objectively and definitively defined; even if its borders are continuously contested; even if its meaning is multiple and indeterminate. It is true that the group's existence is partly constituted by performances, in which the group is produced by being articulated and rearticulated. It is true that the group may be constituted very differently in the future, or maybe not "exist" in the future at all. But that contingency does not make the group less real.[16]

It is worth noting here, too, that while race is not biologically determined, we often use physical characteristics as a way of externally identifying a person's race. This practice can be problematic when it results in discrimination and subordination. Legal scholar Khiara Bridges writes,

"Race has never been simply about describing Asian people as having yellow skin, black hair, and dark eyes; it has also always been about knowing that those particular physical features correspond to severity, haughtiness, and covetousness," dominant stereotypes about race that skew our perceptions and our judgments.[17] But to ignore race and its role in our histories and in our present lives is itself deeply problematic. As we will see in chapter 2, the strategy of colorblindness taken by many whites often backfires in interracial interactions and places emotional burdens on people of color. Moreover, as we will explore more in considering what we can do about our institutions' current approach to racial emotion, without data regarding racial demographics in workplaces it would be difficult to hold employers accountable to their nondiscrimination obligations. One solution to this tension between need for data on the one hand and autonomy on the other is to allow people to self-identify as often as possible.

EMOTION

Much like with race, on the one hand, we all know what emotions are. We experience them in various ways every day. On the other hand, there is more to emotion—and racial emotion, as I use the term in this book— than many of us realize. We will learn about emotion and racial emotion throughout the book. In this chapter, I seek to set some groundwork, to position ourselves so that we can see that, as with race, sometimes our day-to-day narratives about emotions can lead us astray.

Scientists, perhaps surprisingly, don't always agree on a precise definition of "emotion." This is partly because there are so many levels to our affective experiences, from immediate sensory reactions, like when you take a bite of your grandmother's apple pie (or just a bite of apple pie that reminds you of your grandmother), to longer-term affective dispositions, like a melancholy mood.[18] Moreover, some scientists prioritize the physiological basis of emotion, while others are interested in cultural variation in expressing and deciphering emotions.

On the whole, though, scientists tend to agree that our emotions are feelings focused on particular causes or objects. This distinguishes them from the more general affect that we feel throughout the day, such as grumpiness when we haven't had enough to eat or displeasure when we have to force ourselves to get out of bed in the morning. Emotions, in contrast to this more general affect, are built on specific concepts; they orient us to respond to life's specific events. And they are rooted in appraisals, evaluative judgments about whether what someone is experiencing or is about to experience is good or bad, or something in between.

Emotion is often distinguished from cognition, the reasoning processes of the brain. In fact, we often see emotion portrayed as the irrational side of the inner workings of humans as contrasted to more rational, cognitive thought. Greek philosophers drew a sharp distinction between feelings and thoughts, and much of Western thinking follows a similar line, portraying emotions as powerful, involuntary forces. Plato described a battle going on in our brains, with instincts and emotions constantly fighting against rational thought, and the victorious rational thought, when possible, as the way to righteousness and civilization. Some early theorists, like Plato and Kant, saw emotions as at best playing a minimal role in social life—the more we avoided them the better—while others, like Rousseau and Hume, saw emotions as a key source of moral intuition and ethical behavior.[19]

Early "universalists," as they are sometimes called, among them Charles Darwin, thought that emotions were tied to specific, universally recognized physical responses. In his 1872 *The Expression of the Emotions in Man and Animals*, Darwin catalogued a range of different emotions in animals and humans together with their observed "expressive behaviors," from tongue protrusions to body sways.[20] Facial muscle configurations in particular took center stage here, and in the late 1960s, psychologist Paul Ekman took Darwin's claims one step further by studying peoples' ability to recognize various facial muscle configurations as expressing specific emotions.[21] In his studies Ekman presented pictures of people posing the facial muscle configurations commonly associated with six different emotions—anger, disgust, fear, happiness, sadness, and surprise—and he asked individuals living in different countries, and later individuals living in a remote area of Papua New Guinea who did not have access to Western concepts, movies, or magazines, to identify the emotions being portrayed. He and others have interpreted the consistency in interpretations as evidence of the universalist nature of emotions.

This idea that our faces and bodies express our emotions should not surprise us. We use our faces and bodies every day to send signals to those around us. My tears are likely to be interpreted by you differently from my smile, my raised eyebrows differently from my frown. What Ekman and others claimed, however, is not just that we use our bodies to express emotion, but that we are all hard-wired to respond to a discrete set of emotions in our bodies in much the same way, whether we sit at a desk in Silicon Valley or in a hut in a remote area of Papua New Guinea. And that people will recognize those bodily responses in much the same way as well.

We continue to see this view of emotion in a multitude of places, from paintings and picture books in kindergarten classrooms and popular movies like the Pixar hit *Inside Out* to the teachings of the Dalai Lama.[22] Facebook even commissioned a set of emoticons inspired by Darwin's drawings of faces. And tech companies are working on AI that they claim will be able to reliably read emotions from faces.

This view of emotion also leads to our language, a language that often portrays emotions in terms of intrapsychic hydraulics: we "boil over," "blow our top," and "get steamed"; we are "overcome by grief" and "bursting with anger." Our language also suggests that emotion has, as sociologist Arlie Hochschild puts it, "a presence or identity independent of the person it is 'in.'"[23] We say, for example, that our guilt "haunts" us or that our fear "grips" or "paralyzes" us, and generally that emotion "surfaces" in us from events. We talk as if emotion has a physical residence somewhere within us, whether in our heart or our gut, at the ready to take over and control us, or at least to deceive us by outing our desires to others.

The universalist view of emotion has long been controversial, with ethnographers challenging it even when Ekman was conducting his face studies in the 1960s. The view of emotion of late, however, has taken a marked turn toward constructionism. Indeed, while the classical, universalist view of emotion—that there are certain "basic" emotions that are tied consistently to certain neurons firing and are hard-wired to bodily reactions—persists in various realms, including in our language and stories, recent research points to flaws in this view, or at least to a lack of sufficient evidence to confidently sustain it.[24] Psychologist Lisa Feldman Barrett has been most recently at the forefront of this challenge, arguing that the "brute reflex," classical view of emotion is wrong, or at least incomplete.[25] According to Barrett, "Even after a century of effort, scientific research has not revealed a consistent, physical fingerprint for even a single emotion. When scientists attach electrodes to a person's face and measure how facial muscles actually move during the experience of emotion, they find tremendous variety, not uniformity."[26]

Indeed, "constructionists" of emotion would say that, much as with race, there is no such thing as an emotion without the context giving rise to it. Our emotions, in other words, are socially constructed: "They are not universal, but vary from culture to culture. They are not triggered; you create them."[27] When it comes to emotions, there are constructions at work in the brain—systems that integrate our bodies with our brains—as well as social teachings and concepts, but basically what we experience in the world including our emotions is created, not genetically predetermined.[28]

To say that emotions are constructed is not to say that we don't feel something physical with our emotions, a deep sinking feeling in our gut when we feel fear or even lust or grief, for example, or that we don't have physical responses such as facial movements that can sometimes give our emotions away. Nor does it mean that our readings of others' emotions using their facial movements and bodies as cues are entirely off-base. It does mean, however, that emotions, as sociologist Eva Illouz puts it, "originate in the subject's beliefs and desires and cannot be separated from the ways in which culturally encoded social relationships are lived in and by the self."[29] Illouz provides the example of when someone says to you: "You're late again." What emotions, if any, this statement evokes in you will depend not just on the context—is it your boss or your coworker or your child waiting for you after school making the statement?—but also on what you are taught and believe about the relationship that you have with the speaker.[30] Emotions, in this sense, are responsive to what we value.[31] What's more, your emotions will also potentially depend on what you have been taught about the emotion by your family, your friends, and the umbrella institutions that guide our views on lots of things, from the value of governmental support programs to our national identities.[32]

For several decades, research on emotion lagged as social scientists rode a cognitive turn in understanding human interactions, biases, and decision making. Emotion research is currently experiencing its own revolution.[33] Within this revolution, scientists are likely to agree that emotion and cognition are interrelated, that emotion and cognition even share parts of the brain. Neuroscientific studies, moreover, back up Barrett's claim that emotion is variable; it does not result in the same neurons firing each time or same neurons firing in each person.[34]

Historians have also begun to study how emotions have been portrayed and possibly even experienced in past generations, and sociologists are teaching us about the role of power in emotions and emotion rules and displays.[35] Indeed, regardless of how we come down on the debate over universalism and basic emotions, we undoubtedly know more today than ever before about how our emotions work; about how they can display in bodily systems, whether as facial expressions, eye gaze, vocalization patterns, gestures, or postural shifts; and also about how they can affect our longer-term behaviors, decisions, and relationships. We can also be confident that at the very least our emotions are influenced by our social lives, our histories, our cultures, our identities, and our day-to-day interactions, even if they also have a biological, wired-in-how-our-brains-work component.

RACE AND EMOTION

Beyond race and emotion as separate concepts, we also know something about race and emotion together. A good bulk of this research focuses on stereotypes involving race in the United States. In *Biased*, psychologist Jennifer Eberhardt brings years of research together to teach us about how stereotypes affect our thinking.[36] Stereotypes are sets of characteristics that we associate with cognitive categories, and we use them to make sense of the world. With so much information coming at us at any point in time, we all use stereotypes to function. Stereotypes allow us to make quick decisions, in a "blink," as Malcolm Gladwell would say.[37] When I see a sizeable animal coming down the road toward me, my stereotypes tell me that it is likely to be a dog and not a bear. In the same way, I read the body language of other dog walkers—how tightly they tug the leash or whether they cross the street or keep their bodies between me and their dog—to decide whether a dog is likely to be aggressive and bark at mine. These stereotypes can change over time. More and more often these days I take the human behavior to signify that the person is nervous, rather than that the dog is aggressive or even concerned at all. This is because I have learned from experience that when my dog approaches these other dogs, especially when he is off leash, all goes well. Sniffs and wags occur, and no barking or teeth baring. My stereotypes, my expectations based on categorical experiences, have changed over time.

Most, though certainly not all, of our stereotypes about people have to do with our social worlds. We are constantly reading people (and sometimes animals), whether we're standing at a bus stop, driving in our cars, grabbing a coffee in the break room, or walking down a street alone on a dark night. In fact, it is because we are so often reading people that our stereotypes tend to center around socially salient characteristics, those characteristics that have to do with features or traits of people that the world around us says matter. By this I mean that we tend to attach little significance in our stereotyping to some features of people—such as whether they are wearing red or black shoelaces or whether they have a mustache or a beard—and a lot of significance to other features—such as what race we think they are. As much as some people may try to ignore race, race is a socially salient feature of our lives and we all carry with us stereotypes involving race. These stereotypes come to us from our own experiences but also substantially from what those around us tell us or how they behave and also what we see in the media. This can change over time. It may be that in the future race will matter less or in different ways in our mental processing and mustaches and beards will matter more, but today race is a deep part of our social reality in our histories and our present lives and it affects how we see things.

Stereotypes don't just tell us (rightly or wrongly) about a situation; they also affect how our minds process information once we have assigned something to a category. One of the strongest stereotypes involving race is the one that associates Black with crime. Eberhardt tells the story of a police officer who while out working undercover saw a man in the distance "who didn't look right":

This guy looked similar to me—you know, black, same build, same height. But this guy had a scruffy beard, unkempt hair, ripped clothes, and he looked like he was up to no good. The guy began approaching me, and as he was getting closer, I had the feeling that he had a gun on him. *Something's off with this guy*, I thought. *This dude ain't right.*

So this guy is coming down a hill, near the front of a nice office building—one of those big office towers with glass walls. And as the guy is approaching, I couldn't shake the feeling that he was armed and dangerous.

As I got closer to the building, I lost him for a second and I began to feel panicked. Suddenly I see the guy again, but this time he is inside the office building. I could see the guy clearly through the glass wall. He was walking inside the building—in the same direction and at the same pace as I was walking.

Something was wrong. When I quickened my pace, I could see him quicken his pace. And finally, I decided to stop abruptly, turn and confront the guy.

He stops too, and I look at him face-to-face. . . . And when I look in his eyes, a shock went through me. I realized that I was staring at myself. *I* was the person I feared. I was staring at my own reflection through the mirrored wall. That entire time, I was tailing myself; I was profiling myself.[38]

Stereotypes about race and crime can elicit fear of violence when there is no real threat. The stereotype that associates Blackness with crime is so powerful that in some experiments the mere presence of a Black face, even one that appears fleetingly so that the participants say they were not even aware of it, can cause the participants to see weapons more quickly—or to imagine weapons that are not there.[39] In much the same way, stereotypes about race and degree of racial prejudice can elicit skewed evaluations of the emotions of others. For example, a Black man who is excited might appear angry to someone who is relying on the Black-crime or Black-violence stereotype even though the exact same facial cues in a white face would elicit an evaluation of excitement, even joy.[40]

Two emotions have taken center stage in our racial history: lust and anger. Historians have documented the lasting stereotype of the angry, oversexed Black man. Legal scholar Darren Hutchinson details some of these sexualized narratives in his work, noting that the institution of lynching in postbellum South "was justified by the construction of black male heterosexuality as a violent threat to white women."[41] And Black women, too, have often been stereotyped as angry and oversexed, although in slightly different ways. Sociologist K. Sue Jewell traces the media representations of Black women as the Mammy, a large Black woman who is domestic and especially nurturing of her charges; the Sapphire, outspoken, sassy, and emasculating of her Black male partners; and the Jezebel, the bad-Black-girl, who is alluring, arousing, and seductive, yearning for sexual encounters.[42]

These racialized stereotypes involving emotion are tools of power, used to put nonwhites in their place and to instill violence and subordination. It is no coincidence that stereotypes of people of color and emotion are often negative; not just the angry Black person but also the passionate Latina and the emotionless or dragon lady Asian. And the list goes on. Even racial categorization itself can be traced directly to efforts to "control, exploit, dominate, and enslave."[43] And history shows that the stereotypes were and continue to be used in ways that perpetuate whites' fears and efforts to constrain the actions of people of color. A 1974 ad for the drug Haldol, for example, featured a Black man with his fist raised. "Assaultive and Belligerent?" read the ad. "Cooperation begins with Haldol." Indeed, studies suggest that an almost all-white psychiatry profession and client base has led to "lack of attunement to Black expression of emotion," including frequent conflation of distress with anger, and to "an under-diagnosis of major depression, especially in Black men, and an overreliance upon the use of antipsychotic medications."[44]

As we will explore further in a later chapter, research also suggests an emotional stratification along racial lines. The idea here is that emotions are not only raced in the sense that we have racialized pictures of what emotions look like and how they are experienced; the same or similar emotions are also often valued differently in different people. White women's tears, for example, are known to draw out immediate concern for their well-being, especially from other whites, while tears of people of color are seen as weakness, a distraction from the real matters at hand.[45] In much the same way, the stories we tell about reasons for emotion displays are gendered and raced. The same expressions in women and men are attributed to internal emotionality for women and external events for men ("He's just having a bad day.").[46]

RACIAL EMOTION

As I mentioned earlier, I often use the term "racial emotion" in this book to refer to our feelings related to race in interpersonal interaction, especially interracial interaction. This is admittedly just a slice of a broader world of racial emotion that we could explore. For example, we can experience race-related emotion when we are faced with an object in isolation, outside of human interaction, as when we watch a video or other portrayal of abuse or courage. Even as we interact, we can also experience emotion that is more group-based than that of individual-level, interpersonal interaction. We can experience collective pride upon seeing our group as responsible for an important accomplishment or we can experience anger in response to events harming other in-group members even if the events are not harming us personally.[47] There is a long and well-documented history of politicians drumming up and playing to racialized fears, what legal scholar Ian Haney López calls "dog whistle politics."[48] Indeed, there is every reason to believe that emotion regarding race in the United States runs broad and deep. As sociologist Eduardo Bonilla-Silva mapped out in his presidential address to the American Sociological Association several years ago, emotion can be seen as the "skeleton" of racism[49]—and also the root of our hope for progress.[50]

We should, of course, continue to explore these broader group-based emotions across all contexts of our lives, just as we should continue to explore the ways that our policies and practices have been and continue to be structured to the benefit of some and the subordination of others. The government practice of backing loans for whites, with red lines drawn around Black neighborhoods designating their ineligibility, for example, is more than a blip on our policy screen.[51] Welfare, criminality, family, and immigration are just some of the many areas where policies and racial emotion intertwine.

Nor should my emphasis on interpersonal interaction here be read to say that racial stratification is the product of actors' internal states, whether emotion or cognition. As this book will reveal, racial emotion, like all emotion, is structurally situated in the present and through our histories—we do not come to our interpersonal interactions with a "clean" slate nor do we interact in the present isolated from the broader environment in which we find ourselves. We are necessarily reacting to that environment even as we react to and influence the person with whom we are speaking. Racial emotion is therefore part of a "structural perspective on racism" as much as it is a personal one.[52]

Yet it makes sense for us to focus on racial emotion in interpersonal interactions. These interactions present moments for present and future connection—for building relationships or for rupturing them. If we understand discrimination as at least partly a problem of human interaction in the present (albeit within a larger group-based history and context) and if, as research suggests, improving those relations will reduce discrimination and advance equality, then this is one key place to hone our thinking. As I have said, we will see that this emphasis on individuals and interpersonal interaction does not exclude context from analysis or solution. It does, however, situate us to think about day-to-day encounters, interactions, and relationships—as they affect and are affected by context.

2 Racial Emotion and Our Relations at Work

Back in the spring of 1953, while an undergraduate student at Harvard, historian Winthrop Jordan took a course called Prejudice and Group Conflict. The course was taught by Daniel Levinson and Gordon Allport. Levinson, then a junior professor at Harvard, had contributed while a graduate student to the text of a well-known book, *The Authoritarian Personality*, and Allport, as we will see, was a powerhouse on the subject of racial prejudice. He had just completed his *The Nature of Prejudice*, which would be published in 1954. It is said that Jordan was influenced by the course not just for the content and learning that it provided but for what it lacked. In a foreword to Jordan's later, influential *White over Black*, Christopher Leslie Brown says: "[Jordan] doubted the emphasis that the social psychologists placed on cognition—more attention should be given to emotion and the irrational. He distrusted the self-satisfied conviction that prejudices could be expelled if one could learn to think differently. He thought that the emphasis on personality understated the importance of culture. And he suspected that there was a historical dimension to the problem that the social scientists often overlooked."[1]

In this chapter, we explore some of the recent research in the field of social psychology that builds on the insights of Winthrop Jordan from almost seventy years ago. The story reminds us that we are not alone in critiquing a close focus on cognition over emotion, on individual mindsets over cultural influence, including influence by the institutions within which we interact. The research drawn on in this chapter is part of a modern movement toward understanding the role of racial emotion in interracial interactions, whether inside or outside of work.

Almost everyone in the United States today experiences racial emotion—and much of this racial emotion is experienced at work. Work, after all, is the place where we are most likely to interact with members of different racial groups on anything more than a fleeting basis. One person feels uncomfortable making conversation with her coworker of a different race for fear that she will say something that is perceived as biased or offensive; another is anxious that his boss will judge him as less intelligent than the whites on his team. One feels anger at the telling of a racial joke; another feels frustrated when a colleague raises concerns about racial bias during a post-interview debriefing.

These emotions—and the behaviors that give rise to them and respond to them—are sometimes difficult to describe. We lack a rich, shared language of racial emotion in the workplace, in no small part because many of us (especially whites) often prefer not to see it.[2] But racial emotion does exist, and we ignore it to the detriment of not only our individual relationships but also our visions and efforts for equality.

We should be clear from the outset, however, that it is not negative emotions themselves that are problematic, but rather their effect on our interactions and relations. Sometimes negative emotions can result in improved interactions. Other times, what we might think of as positive emotions are grounded in dominance and therefore are negative to our relations even as they may feel positive in the person experiencing them. Therefore, while I sometimes refer to increasing positive emotions in interracial interactions, my eye is on interaction and longer-term relationships more than the precise emotions that are experienced in any single interaction. Moreover, while I talk about negative and positive emotions, as much of the research in this field does, it would be a mistake to insist on a sharp dichotomy between positive and negative. Indeed, research suggests that emotions can blur and that we can experience multiple emotions at once.[3]

In exploring the research on interracial interaction in this chapter, we set the stage for thinking about the role of our institutions in shaping our interactions and our emotions within them. As we will see in part II, law and work organizations create and reinforce emotional repertoires around race and in doing so are likely to shape our own racial emotions and our interracial interactions, but we nonetheless remain active participants in our racial encounters. In this way, the research explored here provides a groundwork for thinking through our individual choices as well as our institutional ones. Just as legal historian Ariela Gross once said about race, racial emotion, too, "is not something imposed from above, imagined by experts and acquiesced in by ordinary people"; it is "created and recreated every day through the workings of community institutions and individuals in daily life."[4]

THE IMPORTANCE OF INTERGROUP RELATIONS
AND RACIAL EMOTION AT WORK

Extensive research has documented the key role of contact for improving intergroup relations.[5] The more often we can interact with members of racial groups other than our own, especially if we can interact cooperatively and as equals with common goals, the more likely we are to break down our prejudices, stereotypes, and biases, to develop cross-group friendships, and even to open up more widely to others who are different from us. The workplace for many people today offers the most potential for these encounters. Schools and neighborhoods remain highly segregated, and while many occupations remain starkly stratified, with whites in jobs at the top and people of color in lower-level positions, most workplaces provide some opportunity for intergroup interaction.[6]

When we think of discrimination at work, we often think about decisions in discrete moments, like hiring and promotion, and we ask whether those decisions may have been biased, meaning that we ask whether the person or people making the decision did so because of the candidate's race. By thinking about discrimination in this way, we tend to narrow our inquiry to a person's state of mind at a precise moment in time. Focusing on intergroup contact, in contrast, brings us to the relational; it gets us thinking not just about the possibility of biased decisions at key moments, but of our interactions and how those interactions can affect our success in work as well as social equality more broadly. Once we understand that the better our intergroup interactions are, the fairer our outcomes at work will be and the less prejudice and anxiety in interaction we will have over time, we cannot help but turn to relations as a site for social justice.

As several excellent books and a mountain of research have shown over the past several decades, our cognitive biases about race can often get us into trouble in our interactions. In their compelling *Blindspot: Hidden Biases of Good People*, social psychologists Mahzarin Banaji and Anthony Greenwald, for example, teach us about the implicit associations test (the "IAT"), which measures speed-associated patterns in our minds and exposes an automatic preference in many of us for white relative to Black.[7] Much of this research focuses on how and why our minds rely on certain stereotypes, often as unconscious categorizing, and how those stereotypes or "pictures in our heads" can lead us astray in our decision making. Biases can also go beyond stereotypes to include things like attribution bias, the tendency to attribute failures of people in an out-group to internal, personal reasons but failures of people in an in-group (those people perceived as "like me") to external causes, such as time pressure. Together, this vast literature on bias tells us that racial bias travels with us wherever we go and affects our brain processing in fundamental ways, making it more difficult for whites to distinguish Black faces, for instance, and to some degree vice versa.

Some of this research on bias highlights interactions and relations. Several studies reveal, for example, that the higher the implicit bias of an interviewer (using the IAT measure), the more awkward the social interaction between that interviewer and an interviewee.[8] Moreover, not only does the interviewer exhibit greater discomfort and more unfriendly behavior toward the interviewee, but the interviewee is likely to replicate the unfriendly behavior. Psychologist Jennifer Eberhardt, as we saw earlier, takes this research more deeply into interactions in *Biased*.[9] There, we see how stereotypes and biases can influence the reaction of a police officer in a split-second encounter with a suspect, or even a more prolonged interchange. *Biased* touches on racial emotion. Bias, we know, can be interconnected with emotions, fear being one of the most obvious ones, especially given stereotypes about Black men and violence.

And yet the dominant story about bias in interactions is also itself incomplete. It turns out that we need to be thinking about biases in interactions, *and also* about emotions in interactions. One of the reasons we need to think about emotions is that they can present another opportunity for improvement—just as with our biases or "blindspots," being armed with knowledge about our emotions can help us better assess, shape, value, manage, and productively respond to them. Another reason is that our institutions currently approach emotion separately from bias, and the way that those institutions approach racial emotion is hindering our efforts at gaining ground on discrimination at work and on racial justice more broadly.

Well-known Black author-activist Audre Lorde once described her experience taking the bus as a child and realizing a white woman did not want to sit by her:

> The AA subway train to Harlem. I clutch my mother's sleeve, her arms full of shopping bags, christmas-heavy. The wet smell of winter clothes, the train's lurching. My mother spots an almost seat, pushes my little snowsuited body down. On one side of me a man reading a paper. On the other, a woman in a fur hat staring at me. Her mouth twitches as she stares and then her gaze drops down, pulling mine with it. Her leather-gloved hand plucks at the line where my new blue snow pants and her sleek fur coat meet. She jerks her coat closer to her. I look. I do not see whatever terrible thing she is seeing on the seat between us—probably a roach. But she has communicated her horror to me. It must be something very bad from the way she's looking, so I pull my snowsuit closer to me away from it, too. When I look up the woman is still staring at me, her nose holes and eyes huge. And suddenly I realize there is nothing crawling up the seat between us; it is me she doesn't want her coat to touch.

Lorde goes on to describe her own emotions in this encounter: "I quickly slide over to make room for my mother to sit down. No word has been spoken. I'm afraid to say anything to my mother because I don't know what I have done. I look at the side of my snow pants secretly. Is there something on them? Something's going on here I do not understand, but I will never forget it. Her eyes. The flared nostrils. The hate."[10]

If this white woman would not even sit closely next to Audre Lorde so that they were touching, and if Lorde noticed how and why she was reacting the way she was, what can we expect of their relationship over time? These two were in a fleeting encounter, albeit one that would have a long-term impact on Lorde, but many people interact (or have the opportunity to interact) with people of different races on a daily, more sustained basis, especially at work, whether as coworkers in the halls or on work teams or in more hierarchical relationships as bosses and subordinates.

What racial emotions can we expect from whites and people of color who are likely to interact in the workplace today on a more sustained basis rather than on the subway in a fleeting encounter? How are these emotions likely to affect our interactions and our longer-term relationships? And, importantly, in what ways might the context for our interactions— where we work and how—impact our racial emotions and also our behaviors and relationships? These are some of the questions that we will begin to explore in this chapter.

The goal of this book bears repeating: Despite an emphasis on racial emotion as race-based emotions experienced in interpersonal interaction, we search here not for ways to ease our own immediate negative emotions, tomorrow or next week—that may be too much to ask—but rather for ways that we can shift our institutions toward creating space for developing positive emotion in our interracial interactions over the longer term. This said, maybe we will find a little bit of both.

CLOSING IN OR REACHING OUT: RACIAL EMOTION IN INTERRACIAL INTERACTION

Research on interracial interaction in the field of social psychology has been under way since at least the early 1900s, though its emphasis has changed substantially over the years. In what is often called the first wave of research on interracial interaction, from the 1920s through the 1950s, the concept of prejudice dominated, with the goal being to identify the factors that cause an individual, especially a white individual, to have a prejudiced personality.[11] Prejudice was seen as something that attached consistently to a person. This was the era of Nazism and World War II, so it should not surprise us that emphasis was placed on distinguishing bad people who were prejudiced from good people who were not. Stigma in this wave too was studied as anomaly—as something attached to people who are not normal in some way. This meant those doing the stigmatizing and also those being stigmatized were considered not just separately from each other but as nonnormal.

Toward the end of this wave, Gordon Allport published *The Nature of Prejudice*, in which he outlined the key contextual factors for intergroup contact to reduce prejudice. Allport emphasized that intermixing alone is not sufficient to reduce prejudice. Rather, the contact hypothesis as framed by Allport states that regular interaction between members of different groups, provided it occurs under favorable circumstances, will tend to reduce intergroup prejudice. According to Allport: "Prejudice (unless deeply rooted in the character structure of the individual) may be reduced by equal status contact between majority and minority groups in the pursuit of common goals. The effect is greatly enhanced if this contact is sanctioned by institutional supports (i.e., by law, custom or local atmosphere), and provided it is of a sort that leads to the perception of common interests and common humanity between members of the two groups."[12]

Throughout this time, including in Allport's work, the focus was largely on whites. The racial experiences of Black people and other people of color generally were not explored. As two social scientists recently put it, Blacks were relegated "to passive objects who are 'reacted to' by Whites, rather than being active agents who may influence the interaction themselves."[13]

During a second wave, research began to emphasize that far from being an anomaly, prejudice and bias are commonplace and can operate even in the well-intentioned. Even so, the focus remained primarily on whites, though with increased attention to interactions.[14]

Beginning in the mid-1990s through to the present, researchers more regularly began to study whites and people of color as active participants in interactions, each with their own biases. Indeed, research in this third wave tends to take a relational approach to studying interracial interaction, making explicit the interdependent nature of white people and people of other races. A key feature of this approach is that not only are people's perceptions of others important; so too are their perceptions of themselves, perceptions of how they think others may perceive them, what is called "metaperception," and, of course, their emotions regarding these perceptions and resulting behaviors.

Taken together, the research on the contact hypothesis shows that intergroup contact reduces prejudice, especially for members of dominant groups. For a 2006 article, social psychologists Thomas F. Pettigrew and Linda R. Tropp conducted a quantitative meta-analysis of the contact hypothesis research literature.[15] The results of their study indicate that contact typically does reduce intergroup prejudice. Moreover, their study suggests that while establishing optimal conditions in the contact situation generally enhances the positive effects of intergroup contact, those conditions are not essential to prejudice reduction. This is good news. Moreover, the wealth of research on conditions and interrelations, especially interrelations as dynamic, tells us even more about what helps and doesn't help when it comes to positive interracial interactions in the long run.[16] We will visit some of this research in chapter 8 when we consider next steps.

Despite the increased focus beyond whites and especially on relations, much of the social science work on racial emotion has focused on interactions between Blacks and whites, only occasionally considering groups of color beyond Blacks or considering the intersection of race and sex or other relevant identity characteristics. This is troubling, to say the least, but much of the research that I relay here nonetheless reflects this reality.

It should also be clear by this point, but is worth reemphasizing: When I talk about the research involving racial emotion in different racial groups in this chapter and elsewhere, neither I nor the research on which I rely asserts that we as members of particular racial groups carry with us inherently different emotions. In other words, racial emotion refers to *any* emotion related to race, regardless of one's membership in a particular racial group at any particular moment in time. This is important because to use the term otherwise—to suggest that whites hold some racial emotions and people of color hold different racial emotions—would instantiate a static understanding of racial emotion as something that is bound within each of us depending on our race, and this would be not just plain wrong but also dangerous to our progress toward racial equality and justice.

HOW WE FEEL: COMMON RACIAL EMOTIONS

Before digging into the research in this area, we should acknowledge that generalizations from research on racial emotion cannot determine how any one person will feel or act in their own interracial interactions. We are each unique, with our own personalities, histories, and contexts for our interactions. Yet we can draw from the research some sense of what we might expect on the whole when it comes to racial emotion in the workplace. And here we can safely say that the research on interracial interactions suggests that we should expect negative emotional experiences in interracial interaction in most workplaces today. In general, we should expect emotions like fear, shame, anger, frustration, humiliation, and anxiety on the part of people of color at perceived discrimination and expectations that they will be judged according to stereotypes and biases. And we should also expect emotions like fear, anger, frustration, shame, and anxiety on the part of whites at the prospect of losing group-based advantage and being perceived as biased or labeled racist. I map the research along group lines here not because we are inherently different (indeed, some of these negative emotions stem from common concerns, such as concerns about how others view us), but because our experiences as members of various racial groups often *are* different. Moreover, racial emotion, like race, is experienced, valued, and shaped relationally, not in silos of statically conceived groups.[17] Whether we experience positive or negative racial emotions in interracial interaction depends in part on how our emotions are treated and shaped not just by ourselves but also by the world around us.

PEOPLE OF COLOR AND RACIAL EMOTION

We don't all see the world in the same way. Our experiences, our hopes and our fears, are different from one person to the next. We occupy different spaces—often racially segregated spaces, especially whites—and we tell different stories to ourselves and to others about racial discrimination and generally about how race is relevant in our lives. In "Perceptual Segregation," legal scholar Russell Robinson describes the voluminous literature that supports this point.[18] In survey after survey, including the most recent Gallup Poll, Black people report expecting discrimination against Blacks at a much higher rate than whites do.[19] Black people are also more likely than white people to interpret scenarios involving slow seating at a restaurant, refusing to show an apartment for the reason that it has "already been rented," and being turned down for a date by a white person as due to discrimination.[20]

Robinson says that we see these high numbers because Black people are likely to interpret the scenarios through an informational lens that suggests that discrimination is prevalent and through a definitional lens that includes as discrimination subtle forms of bias and insensitivity in addition to overt racial hostility.[21] He provides an example of a restaurant experience:

> Imagine that I conducted an experiment in which I randomly selected ten white people and ten black people and asked them to watch a scenario involving potential discrimination. The setting is a mostly white, fancy restaurant situated in a suburb at 8:00 pm on a Saturday. The only all-black party is an African American family, which is seated near the back of the restaurant. The parents try in vain several times to flag down the waiters to ask for menus and to order food. This goes on for ten minutes.

Based on existing research, Robinson predicts:

> If we asked our ten black and ten white people whether it is likely that race played a factor in the restaurant staff failing to attend to the black family, the black participants would be significantly more likely to reply that race was a factor. Specifically, the black participants would tend to recognize, recall, and consider different information than the white participants. For instance, the blacks might be keenly aware that the restaurant is dominated by white staff and patrons and the black family was seated near the back, while the white participants might say that they did not even notice race or think that the placement of the family's table might have correlated with race. The black participants might also take note that this is an upscale restaurant in a wealthy suburb, where black patrons might be relatively unusual, and potentially less welcome. By contrast, the white participants might focus on a race-neutral explanation: the fact that the incident occurred during prime dinner hours on a weekend and the possibility that staff may have just been busy, rather than racially motivated.[22]

We do not need to determine whether these interpretations are in any sense objectively true to understand that Black people and other people of color may come to interactions with an expectation of bias and discrimination.[23]

And from there, it is reasonable to expect people of color to experience negative emotions, emotions like anger and frustration, or shame and humiliation, when interacting with whites whom they perceive as biased, bigoted, or discriminating against them. The same is as true in the workplace as it is in the restaurant. We can expect a range of intensity in these emotions, just as we can expect a range of behaviors perceived as discriminatory or racist. A supervisor's use of a racial epithet or telling of a racial joke might involve stronger emotional reaction, for example, than a team member's one-time, subtle resistance to providing credit for contributions to a project. Even if a person of color does not attribute a specific outcome, such as a denial of a promotion, to discrimination, they may perceive the white person's actions as biased or racially hostile, which is enough to trigger negative emotions.

Research further suggests that people of color are likely to experience anxiety and fear before and during interracial interactions arising out of concerns about being judged according to stereotypes or otherwise of conforming to commonly held stereotypes about their group. This is the "metaperception" concept mentioned earlier. We not only perceive others in our interactions; we worry about those others' perceptions of us. Blacks, for example, expect whites to view Blacks generally as untrustworthy, aggressive, and not hardworking, and they expect whites to apply those stereotypes in interracial interaction.[24] In the same way, Asian Americans are aware that others expect them to be intelligent but unsociable, and Latin Americans believe that others perceive them as unintelligent or low-skilled and lacking in character.[25]

Social psychologist Claude Steele and colleagues spearheaded a wealth of research in this area, identifying what they call "stereotype threat."[26] Steele was interested in the implications of stereotype threat for everything from performances in the classroom and on the athletic field to how we feel in interracial interaction. Much of the early research focused on its role in understanding underperformance of women and people of color in academic settings. Steele found that when meta-stereotypes were triggered, when women were told, for example, that a task measured mathematical ability before they performed the task, they would underperform on the task. When those meta-stereotypes were dampened, in contrast, for example, when the same women were told that the task did not reveal differences in mathematical aptitude, they would perform equally as well as men.

Importantly for our interactions, the effects of this stereotype threat go beyond performance on specific tasks. Concern on the part of people of color about being judged according to stereotypes can lead to anxiety and other negative emotions prior to and during interactions with whites.[27] This anxiety may be variable, related to how heightened these meta-stereotypes or expectations of prejudice are. In one study, for example, the more a Black college roommate expected their white college roommate to be prejudiced against them, the more negative emotion they reported in interactions.[28]

WHITES AND RACIAL EMOTION

White people also assess behavior in interactions through particular informational and definitional lenses, and, like with all of us, these assessments affect the emotions that are experienced during interaction. Whites, in contrast to Blacks and other people of color, tend to believe that discrimination is not prevalent and to define discrimination narrowly as incidents involving overt expressions of racial hostility. Some of the recent research on this issue is especially concerning. The results of one survey from 2015, for example, suggest that 50 percent of whites in America believe that discrimination against whites is a problem equivalent to that of discrimination against Blacks. I say this is concerning because data on jobs and other measures of success and well-being overwhelming suggests otherwise: The statistics continue to indicate drastically poorer outcomes for Black Americans than for white Americans,[29] and there is plenty of research to suggest that discrimination continues to be one cause of these outcomes.[30]

Nonetheless, when we think about the racial emotion that we should expect in whites, because they perceive less discrimination generally and because they are less likely to attribute specific situations to discrimination, whites are likely to experience exasperation, frustration, and anger when Blacks or other racial minorities raise concerns about discrimination. Drawing on racial stereotypes, they may see people who raise these concerns as overly emotional or unduly angry. And they may interpret stated discrimination or racial bias concerns as "playing the race card" or otherwise trying to benefit from racial status.[31]

Related to this, whites can also experience fear and anxiety arising out of group-based perceived threats to social dominance.[32] As Gordon Allport put it back in 1954, "The hunger for status is matched by a haunting fear that one's status may not be secure. The effort to maintain a precarious position can bring with it an almost reflex disparagement to others."[33] Recent research, for example, finds greater negative emotion and favoring of more conservative policies and politicians when diversity is emphasized.[34] There is also a large body of research on what is called "social closure," meaning drawing boundaries around in-groups and setting others outside of those boundaries.[35] Job requirements and tests that match qualities of in-groups rather than actual requirements for doing a job well and information networks that advantage some over others are examples of structural results of these behaviors. We also see these behaviors in more microrelational encounters when, for example, people exhibit warmth toward the high-status in-group and coldness toward those outside of that group or, in extreme cases, when in-group members use harassment to build feelings of power and status.

We may also see pleasure as an emotion experienced by whites in interracial interactions, for while pleasure is understood as a positive emotion, in the race context it can emerge from dominance, which makes it overall a negative for relational outcomes. As sociologist Eduardo Bonilla-Silva describes, "Whites, whether consciously or not, participate in various ways in maintaining racial order, and, hence, on occasion, derive a degree of satisfaction from enforcing racial boundaries."[36] In extreme cases, like group-based harassment, this satisfaction can involve the racial emotion of pleasure.

In addition, whites—like their Black relational counterparts—experience negative emotion from social identity threat. In the case of whites, however, especially for whites who profess to subscribe to an egalitarian ideal, the meta-stereotype is that whites are racist or hold discriminatory biases. Whites therefore fear that they will act or be labeled as racist or biased in interracial interaction.

Social psychologists Samuel Gaertner and John Dovidio explain this anxiety as a product of "aversive racism."[37] The idea is that as more whites publicly and even privately subscribe to an egalitarian ideal, they are more likely to discriminate not in the old-fashioned, bigoted ways, but by making decisions in favor of whites when there is ambiguity. Moreover, because whites generally have less experience than Blacks and other people of color with interracial interaction, their own self-efficacy can be low, which further contributes to heightened anxiety.

In short, white Americans tend to find interracial interaction uncomfortable; they report experiencing negative affect and anxiety before and during interracial interaction, particularly when interacting with Black people. Indeed, whites are more likely than their Black relational partners to report that an interracial interaction was "uncomfortable, awkward, forced, and strained."[38] A meta-analysis of forty years of research on interracial interactions shows that although whites' expressed attitudes about their interracial interaction partners have become increasingly egalitarian, whites continue to report experiencing a negative emotional state during interaction.[39]

WHAT WE DO: ANTAGONISM, AVOIDANCE, AND ENGAGEMENT

Even more important than what we *feel* in our interracial interactions is what we *do* in response to and as part of those feelings. Our behaviors, after all, are what will determine whether our interactions are positive or negative over time. People experience emotion in interracial interaction as part of a dynamic interchange. They process and react to feelings in verbal and nonverbal ways that can affect the interaction in the moment and also the relationship in the longer term. In trying to understand racial emotion and the effects of racial emotion on our working relationships, it makes sense then to look at the research on our behaviors—sometimes called "coping strategies"—used in response to or in conjunction with our racial emotions. The language may be misleading here, for it tends to exaggerate cause and effect. In reality, it's not necessarily that emotions beget action; the two are almost always intertwined. Yet this research suggests that people tend to use one of three strategies in experiencing negative emotions (or sometimes even expected negative emotions, without even waiting for the emotions themselves to kick in) in interracial interaction: antagonism, avoidance, and engagement.

Antagonism

One way that we can manage our negative racial emotions like fear-related anxiety, frustration, or anger is by lashing out. This is when we get defensive and say something degrading about the other person to try to shift the focus away from ourselves and the emotions that we are feeling. We can easily imagine the extreme relational outcomes of antagonism as it emerges from negative racial emotion. In the workplace, antagonistic behavior might take form in sabotage, ridicule and harassment (including telling racial jokes and using racial epithets), poor reviews or write-ups for not following rules, disobeying orders, even physical altercations.

Antagonism is not always so obvious, however, and it can emerge out of something as simple as sensing reluctance on the part of the person with whom we are interacting. In one study, researchers conveyed to Black and white participants negative or positive feedback about their partner's openness to an interaction.[40] Both Black and white participants who received the negative feedback reported more anger and other-focused blame than did participants who received positive feedback. In a follow-up study, participants receiving the negative feedback about their partner's openness to an interaction also engaged in more hostile behavior—assigning them harder, less useful letters in a word-building task in which their partner would earn money for building words—even when they anticipated that their partner would be angry with the letter allocation.

These behaviors were studied in a lab so that the researchers could isolate a specific question for study. More subtle antagonistic behavior in the workplace might include not helping someone with an assignment when they ask or appear to need it, not being willing to cover them for a shift, or excluding them in meetings or keeping them out of the loop for knowing about promotional opportunities. People of color as well as white participants in interracial interaction can resort to antagonistic and hostile behavior, of course, but research suggests that whites, who are in positions of power more often than people of color in many workplaces, are more likely to turn to antagonism as a coping strategy.[41]

Avoidance

When people feel threatened in or by an interaction, the most common behavioral strategy for reducing the threat—and the anxiety that goes along with it—is avoidance. People avoid interactions that they expect to trigger negative emotions.

In one study, white Americans who had previously completed a questionnaire measuring intergroup anxiety came to a lab for a study that they were told involved either different-race or same-race interactions.[42] Once the participants arrived and were told about the study, the researchers feigned technical difficulties and asked the participants to reschedule their session for a later date. Participants whose questionnaire results indicated they were highly anxious about interacting with African Americans were three times more likely to be "no shows" the following week when they believed the session involved interacting with African Americans than when they believed that the session involved interacting with whites.

Legal scholar Sheryll Cashin tells a story that tees up this reality in a more anecdotal way in *The Failures of Integration*.[43] Cashin and her husband (both African American) joke that when they arrive late to a flight where seating is unassigned, they hope that there is a Black male at the front of the line and that he will take one of the seats up front in the plane when he boards. "At least four out of five times, we can depend on the seats next to that black person being empty, even if his row is far up front, begging for the taking. . . . I smile warmly at my black brother as I plop down next to him."[44]

Avoidance can also take more subtle forms. Interaction in many settings may be difficult to avoid altogether, but individuals with an underlying desire to avoid or escape the interaction may engage in other avoidance-related behaviors, such as decreased eye contact, less smiling, greater fidgeting, more hesitant speech, and physically moving away.[45] People engaging in avoidance behavior are also more likely to have shorter interactions, closing them out as soon as possible.

In addition to awkward, misunderstood signals in interactions, avoidance might also take form as hesitancy to interact in informal settings, such as waiting until someone is out of the kitchen prep area before heading in, or deciding not to go to a group lunch. As one Black female nurse noted in a study on race and hierarchy in the hospital setting, "I've become just . . . not nearly as open as I used to be with my colleagues."[46] Even understanding that we often have to interact across racial lines at work, those interactions might be shorter and less productive if we are engaging in avoidance behaviors as our coping strategy.

Whites, moreover, are likely to engage in the microsocial strategy of colorblindness, refusing to acknowledge or mention race even when it is relevant. This is another form of avoidance. Research suggests that perceptual differentiation of race emerges in humans as young as three months of age, yet many parents avoid talking about race, and white parents tend to teach their children that it is wrong to see race.[47] Studies suggest that white adults are especially likely to refuse to "see" or mention race in interracial interactions.[48] In one study of adults, researchers had people engage in a photo identification task in pairs. One person would be asked to describe a person while the other would try to identify the person's photo from several. When a white person was paired with a Black partner, they often avoided mentioning race, even when race was helpful in identifying the photo requested. Further studies suggest the more worried a white person is about appearing nonbiased, the more likely they are to avoid mentioning race in an interracial interaction.

Avoidance, while not as extreme as antagonistic behavior, can also have disastrous effects on interactions and relationships. Whites who adopt avoidance, including colorblindness, as their strategy for coping with anxiety in interaction view the interaction as unpleasant and report that they want to avoid future interactions with their partners.[49] Ironically, they also come across as prejudiced and avoidant to their partners, which in turn can lead to avoidant behavior by the partner.

Other studies show that even something as simple as priming experimental subjects with Black or white faces before an interview affected whites' avoidant behavior (they engaged in more avoidant behavior when they were shown a Black face prior to the interview) and provoked avoidant behavior in their interaction partners. Indeed, not only is avoidant behavior more likely to be perceived as biased by Black interaction partners; whites and Blacks alike are likely to attribute avoidant behavior in others to personal rejection and social exclusion. In one recent study, for example, Blacks and whites both tended to explain their own avoidance in interracial interactions "in terms of fear of personal rejection due to their race," but to explain out-group members' avoidance of interracial interactions "as due to lack of interest."[50]

Finally, avoidant behaviors can lead to "downward spirals" into hostility and distrust as each person in the relationship distrusts the other and misinterprets the other's behavior as hostile.[51] "He doesn't seem to like me" turns into anger at the rebuff and ensuing altercations or other antagonistic behaviors.

Engagement

Some individuals who experience anxiety in interracial interactions seek not to antagonize or avoid the interaction but to engage. And high levels of engagement can result not just in more interracial interactions but in more positive impressions during those interracial interactions. Indeed, some research even suggests that high anxiety in whites about appearing biased in an interaction, together with low desire to antagonize or avoid the situation, leads to more pleasant interactions for interaction partners than lower anxiety. The more we worry that we will be judged as prejudiced, in other words, the harder we may try to show that we are not prejudiced.[52]

Yet individuals also vary on their willingness to engage. While some surveys suggest that there has been an overall shift away from express color-conscious supremacy views on the part of whites, we have also seen a rise in white supremacy groups in recent years. The Southern Poverty Law Center has documented an increase in alt-right groups that expose views that the "white identity" is under attack and that use rhetoric that is specifically "racist, anti-immigrant, anti-Semitic, and anti-feminist."[53] Believing strongly in these racist ideologies will, of course, affect racial emotions and behaviors in interracial interactions.

Whites who are personally motivated (rather than externally motivated) to be nonprejudiced are also more likely to engage.[54] Internally motivated people seek to act and appear nonprejudiced out of dedication to egalitarianism, while externally motivated people act from a fear of negative social consequences. It turns out that internally motivated people generally tend to focus on their relational partners' concerns, while externally motivated people tend to focus on themselves and their own behaviors. In fact, some research suggests that internal motivation may be especially helpful because it may lead whites to be more respectful in interactions with Blacks. Generally speaking, given awareness of stereotypes, whites are concerned about being liked in interracial interactions while Blacks are concerned about being respected.[55] These different "impression management goals," as researchers call them, can lead to incompatible behaviors. A white person might try to elicit liking with flattery, for example, and this may appear patronizing to a Black person who is trying to elicit respect. When whites are internally motivated, researchers found that they were more likely to be concerned about showing their Black partner respect in an imagined interaction.

Expectations about one's ability to make a desired impression in interracial interactions and about the likelihood of an out-group member responding positively also influence anxiety and avoidance behavior. In particular, people who perceive their personal resources for coping with a perceived identity threat are high—meaning they believe that they can overcome the meta-stereotype—are more likely to respond by expending effort and energy to achieve a positive outcome.[56]

Context also plays an important role. By context, I mean the environment in which an interaction takes place. Context can be in time, physical space, relation structures, such as status, or overarching culture, such as in framing of work or goals; it is often a combination of all of these and more. For years, sociologists have been emphasizing demographics in the area of stereotyping and bias. People of color are less likely to be judged according to stereotypes when they are one among many people of color than they are when they are one among just a few.[57] Dividing people physically into racial groups can also result in people preferring to interact with in-group members and avoiding contact with out-group members. Indeed, the spatial features of our workplaces affect the frequency, duration, and conditions for our interactions. Segregation, not surprisingly, and also the simple architectures of our workplaces, including layouts, offerings like food and childcare spaces, and temperature, among other things, have been shown to affect relations at work.[58]

Beyond demographics and physical context, framing for the interaction can also influence emotions and behaviors. Social psychologists Jennifer Crocker and Julia Garcia, for example, find that getting individuals to frame goals in terms of an ecosystem (in which people focus on their connection to others) rather than in terms of an egosystem (in which people focus on their own desires or needs) can reduce identity threat and lead to engagement and more positive emotions toward others, such as feelings of compassion, love, and empathy.[59] Other research in this vein suggests it helps when whites adopt learning goals for an interaction. In one recent study, researchers asked whites to focus either on learning about their partner during their interaction or on presenting themselves to their partner. The researchers then observed and coded participants' nonverbal behavior during an interaction with either a white or Black partner. Particularly when discussing a race-sensitive topic with a cross-race partner, "participants who were instructed to focus on learning maintained longer eye contact, averted their gaze less often, used fewer speech dysfluencies (e.g., 'like,' and 'umm'), and exhibited fewer fidgeting behaviors than those who were instructed to focus on how they present themselves to their partner."[60] Along the same lines, "If White and Black students focus on their common group membership as students of their university instead of their racial group memberships, then the dynamics of their interactions are likely to be more positive."[61]

As we will see in part II, context can also be a matter of institutional constructs for emotion. As institutions approach racial emotion, they value some over others and create and support racial emotion repertoires that benefit some emotions and actions over others. This is why looking closely at our institutions' approach to racial emotion is so important.

A positive interaction is not necessarily an interaction without negative emotion, but one where negative emotions are lessened and especially where relational partners can leverage their negative emotions to engage in more positive ways. Over time, as interactional partners do more engaging and less antagonizing and avoiding,, we should expect fewer and less intense negative emotions in interactions with that same partner and possibly beyond. Moreover, we should expect that when negative emotions do arise in an interaction—when, for example, a sensitive racial topic emerges or mistakes are made—the parties will be better equipped to engage in conversation about that topic without rupturing the relationship. One activist of color in a study of white antiracist practices put it this way:

> Because many people are not willing to expose themselves and be vulnerable to misunderstandings, which is part of the game, then they develop a shield and never really go beyond sort of appearances and always remaining sort of aloof. That sense of aloofness has always been an issue in developing true interracial organizations and struggles. So you need to break those barriers and the only way is by making mistakes, by saying silly things occasionally, and then getting mad and then sort of getting smart and then moving on.[62]

There is little reason to believe that learning about our racial emotions alone will lead to more, or more positive, interactions. Instead, we will need to actively engage in interracial interactions, and we will need to act beyond our interpersonal relationships to build the kinds of context and space at work that better allow for our productive engagement. This is where our institutions come in. Institutions, it turns out, may be one of the best places to start changing our relations.

PART II OUR INSTITUTIONS
        AND RACIAL EMOTION

In part I, we learned about racial emotion, including some of the racial emotions we might expect in interracial interactions in the workplace, emotions such as frustration, shame, and anger, and what these racial emotions may mean for our relationships at work. The next part exposes how two of our institutions—employment discrimination law and work organizations—approach racial emotion at work today. At this point, we take a turn decidedly away from the micro (our feelings and behaviors in individual, interracial relationships) to think about how our institutions affect our racial emotions and relationships.

We start this part with a focus on racial emotion in legal cases brought under Title VII—the employment discrimination provision of the federal Civil Rights Act of 1964. Racial emotion in particular is misunderstood in especially troubling ways in law, which sends signals to employees about discrimination and their rights and also to employers about what amounts to discrimination and what can and should be done about it. The statute itself says little about what discrimination means or how it can be proved in court. Instead, years of judicial interpretation, including by the U.S. Supreme Court, have set down some parameters for these cases.

The next two chapters address some of those legal parameters, but the goal is much larger and more holistic: to expose how some judges react to racial emotion when it is revealed in employment discrimination cases brought under Title VII. Not all judges will react in the same way, but these cases show judges closing racial emotion out of antidiscrimination concern. By this I mean that their conceptions of discrimination prohibited by Title VII focus on states of mind at discrete, static moments in time and on cool, cognitive processing and stereotyping over hotter emotional impulse and feeling. We also see judges favoring some racial emotions over others, erecting a high barrier for people of color and yet coming quickly to the defense or protection of whites who may perceive themselves as accused of being biased or racist. Moreover, we will begin to see the burden that this approach places on people of color.

Our work organizations are likely to take a similar approach to racial emotion, albeit in somewhat different ways. Here we can look both at the managerial literature and at research based on that literature to discern how organizations are likely to treat emotion and racial emotion. We can also look at recent research on what organizations are doing in response to increased calls for managing diversity as well as research on what organizations do in response to complaints of bias or discrimination.

The Law and Racial Emotion

In the next two chapters we delve into the law's current approach to racial emotion. A quick note on methodology: Several of the cases discussed in these chapters are well-known Supreme Court cases, although often their deeper stories have not yet been told. To find many of the lesser-known lower court decisions in these chapters, I ran multiple searches in online databases of decided legal cases using various search terms and also combed legal scholarship for relevant cases. Sometimes additional cases were located from citations in judicial opinions. I use the cases in these chapters to illustrate what some judges are doing. Many cases go through trial or otherwise resolve (including through settlement but also nonjudicial settings such as arbitration) without written judicial opinions that show up in a legal database. In cases with facts similar to those that I discuss here, another judge may have come out another way. Moreover, because of the nature of the database search approach (using keywords like "epithet" or "N-word" or "altercation"), the cases tend to be on the more extreme end of racial emotion and relational consequences. Some of the cases are also older, especially the Supreme Court cases, even as many are quite recent, decided within the last several years. Older cases can be worth considering when they are Supreme Court cases laying down the law (or rationale for the law) and also because even seemingly run-of-the-mill lower court decisions can have a ripple effect on later positions.

One other note, this one cautionary: Some of the cases in the next two chapters involve extreme racialized behavior, including use of racial epithets. For the most part, except in a few situations where the word was used with emphasis on meaning or with intention by the author or speaker, I have edited to use "n——(s)" rather than the full word. Nonetheless, together, and even separately, many of the cases relayed here will evoke strong emotions in readers.

3 Law: Closing Racial Emotion Out of Antidiscrimination Concern

Law does not sit idly by while people go about their lives. It sets rules for our behaviors, from limits on how much we can drink before we drive to when a killing can be justified, and it also sets sometimes explicit expectations about the feeling and display of emotion. These feeling rules include things like shifting the severity of a crime when killing is spurred by a fit of rage, or easing penalties upon showing of remorse. But the influence of law in constructing emotions and emotion repertoires is often subtler than that. For example, through its rules on who can marry, law shapes expectations about who is capable of romantic love, and through its rules and rulings in rape and domestic violence cases, it constructs repertoires about what rape or domestic violence victims ought to feel and how they ought to express their feelings.[1]

In short, a key point at the outset here is that law is not only constructing and shaping our views about rights and responsibilities around discrimination in work, including what can be done to reduce discrimination; it is playing a role in constructing our emotions, their desirability, who is responsible for them, and how they should be managed and expressed. This has always been true for law and emotion and it is no less true when it comes to law, racial emotion, and discrimination.

We often think of law as legal rules, sometimes but not always passed by Congress in the form of statutes. Title VII of the Civil Rights Act, though, is a statute that leaves a substantial amount of room for judges to decide what the legal rules are.[2] Moreover, as with any statute (or even a law made entirely by judges), judges are human beings who inevitably interpret and define the law on a case-by-case basis as they make decisions about whether a case should be dismissed at an early stage or whether it should go to trial, among other things. In this chapter, we see three often interrelated and overlapping ways that judges close racial emotion out of antidiscrimination concern in their interpretation and application of Title VII law: (1) by refusing to see racial emotion when it occurs; (2) by categorizing emotion in interracial interaction when they see it as "personal" and thereby nonracial; and (3) by judging the racial emotion that they do acknowledge as unreasonable.

IGNORING RACIAL EMOTION: "I'LL TELL YOU WHAT I SEE"

One way judges close racial emotion out of antidiscrimination concern is by narrowing legal inquiries to focus closely on certain moments and behaviors. I call this "I'll Tell You What I See" because it reflects judicial power in determining what counts in proving (or defending) discrimination claims. Judges use this power to ignore relations generally, and in doing so they also ignore racial emotion as it arises in those relations. In these cases, the judges often don't even get to the point of considering the racial emotion experienced in interaction because it falls entirely outside the view of their lens.

A Mind and a Target

Title VII of the Civil Rights Act makes it unlawful for an employer to make employment decisions "because of" a person's race.[3] The statute doesn't require that bias be operating in the mind of the final decision maker, such as the supervisor who makes the promotion decision. It would be enough, for example, if a Black employee received poor reviews because he was

Black, especially if those reviews resulted in a negative promotion decision. This is clear law laid down by the Supreme Court in numerous decisions.[4] In application of the law, though, judges have often had a hard
time seeing past the state of mind of the final decision maker at the precise
moment when the decision was made. They find a variety of ways to
narrow the inquiry to this place and time (a single mind and moment in
time), thereby closing the emotion experienced in day-to-day interactions
(racial or otherwise) out of their legal inquiry and of our antidiscrimination conversations.

Plaintiffs sometimes seek to prove discrimination with statements of a
decision maker that reflect that decision maker's racial bias. Often these
statements occur in the context of an interaction between the plaintiff and
the decision maker. One way judges ignore racial emotion is by downplaying or excluding these statements.

The case of *Ash v. Tyson Foods* shows judges doing this and at the same
time shows how language and behavior can evoke racial emotion in relations, which makes it a good case to start with.[5] The case involved claims
of race-based discrimination brought by two Black men, Anthony Ash and
John Hithon. Both men worked as superintendents at a Tyson Foods poul-
try processing plant in Gadsen, Alabama. In 1995, Ash and Hithon
applied for promotion to two open shift manager positions. The positions
went to white men.

In support of his claim of discrimination, Ash submitted evidence that
Thomas Hatley, a white man and the plant manager responsible for the
promotion decisions, called Ash and Hithon each "boy" at least once in
their working relationship. On one occasion, Ash and his wife, who also
worked at Tyson Foods, heard Hatley use "boy" to refer to Ash in the workplace cafeteria. When Ash's wife told Hatley that her husband was not a
"boy," Hatley "just looked at [her] with a smirk on his face like it was
funny and then he walked off."[6]

What emotions might Ash and Hatley have experienced in this and
other encounters where Hatley referred to Ash as "boy"? Let's start with
Ash. How might Ash have felt in being referred to as "boy" by his white
supervisor at the plant? We can draw some insight on this question from
later testimony of Ash in a rehearing of Hithon's case. The testimony goes
like this: "It was break time, it was lunch time. And we were just sitting in

the cafeteria having lunch. And Mr. Hatley walks up to the table without saying anything, but he just said, 'Boy, you better get going.' So I looked at him. I was shocked that he said it, because, you know, I felt like he said it in a mean and derogatory way."

Ash also testified that Hatley's use of the word was offensive to him:

ASH: Because, you know, being in the South, and everybody know[s] being in the South, a white man says boy to a black man, that's an offensive word.

QUESTION: What do you equate that to, using the word "boy" to a black man?

ASH: I equate that to just a racial comment because you might as well use the "N" word if you are going to say that.[7]

Of course, we cannot know with certainty what specific emotions Ash or Hatley experienced during this interchange or in future interactions, but from this testimony we might expect Ash experienced racial sadness, shame, anger, or frustration at the use of the term. At a later point in the case, a group of prominent civil rights leaders submitted a brief describing the term as a "racial epithet," which "if not a proxy for 'n——' is at the very least a close cousin."[8] They detailed the use of the term during slavery and segregation to reinforce African Americans' "racially subordinate status" and to "intimidate them and to 'put them in their place' when they threatened the racial order." The brief also quoted Dr. Martin Luther King's "Letter from Birmingham Jail" in which he wrote: "When your first name becomes 'nigger,' your middle name becomes 'boy' (however old you are) and your last name becomes 'John' . . . then you will understand why we find it difficult to wait."[9]

What about Hatley? Thinking about the "smirk" on his face and assuming that he did say it in a "mean and derogatory way," we might expect Hatley to have experienced something like racial pleasure at his use of the subordinating and racially charged term, and maybe anger or annoyance in response to Ash's (or his wife's) objection. Again, we cannot know for sure what racial emotions either man experienced in these encounters. But we don't need to know with certainty to understand that this interchange may be relevant to Ash's claim of discrimination in the promotion decision made by Hatley.

What then did the judges do with this evidence? It's actually a long story, but here's the short of it:

Ash's and Hithon's claims went together to a jury. The men presented a variety of evidence, including that Hatley did not base his decisions on the written qualifications for manager laid out at the plant, that Ash and Hithon were more qualified than the white men placed in the positions, and that Hatley had called them "boy" on several occasions.[10] The jury decided in their favor, awarding them each $250,000 in damages. The trial judge in the case, at the request of Tyson Foods, then used a procedure known as "judgment as a matter of law" to overturn the jury's decision and to grant judgment in favor of Tyson Foods. Judges are allowed to do this so long as they find that no reasonable jury could have found in favor of Ash and Hithon on the evidence presented at trial. In granting the judgment, the judge ignored the evidence that Hatley called Ash "boy," stating that "even if Hatley made these statements, it cannot be found, without more, that they were racial in nature."[11]

Ash and Hithon appealed the trial judge's decision to a panel of three judges in the appellate court. These judges affirmed the trial judge's decision on Ash's claim, stating, "While the use of 'boy' when modified by a racial classification like 'black' or 'white' is evidence of discriminatory intent, the use of 'boy' alone is not evidence of discrimination."[12]

Ash appealed this decision to the Supreme Court of the United States. The Supreme Court does not have to take the cases that are appealed to it; it gets to decide whether to take them. The Court took this one, and reversed the court of appeals decision, sending the case back for further consideration. In doing so, it issued a short, unanimous opinion in which it expressed concern about the seemingly bright line drawn by the court of appeals, that "boy" is only racial when modified by "black" or "white." According to the Supreme Court, "The speaker's meaning may depend on various factors including context, inflection, tone of voice, local custom, and historical usage. Insofar as the Court of Appeals held that modifiers or qualifications are necessary in all instances to render the disputed term probative of bias the court's decision is erroneous."[13]

When the court of appeals revisited Ash's case, however, it again granted judgment for Tyson Foods, this time using a different tactic. The panel of three judges began by reasserting their view that the "usages were conversational" and "non-racial," and then they went on to find further reason to downplay the evidence. They said: "Even if somehow construed as racial, we conclude that the comments were ambiguous stray remarks not uttered in the context of the decisions at issue and are not sufficient circumstantial evidence of bias to provide a reasonable basis for a finding of racial discrimination in the denial of the promotion."[14]

This second decision by the court of appeals stood, and Tyson Foods therefore won the case brought by Ash. For other reasons, the Hithon case was retried, and after two more appellate decisions, a jury verdict in favor of Hithon was upheld.[15] We will talk more about Hithon's case later in this chapter. What's more important than the outcome for either of the cases is to see that by labeling Hatley's comments as "ambiguous stray remarks," the judges in Ash's case narrowed their lens to focus closely on the time of the promotion decision. In doing so, they closed the relationship between Ash and Hatley—and any emotion experienced as part of that relationship—entirely out of the discrimination inquiry.[16]

One more example: In this earlier case, the court described the Black male plaintiff, James Bolden, as "a sensitive and serious person working in a shop filled with boorish churls."[17] Bolden worked as an electrician for PRC, Inc., for eight years. The court acknowledged that Bolden was "badgered frequently by several of his coworkers" but pointed out that "only two of his coworkers made overtly racial remarks." One of those coworkers warned Bolden, "You better be careful because we know people in [the] Ku Klux Klan," and used terms like "honky" and the "N-word" in Bolden's presence. He also drew a cartoon in front of Bolden that Bolden perceived to be race based. Other coworkers called Bolden "dickhead," "dumbshit," and other similar names, and one rigged his chair during a lunch break so that the back would fall off when Bolden leaned against it. The court of appeals affirmed the district court's grant of summary judgment for the defendant in the case. Similar to judgment as a matter of law after a trial, the summary judgment procedure allows a judge to grant judgment for a defendant prior to a jury trial if the judge finds that no reasonable jury could find for the plaintiff. In affirming the trial judge's grant of the motion, the appellate judges reasoned that the "overtly racial remarks" by the two coworkers were not sufficiently pervasive and therefore were not actionable. "Instead of sporadic racial slurs," said the court, "there must be a steady barrage of opprobrious racial comments."[18] Moreover, according to the court, because the racialized comments were made two years prior to when the "general ridicule became prevalent," it was not reasonable to infer that the "general torment and taunting" was racially discriminatory.[19]

Targets

Some judges also confine their inquiry to behavior or comments made in the plaintiff's presence. This protects white racialized behaviors so long as they are performed behind closed doors or are general rather than targeted at the person who brings the lawsuit. For example, in *McCann v. Tillman*, the plaintiff, a Black woman and corrections officer for Mobile County, Alabama, claimed that she suffered a race-based hostile work environment in the county sheriff's office.[20] She alleged she was called "girl" by her supervisor, and two Black male officers were called "boy." She also alleged the sheriff referred to a former employee as a "n—— bitch," and remarked that "he had never received the 'n—— vote' and that he didn't want it." In granting judgment for the defendant, the court found it significant that the remarks made by the sheriff were not directed toward McCann or made in her presence.[21]

In some jurisdictions, courts of appeals have expressly held that statements or behavior need not be targeted at the plaintiff to be considered as evidence of discrimination, and the trial court judges in those jurisdictions must follow this holding. But even in these jurisdictions, cases similar to *McCann* still arise. Another recent case, for example, involved a claim of racial harassment by a Black man at a concrete plant.[22] In addition to other evidence, he presented evidence that a white coworker who was assigned to clean an area called "the pit" told coworkers that he wouldn't do it and declared in writing on his assignment sheet, "that's a n—— job." The judge in the case granted judgment for the employer, stating that "the severity [of racial epithets] is reduced when the slur is not directed at the plaintiff himself." The judge went on to explain that there was no evidence "that [the white man] wrote the note for Plaintiff specifically, as opposed to writing it for the whole mixing department to see."[23]

When Tempers Flare: Unreasonable Conduct and Insubordination

So far, we've seen judges ignoring racial emotion by narrowing their inquiry to specific individuals—often a specific decision maker's state of mind—at a precise moment in time, excluding or downplaying what they call evidence of "stray remarks" on the part of a decision maker and harassing behavior that is not directly targeted at the plaintiff. Another way judges ignore racial emotion ("I'll Tell You What I See") is by focusing in closely on the behavior of the plaintiff without any consideration of the relations that may have given rise to that behavior.

It shouldn't surprise us that we sometimes see antagonistic behavior associated with racial emotion in interracial interactions, especially when the interactions are charged with insults or racial epithets. Here is an example, from a much earlier case than many here, but still helpful for illustration:

Donald Edwards, a Black man, worked at a manufacturing plant in Hayward, California.[24] The plant manager and Edwards's boss at the time, Donald Johnson, was a white man, and Edwards and Johnson had a difficult relationship. Edwards complained several times that Johnson was "criticizing the manner in which he worked, unfairly allotting overtime, and unfairly assigning routes." Meetings between the union, NAACP, and president and vice president of the company resulted in a recommendation that Johnson and Edwards "should attempt to work out their problems." One day later, Edwards walked into the break room at the plant when Johnson was having coffee with another employee. Johnson greeted Edwards, "Good morning, sunshine." Edwards responded, "Don't call me 'sunshine,' you motherfucker. My name is Donald Edwards." Johnson responded, "You're fired. You're fired for gross insubordination. Go home." Johnson and Edwards proceeded to Johnson's office, where Johnson said to Edwards, "I finally got you, you n—— bastard." Johnson and Edwards were next seen coming out of Johnson's office. Edwards threw Johnson against a wall, over a desk, and onto the floor. Edwards was fired directly after the incident.

The judge in the case found that Edwards was fired for a nonracial reason, attacking a superior at work, and not because of his race. Under the union contract, Edwards could not be fired for uttering the obscenity to Johnson, and the president of the company testified at trial that he would have reversed Johnson's decision if he had been given the opportunity. But, according to the court, "Plaintiff did not give defendant an opportunity to review Johnson's initial action because instead of following normal grievance procedures as he was required to do, plaintiff attacked Johnson within minutes after he was fired by him." The court took no note of the fact that Johnson had uttered the racial slur right before Edwards attacked.

Courts take a similar approach in cases involving claims of retaliation, where the plaintiff alleges their conduct was part of their opposition to racially discriminatory treatment, whether their own or others'. While Title VII protects employees from retaliation for opposing discriminatory practices by their employers,[25] most courts require that the plaintiff's opposing conduct be "reasonable" in order for retaliation in response to that conduct to be unlawful.[26] Judges often do not take into account the history of a relationship in determining whether the plaintiff's opposition conduct was reasonable, even when that history is highly racially charged.

In other cases, the plaintiff engages in what a judge believes is "insubordination" in an interaction. Kenneth Clack, a Black man, worked as a line worker at a Rock-Tenn recycling plant in Chattanooga, Tennessee, for almost twenty years, from 1986 to 2005.[27] For the first ten years of his employment, things seem to have gone relatively smoothly, but starting in 1995, Clack filed numerous grievances with his union steward and ultimately a federal lawsuit alleging discrimination. In 2000, Clack and Rock-Tenn entered into a confidential settlement agreement, though Clack filed several more grievances over the next few years, including one against his foreman, Bill Murphy.

On February 1, 2005, Murphy instructed Clack to clean up some debris that had fallen near the machine where Clack was working. Clack considered the work outside of his job duties and saw Murphy's action as race-based harassment. Clack objected to doing the work, and when Murphy insisted, Clack walked off of the floor to contact his next-in-line supervisor about the incident. Murphy wrote Clack up for insubordination and submitted the write-up to the general manager of the plant, William Lancaster.

The next day, Lancaster met with Clack to "get his side of the story," and then terminated his employment. Clack filed suit claiming the termination was discriminatory.

During the trial phase of the lawsuit, Clack presented testimony of Ted Bonine, a former foreman at Rock-Tenn who had worked with Murphy from 1999 until approximately 2002. Here is what Bonine said:

> [Murphy] repeatedly expressed his opinion that the black employees were generally lazy and "Good for nothing".... As a general rule, Mr. Murphy would always treat the African American employees more harshly than white employees in almost every nuance of the job. [He] also seemed to single out Mr. Kenneth Clack for his racially based rage. [He] was aware of the outcome of Mr. Clack's previous lawsuit and spoke of it on several occasions. It seemed to make him angry. On one occasion I went with Mr. Murphy to Norcross, Georgia for training. During that trip, Mr. Murphy repeatedly spoke of Mr. Clack on a racially offensive level. Both on the above trip and at other times, Mr. Murphy made the comments "KC is nothing but a fucking n——" and "I am going to get rid of him." Mr. Murphy also referred to Mr. Clack as a "black mother fucker." On one occasion in 2001, Mr. Murphy made the comment that he was going to throw Mr. Clack in the pulper and make him into paper. On another occasion, Mr. Murphy stated he wanted to "string him up." I complained to management about Murphy but to my knowledge nothing was done about it. It was my observation, experience and belief that Murphy's general attitude and feelings were known throughout the facility. As a foreman, I believe that I respected all of the employees and felt that I had a good relationship with the black employees. This made Mr. Murphy angry and he commented that I was too friendly with the black employees. He would also become angry when I would defend a black employee or ask him to stop his offensive language.[28]

The trial judge excluded Bonine's testimony on the ground that it involved behavior of Murphy that took place several years before the 2005 incident and on the ground that it reflected bias by Murphy, and not bias by Lancaster, the ultimate decision maker. The judge granted judgment as a matter of law for Rock-Tenn, ruling that no reasonable fact finder could find in favor of Clack.

On appeal, the three-judge panel affirmed the trial decision, but on slightly different grounds, and with a dissenting opinion. Two of the judges on the three-judge panel held that Lancaster's independent investigation and ultimate decision that Clack was insubordinate rendered Murphy's race-based actions irrelevant.[29]

In her dissent, judge Karen Nelson Moore insisted the judges should have used a broader lens to inquire whether Lancaster should have investigated the possibility that Murphy's racial animus may have played a role in the incident and subsequent write-up, especially given the evidence that McDougal and Lancaster knew of prior racially hostile behavior by Murphy generally and specifically toward Clack. According to Judge Moore: "Instead, they conducted an investigation with blinders on, narrowly focused on the details of Clack's conduct. . . . [They] never inquired into what role, if any, Murphy's racial animus may have played in the incident. Not surprisingly given the limited focus of the investigation, Lancaster's explanation of his decision to terminate Clack had a similarly narrow focus on Clack's alleged misconduct, without any discussion of the potential role of Murphy's racism."[30]

CATEGORIZING RACIAL EMOTION:
IT'S PERSONAL, NOT RACIAL

In this second category of cases, judges do see the emotion in interactions, especially when the emotional responses are high. When some judges see emotion in interracial interaction, however, they reach to categorize it as solely personal and thereby not racial.

Legal scholars have amply documented a growing reluctance on the part of courts to infer discrimination based on a plaintiff's evidence showing that the reason put forward for a decision by the employer is false.[31] For example, a Black person might be fired, and the employer says it is because she was late five times in violation of company policy. If she could show in her HR record that she was late only three times, a judge might infer from the fact that the employer put forward a false reason that race-based discrimination was a reason for the decision. Data suggests that judges are less willing to draw this inference today than they were twenty or thirty years ago.[32] The decisions in the district court and court of appeals in *Ash v. Tyson Foods* discussed earlier show a similar unwillingness on the part of judges to construe use of the term once readily understood as race based, such as "boy" to refer to a Black man, as racial. Categorizing emotion in interracial interaction as personal and thereby not racial fits this basic mold.

But judicial assumptions about emotion go further than a general reluctance to characterize emotion as racial. When some judges see emotion in interactions, particularly negative emotion as it spills over into friction and acrimonious relationships, they take the "personal" nature of that emotion as evidence that the emotion was not racial. Another way of saying this is that the rawness of our emotions in our individual relationships can be used against us as reason to believe that the relationship went awry for nonracial reasons. When judges do this, they may be drawing on their own (mistaken) views of discrimination as driven solely by emotionless, generalized, group-based bias or animus. These judges miss that emotion can be both highly personal *and* racial.

The Supreme Court's opinion in a case called *St. Mary's Honor Center v. Hicks* arguably set the stage for judicial willingness to categorize emotion as personal and thereby nonracial.[33] The case involved a claim by Melvin Hicks, a Black man, who worked in corrections at St. Mary's Honor Center, a minimal-security correctional facility operated by the Missouri Department of Corrections and Human Resources. Hicks claimed he was demoted in his position and later discharged because of his race in violation of Title VII.

Hicks was hired in 1978 as a correctional officer, and he was promoted to a supervisory position two years later. Several years after that, the head of the department instituted several supervisory changes that resulted in John Powell, a white man, becoming Hicks's immediate supervisor and Steve Long, another white man, becoming the new superintendent, who oversaw them both. After Powell and Long came on board, Hicks's disciplinary record took a downward turn. He was cited for several violations and demoted. When Hicks was notified of his demotion, he "was shaken by the news and requested the rest of the day off." His request was granted, but as he was leaving, he got into a heated exchange with Powell, which resulted in Hicks asking if Powell wanted to "step outside." Based on this incident, Hicks was discharged.

The trial judge heard the evidence in the case and found that the reasons put forward by the correctional facility for Hicks's demotion were fabricated by Powell and Long and that Powell provoked the threat that formed the basis of the discharge. Nonetheless, the judge said while Hicks had proven "the existence of a crusade to terminate him," he had not proven "that the crusade was racially rather than personally motivated."[34] The court cited no evidence suggesting a nonracial source of the acrimonious relationship between Hicks and Powell. Indeed, Powell had testified that he harbored no personal animus against Hicks.

Legal scholars have shown that courts after *Hicks* shifted toward presuming personal, nonracial bias in cases where plaintiffs seek to prove discrimination by showing the employer's reason false.[35] The law has long allowed plaintiffs to succeed in an employment discrimination case by proving the employer's provided reason false, but after *Hicks* courts started requiring evidence of racial bias in addition to any proof that the reason provided was false. The Supreme Court ultimately held that no racial bias evidence is required.[36] Yet courts continue to presume personal animosity if evidence of racial bias is not submitted.

As I mentioned earlier, though, this presumption about emotion in interracial interactions goes further than a mere tendency to label interpersonal difficulties nonracial. Some judges seem to think that animosity and antagonistic behavior in interpersonal, interracial relationships means the emotion (and related behavior) *can't* be race based. It's as if when people don't like each other, their dislike must be tied to something other than race. Here is an example:

Judith Sweezer, a Black woman, worked as a prison officer at the Michigan Department of Corrections.[37] She filed a lawsuit claiming she had been subjected to a racially hostile work environment in violation of Title VII. Among other evidence of a hostile work environment, including that her subordinates refused to follow her orders and that her supervisors refused to back her up, Sweezer presented evidence of harassment by Wayne Allen, a white man.

In one incident, Allen saw Sweezer at a local restaurant and called out, "Hey, there's a new colored woman in town." Back at the workplace, Allen recounted this incident in Sweezer's presence to officers who were supervised by Sweezer. Several months later, Sweezer took disciplinary action against Allen for abusing an inmate. After a hearing on the disciplinary action, Allen and others harassed Sweezer by calling her a "bitch" and

"N--" and "making other remarks." Allen also blocked Sweezer in the parking lot with his truck and spit at her several times as she walked by. When Sweezer arrived at work, Allen would "follow her to where she parked her car, block her in with his car, display weapons, and follow or try to hit her with his vehicle."

The trial judge in the case granted summary judgment to the defendant, meaning that the case would not go to a jury. In the judge's view, no reasonable jury could find discrimination in the case because while Allen's behavior was "indisputably improper, Allen's comments were brief and isolated, and [were] more indicative of personality conflict than racial animus."[38]

This tendency of judges to view an emotionally charged, acrimonious relationship as solely "personal" and thereby "nonracial" is arguably reinforced by a sense generally that discrimination is the product of cool, unconscious bias and stereotyping rather than the product of hotter emotion in interactions and relations. Racial animus in this account is seen as consistent and group based. It is not seen to drive acrimony in individual relationships.

In another case, for example, the judge pointed to the fact that the plaintiff "admitted" in his pre-complaint counseling form that the supervisor who he alleged had discriminated against him had been "very, very mean" to him.[39] The judge seemed to think the plaintiff's acknowledgment that his supervisor was "mean" to him amounted to an admission that the supervisor was mean simply because he "disliked" the plaintiff and not for reasons involving race. In yet another case, the judge granted judgment against the plaintiff, stating that the plaintiff "offered no evidence of discriminatory animus and conceded . . . that [her supervisor] 'had a personal problem' with [her]."[40]

JUDGING RACIAL EMOTION: GRANTED, THERE'S EMOTION, AND IT'S RACIAL, BUT IT'S UNREASONABLE

A third way judges close racial emotion out of antidiscrimination concern is by acknowledging emotion as racial and then rejecting it as unreasonable, especially in hostile work environment cases. We tend to think of harassment these days as a sex-based phenomenon, but the Supreme Court long ago recognized that a racially hostile work environment can amount to a Title VII violation as well.[41] In fact, one of the earliest hostile work environment cases involved an optometrist office where the doctors insisted on segregating patients along national origin and racial lines. Josephine Chavez, a "Spanish-surnamed" employee in the office, filed a claim of discrimination. The doctors' office argued that segregating its patients could not amount to discrimination against Chavez, but the Fifth Circuit Court of Appeals disagreed. According to the court, the phrase "terms, conditions, or privileges of employment" in U.S. statutory antidiscrimination law, Title VII, "is an expansive concept which sweeps within its protective ambit the practice of creating a working environment heavily charged with ethnic or racial discrimination."[42]

Hostile work environments often build over time, and this extended temporal frame arguably offers greater potential for recognizing the role of racial emotion in discrimination, whether emotion in the person or persons creating the hostile environment or in the person or persons experiencing it, or both. Nonetheless, both the law of hostile work environment and judicial application of that law tend to close racial emotion out by setting a high bar for reasonableness.

A brief background on the law of hostile work environment is helpful here. In 1986, the Supreme Court held that discrimination in violation of Title VII includes hostile work environments as well as discrete decisions, like a hiring or promotion decision.[43] In that same case, the Court established that to succeed on a hostile work environment claim, a plaintiff must show that the discriminatory conduct was "sufficiently severe or pervasive to alter the conditions of [the plaintiff's] employment and create an abusive working environment."[44] An employee's conditions of employment are altered, held the Court several years later in a case called *Harris v. Forklift Systems*, "so long as the environment would reasonably be perceived and is perceived, as hostile or abusive."[45] This means that to succeed on a claim of hostile work environment, a plaintiff must show both that they found the environment hostile or abusive and that a reasonable person also would have found it hostile or abusive.

This requirement from *Harris* that an environment "would reasonably be perceived . . . as hostile or abusive" is not itself necessarily problematic. The law often uses "reasonableness" standards, and an inquiry into whether an individual's "terms, conditions, or privileges" of employment were affected by discrimination makes sense given the statutory language of the Civil Rights Act. However, the standard has been used as a thick filter. Some judges, in other words, are applying the reasonable person, severe or pervasive requirement to set a high bar for recognizing racial emotion in antidiscrimination law.

In *Pratt v. Austal, USA*, for example, the plaintiff testified that he overheard three white coworkers saying "how him and the n—— got into it yesterday, and he'll hang that n—— and shoot that n——, and all that kind of stuff. Just going on and on. And . . . calling them 'monkeys' and stuff like that."[46] He also presented evidence that several white workers wore T-shirts and bandannas bearing the confederate flag to work and that he saw racial epithets in graffiti on the bathroom walls and stalls and toolboxes, including things like "How many n—— do you see here wearing white hats" and "Why don't n——s use aspirin? Because they don't want to pick the cotton out of the top." The court held that although there was sufficient evidence that the plaintiff subjectively perceived his work environment to be racially hostile, the plaintiff's perception was not objectively reasonable.

In *Barrow v. Georgia Pacific Corp.*, Curtis Green testified that he had seen displays of the rebel flag on hard hats, the letters "KKK" on a bathroom wall and on a block-saw console, and a noose in another employee's locker.[47] He also testified that a superintendent "called him 'n——' three times in one year, repeatedly called him 'boy,' and told him two or three times that he was going to kick Green's 'black ass'"; and that another supervisor "called him a 'n——' and told him that if he looked at 'that white girl' he would 'cut' him."[48] The court of appeals affirmed the district court's grant of summary judgment to the defendant. According to the court, although the incidents relayed were "discriminatory and offensive," Green had not presented sufficient evidence that the workplace was "permeated with 'discriminatory intimidation, ridicule, and insult' that is 'sufficiently severe or pervasive to alter the conditions of [his] employment and create an abusive working environment.'"

Numerous judges have held that "occasional use of the N word" is not enough for a Black plaintiff to get to a jury.[49] Indeed, even the Supreme Court has suggested as much. In a 2002 opinion, authored by Justice Clarence Thomas, the Court indicated a belief that harassment "occurs over a series of days or perhaps years," and referred to an earlier statement that "mere utterance of an epithet . . . which engenders offensive feelings in a[n] employee . . . does not sufficiently implicate the conditions of employment to implicate Title VII."[50]

In another recent case, decided in 2020, a judge held that three white women telling a Black woman they were "rednecks" and "flew the confederate flag" is not enough,[51] and in yet another case, a panel for the Fifth Circuit Court of Appeals held that graffiti of the N-word and two painted swastikas, plus Black employees being called "boy," was insufficient to amount to a hostile work environment.[52] These judges often use other, even more extreme cases in comparison to deem the case before them insufficient. They declare things like "not one of the incidents was physically threatening"[53] and "plaintiff's allegations do not come anywhere close to the number of racial incidents in [another case]."[54] As one court put it in a case involving a reference to a Black customer as the N-word, a racial joke, and a reference to the office where the plaintiff worked as the "ghetto" and a "FEMA trailer," the plaintiff's race-based incidents "'pale in comparison, both in severity and frequency,' to the kinds of verbal harassment that this court and other circuits have held would support a Title VII claim."[55] The court cited for comparison three cases: one in which the plaintiff submitted evidence of, as the court put it, "years of inflammatory racial epithets, including 'n——' and 'little black monkey'"; another in which the plaintiff "was subjected to 'n—— jokes' for a ten-year period and the plaintiff's workstation was adorned with 'a human-sized dummy with a black head'"; and a third "where the plaintiff suffered 'incessant racial slurs' including 'n——' and 'dumb monkey.'"[56]

.   .   .   .   .

Together, these cases and others like them tell us something about the judges' views of not just what the law prohibits but also of when and how racial emotion is of antidiscrimination concern. Racial emotion in interracial interactions, especially racial emotion in people of color, is ignored and devalued by these judges and the law that they create. Racial emotion is something that people of color must bear, with consequences not just for their own mental and physical health but also for their success at work and our country's efforts at advancing racial justice and equality. We will turn to these costs and others in chapter 7. First, though, we should complete the story of our institutions' approach to racial emotion, including a look at how some judges treat some racial emotions in whites, and also at what our work organizations are doing about racial emotion.

4   Law: The Racist Call and Caring for Racial Emotion of Whites

There is a gaping exception to the law's tendency to ignore, categorize, and judge racial emotion in antidiscrimination cases in ways that close racial emotion out of antidiscrimination concern: the racist call. Indeed, juxtaposed against the law's approach to racial emotion generally, which often means racial emotion of people of color, as we saw in chapter 3, is the law's approach to racial emotion of whites, especially racial emotion tied to concerns about appearing racist. When it comes to these racial emotions, emotions like shame, guilt, and embarrassment, we see something different. Where the law generally tends to close racial emotion out of antidiscrimination concern, it simultaneously protects whites from at least some of their racial emotion. In this chapter, we see judges proclaiming whites' innocence and taking care to help whites avoid emotions tied to being called or perceived as racist.

Nowhere is it easier to see this urge to protect whites from racial emotion than the Trump administration's directive regarding diversity training in workplaces. On September 22, 2020, just as organizations were implementing a new wave of racial justice–oriented diversity training after the murder of George Floyd, then-president Trump issued an executive order in which he directed the U.S. attorney general "to assess the extent to which diversity training that teaches divisive concepts . . . may contribute to a hostile work environment and give rise to potential liability under Title VII of the Civil Rights Act."[1] The order cited as problematic a Smithsonian Institution museum graphic that stated, "Facing your whiteness is hard and can result in feelings of guilt, sadness, confusion, defensiveness, and fear."[2] Notable in the "divisive concepts" list of the executive order was training suggesting that "any individual should feel discomfort, guilt, anguish, or any other form of psychological distress on account of his or her race or sex."[3] In short, drumming up negative emotions in whites, emotions associated with our country's racial history or even with current research on the operation of racial bias, according to Trump, may itself create a legally actionable hostile work environment at work—for whites. When someone asked Trump in a presidential debate why he sought to end diversity training that might raise negative emotions in whites (especially any trainings that include the concepts of white privilege or critical race theory), he responded, "I ended it because it's racist."

There's a lot going on here.[4] Drilling down to racial emotion specifically, while a noose, proud mention of family members in the KKK, and several-times use of the N-word in some cases cannot amount to a racially hostile work environment, as we saw in chapter 3, diversity training that evokes negative emotions in whites can, even when those trainings merely provide information about history, systems of subordination, or the ways that stereotypes and other biases can lead to biased behaviors. This seems a pretty obvious difference in the law's treatment of the racial emotion of whites and people of color, and it is not a thing of the past. Although the Biden administration revoked the Trump executive order, states have been picking up the call. By one count legislatures in twenty-four states had introduced bills between January and September 2021 banning the teaching of "divisive concepts" in state agencies and schools, including the idea, as a Rhode Island bill puts it, that "the State of Rhode Island or the United States is fundamentally racist or sexist."[5]

Even apart from this obvious effort to control learning about our country's racial history and its contribution to present-day racial injustice, Trump's use of the word "racist" is notable as we think about the law's approach to racial emotion. Over the past couple of decades, the term "racist" has come to be seen as a racial epithet, at least in the eyes of some, and this move seems closely tied to concern in the law for racial emotions of whites. Not only is "racist" a racial epithet; it is considered by some the equal of using the "N-word" and when used to call out concerns about racial bias in whites it is itself considered "racist." As a pair of commentators put it recently, "Many white Americans [today] understand the allegation of racism to be a form of racism directed at them; an allegation so damning it is 'like the N-word for white people.'"[6]

To understand what's going on with this claim, we need to take a step back in history to see a battle unfolding. Recall that in the 1940s, the emphasis in the social sciences was on identifying personality or psychological traits that made some people good people and others bad people. The word "racist" was coined in this period as a word that referred to a particular identity status or belief. It was framed by opponents of Nazism to call out the false ideology that drove the Nazis and their theory of race, as one British sociologist explains it, to "expose falsehood and to discredit the person to whom it was applied."[7] By the 1970s "racist" was being used largely as a synonym for "prejudiced." But it wasn't the soft kind of "prejudiced" that we sometimes talk about today, referring to implicit biases and stereotypes as well as conscious belief in difference. A racist or prejudiced person was someone who explained Blacks' social standing as the result of their biological and/or moral inferiority. Some people were racist; others were not.

As our study of race and racism evolved, however, we began to acknowledge that systems often enact and entrench disadvantage, and in this way it's not just people who are racist but systems and practices and even individual actions that are racist, even if the specific person is not. Racism in this way became a term to describe practices, not just people. This was an idea that had been percolating since the 1960s when Stokely Carmichael and Charles Hamilton introduced a concept of institutional racism alongside Black Power.[8] Although Carmichael and Hamilton did not expressly use the term "institutional racism" at the time, they did stress that institutions and actions within and by them were a causal force in keeping Black people impoverished. Sociologists later more fully developed the concept.

It's not that sociologists and others sought to manipulate the term "racist" as it applies to people, an identity status, but rather to expose the breadth of racism to include practices, practices that people today continue to engage in, practices that continue to keep Black and other people down. In his important and powerful *Racism without Racists*, sociologist Eduardo Bonilla-Silva, for example, describes the modern phenomenon of "colorblind racism," whereby whites rely on colorblind justifications for racial inequality to maintain their innocence and to distinguish themselves from "racist" people who "explain Blacks' social standing as the result of their biological and moral inferiority."[9] Bonilla-Silva does not redefine the old "racist"—hence the title *Racism without Racists*—but expands the idea of racism beyond individual, color-conscious mindsets.

At the same time, conservatives doubled down on the idea of a "racist" as an identity status or belief system involving race distinctions. George Wallace's early image in the early 1960s as a racist politician gave way to "coded" racial politics in his 1968 presidential run, and Ronald Reagan supplied the press with numerous "photo opportunities" to display his "enlightened" racial attitudes.[10] Before we knew it, any call that an action was biased or racist—note the *action* as racist, not the person—immediately became a racial insult. Even allegations of subtle racial bias, which we know can occur in well-meaning people who subscribe to egalitarian ideals, are frequently construed by whites as insult: "Are you calling me a racist?"

In this context the modern claim emerged that the word "racist" for whites is like the "N-word" for Blacks. In *How to Be an Antiracist*, Ibram X. Kendi emphasizes this call as an effort to take the word "racist" from descriptive to pejorative. In Kendi's view, a racist is "one who is supporting a racist policy through their action or inaction or expressing a racist idea."[11] It is not a slur according to Kendi because it does not call into question someone's self-hood or identity but rather only their actions (or inactions). He calls the conservative move toward identifying the call of "racist" as a slur an attempt to close down conversation, to freeze us into inaction. If, as he says, "the only way to undo racism is to consistently identify and describe it—and then dismantle it," then turning every attempt to identify it into a slur is an effective way to keep things as they are.[12]

Kendi makes a good point. The accusations are inherently different because one is calling out potential unequal treatment while the other is always mere epithet. But there is something beyond the turn (back) to pejorative at play in this move—and that something is racial emotion. The claim of racist-as-equivalent-to-the-N-word is a marking of concern for the racial emotions of whites. By this I mean that to call someone a "racist" is not just a pejorative or insult, like calling someone "stupid"; it is perceived as an instrument of racial "assaultive speech." Again, this is in the minds of some, not all. Racist-as-like-the-N-word raises the salience—and legitimacy, or value—of whites' racial emotions. "I am not a racist" is thereby made emotional; it is an honor call, an honorable defense of one's personhood driven by one's emotions.

This is the emotional repertoire we see time and again from whites around the word "racist." When congressman Mark Meadows, who had frequently declared that then-president Barack Obama should "go back to Kenya," during a congressional hearing involving testimony of Michael Cohen about Trump's racially derogative comments about Black people, called an African American lawyer to stand behind his chair as "living proof that President Trump was not a racist," congresswoman Rashida Tlaib said that using a Black woman as a prop was a "possibly racist" act. Meadows stopped the hearing to insist that Tlaib and committee chair Elijah Cummings affirm that they did not believe that Meadows was a racist.[13] During his presidency, Trump regularly insisted that he was not a racist, that he "[did] not have a racist bone in [his] body."[14] Even Richard Spencer, a self-avowed white supremacist, identifies as "not racist."[15]

It is worthwhile here to consider the "N-word" to understand why it is widely understood to be so powerful a racial insult. As scholar Debra Walker King explains, "History distinguishes nigger as a racial insult from other words of 'mere insult' and ultimately renders it a word that wounds."[16] It is a word with a social history "that it can never escape," arriving in our language as a seventeenth-century invention by people who were just beginning to consider themselves "white" and used to connote "inhuman and barbarian inferiority" to justify slavery and the inhumane treatment of African Americans. For a white person to call a Black person the N-word is to label them, to exert power over them, for what they are not, not for what they have done. When used by whites toward Blacks, it is considered one of several "insults of such dimension that they either urge people to violence or inflict harm." It is, in other words, an instrument of "assaultive speech," in some sense a fighting word.

And it is the history, not in the abstract but in the collective memory of the word, that drives its assaultive power. In *The Many Costs of Racism*, sociologists Joe Feagin and Karyn McKinney asked people why the word is so often an "irritating and painful experience" for Black people.[17] One respondent explained that when he hears the N-word, in the back of his mind he sees a Black man hanging from a tree. He is aware of the way that the word has been used and continues to be used as power—putting someone in their place—and he associates it with subordination and violence against Black people. From this, we expect, rightly so, strong racial emotions in Black people when whites call them the N-word. Indignation, humiliation, shame, and anger all come to mind.

To say, then, that the word racist is "like" the N-word is to call to the racial emotions involved. The idea is that whites feel these or similar emotions when they are called "racist," and therefore the act of calling them racist is itself "racist." That some people make this claim does not mean that we must accept it, however. In chapter 8, we will revisit these words and consider again why the N-word and the word racist should be understood differently. There is the not-so-small difference in history, after all, as well as Kendi's point taken above. For now, it is enough to understand the claim and where it gets its power: from concern about racial emotion of whites. From there we can better see the various ways that law protects whites from racial emotion, including but not exclusively in cases where people of color allege discrimination.

Legal scholar Kim Shayo Buchanan and social psychologist Phillip Atiba Goff have done some important groundbreaking work in this area, framing their analysis through a lens of what they call "racist stereotype threat."[18] According to Buchanan and Goff, "selective empathy" by judges for whites and their racial emotions may be the product of white judges' own stereotype threat, their fear of being called racist and thereby their empathy with other whites who are called racist. While Buchanan and Goff do not situate their argument expressly around racial emotion, they deftly illustrate judicial concern for the racial emotion of whites. For example, they point to the recent voting rights case, *Shelby County v. Holder*, in which the Supreme Court of the United States "proclaimed a novel constitutional equality interest, enjoyed by state governments, which is infringed by federal judicial oversight that is premised on suspicion that state entities might discriminate."[19] And in other cases, justices "defend the honor of states," as Buchanan and Goff put it, such as when several justices objected to mention of the historical origin of a state's switch to non-unanimity in criminal jury verdicts—a way of "maintaining the supremacy of the white race" by diluting the influence of nonwhite jurors—because the mention of that history "tar[red] Louisiana and Oregon with the charge of racism" and was therefore inappropriate.[20]

Justice Powell, in the affirmative action case *Regents of University of California Davis v. Bakke*, also portrays whites as innocent, questioning any assumption that whites as a group would subordinate others as "unfair."[21] And while whites in these cases are often cast as innocent, the motives of people of color are questioned. In *City of Richmond v. J.A. Croson*, Justice O'Connor expressed concern in her majority opinion that because Blacks constituted approximately 50 percent of the population of the city and constituted five of the nine seats on the city council, the Black "political majority will more easily act to the disadvantage of a [white] minority based on unwarranted assumptions or incomplete facts."[22] In another, more recent case involving a challenge by whites to a decision of the City of New Haven not to certify test results because of the disparate impact of the results on people of color, Justice Alito in his concurrence highlighted the racial identities of politicians in the city at the time and implied that they may have been involved in discriminatory pro-Black advocacy.[23] And during oral argument for a case involving affirmative action in 2006, Justice Scalia declared that he "was not . . . prepared to accept that the school board's [voluntary desegregation] plan stemmed from good intentions." He asked, "Do we know the race of the school board here? . . . [H]ow do we know these are benign school boards?"[24]

We can see a similar effort to protect whites from racial emotions associated with being called or perceived as racist in some otherwise run-of-the-mill individual cases of discrimination brought by people of color. In one case a Black woman, Antonia Wilcoxon, worked for a nonprofit organization providing services to low-income residents in Minnesota.[25] She complained to her supervisor that she thought Black managers were not appreciated and also to the executive director that one of the supervisors, Kathy Klumb, who had been recently promoted, had made biased comments. Earlier in the year, Klumb had used the term "KKK" in a lesson on phonics. When Wilcoxon questioned Klumb about the incident, Klumb "professed ignorance about the civil rights movement, claiming to

have been out of the country at the time, and asserted that she was referring to her initials."

Wilcoxon was discharged after a meeting with her supervisor, Morris
Manning, in which she complained again about what she thought was
discrimination within the organization, especially in the way it treated clients who were children of color. In his discharge letter, Manning noted,
"You recently called me a racist. . . . I have zero toleration for that kind of
characterization applied to me. . . . I no longer trust your professional
judgment." The judge granted summary judgment for the defendant, noting that Manning "believed that Wilcoxon was overly focused on race . . .
and was unwilling to recognize that her behavior, tone, or manner might
be creating tension among the staff." As the judge saw it, "there is simply
no evidence that Wilcoxon's alleged termination was due to or based on
her race." Rather, according to the judge, "it is very clear . . . that her termination was based on an irresolvable personality conflict between
Wilcoxon and Manning."[26]

In another case, the plaintiff, a Black woman, was asked by her supervisor to inform another worker, also a Black woman, that she was not in
compliance with the employer's appearance policy because she was wearing unauthorized beads in her hair.[27] Plaintiff did as she was ordered, but
the next day she complained to her supervisor that she thought the request
was based on race, that she had been asked to talk with the Black woman
about her hair because they were both Black women. She was written up
for calling her supervisor a "racist" "in front of subordinate staff," after the
supervisor directed her to "watch what she was saying." The judge granted
judgment for the employer on the ground that calling her supervisor racist
was "defamatory" and a legitimate basis for the write-up and that plaintiff
did not provide any evidence that she received the written reprimand
because of her race.

Judges have also held that calling a supervisor or employer "racist" or
discriminatory generally does not qualify as protected activity for purposes of a retaliation claim. In one case, the plaintiff stated in his response
to a required HR goals memo: "I . . . don't have any dreams of advancing
on this job. I view this department as a place where dreams go to die. I
have encountered all kinds of discrimination on this job, and I have made
up my mind that this is a racist department. I just want to be left alone

and allowed to do my job as a firefighter." The judge held that this was not sufficiently specific to qualify as protected activity, which meant that he could be fired for making the statement.[28]

Other judges seem to think that a plaintiff's admission that an employer is "not racist" diminishes substantially the likelihood that discrimination took place. Recall that treating people differently on the basis of race violates Title VII. In *Felder-Ward v. Flexible Staffing*, however, in explaining his reasoning for why the plaintiff could not get to a jury on her discrimination claim, the judge noted that the plaintiff had testified "that [the employer] was not 'racist' and that they 'hired a whole lot of blacks,' and [the plaintiff] concludes only that they treated African Americans 'differently.'"[29] Similarly, in *Vance v. Ball State*, a case that made it to the Supreme Court, Maetta Vance, a Black woman, alleged that her supervisor acted in a threatening manner toward her and treated her "more poorly than her co-employees by yelling at her [and] giving her less desirable shifts." The trial judge in the case noted that there was testimony that the supervisor was difficult to work for and "play[ed] favorites among employees," but saw no reason to attribute his behavior to Vance's race, noting that one worker testified that she had "never heard or seen [the supervisor] do or say something that indicates he is a racist, and I do not believe he is a racist."[30]

Another way judges protect whites from this racial emotion is through close inquiry on what someone meant by the words or actions that they used. We saw in chapter 3 that narrowing the legal inquiry to a single state of mind is one way judges close racial emotion out of antidiscrimination concern, but judges also sometimes note that the person engaging in a challenged action did not "intend" to harm. We see this regularly when it comes to public responses to allegations of racist behavior, from black face to use of the N-word and other racial epithets.

Judges employ a similar move in race-based discrimination cases, emphasizing what actors "intended" over the action itself. In *Tademy v. Union Pacific Corp.*, for example, the trial judge granted summary judgment to the defendant on the ground that no reasonable jury could find a noose hanging from a clock was racially motivated, "given the explanation" of the white man who hung it there.[31] And in *Ash v. Tyson Foods*, described in detail in the previous chapter, the appellate court reviewing the retrial for Hithon with Ash's testimony about what "boy" indicated to him noted that such evidence was not helpful because it did not go to the state of mind of Hatley, of what Hatley was thinking when he used the term.[32]

The cases discussed in this chapter, taken together with those in chapter 3, mark an institution—the law—that is itself arguably driven and sustained by racial emotion. These decisions suggest that our judges, who are mostly white men, especially in the federal judiciary, may not only empathize with whites who perceive themselves as called racist; they may themselves desire to "move past" racism and protect themselves from their own racial emotions.[33] One way they may seek to do this is by ignoring racial emotion and denying the realities of the experiences of people of color even as they protect whites from their racial emotion, at least in some contexts.[34]

Work Organizations and
Racial Emotion

If the law generally tends to close racial emotion out of antidiscrimination concern and protect whites from racial emotion associated with being called racist, what about the organizations in which we work? Is there reason to expect that our work organizations are providing conditions for positive interracial relations and emotions? It would be reasonable to expect that most employers prefer positive relations to negative. A workplace where people get along, after all, is generally understood to be more productive than one where they do not. The recent rise of the business case for valuing and managing diversity, together with widespread claims by organizations that they care about racial justice, might also lead us to expect that organizations are already attentive to the realities of racial emotion and working to develop conditions for positive interracial relationships at work.

Yet, despite the expectation that organizations would prefer positive to negative interracial relations, there is little reason to believe they are actually acting to that end. The next two chapters take a closer look at the organizational approach to racial emotion at work, setting the stage for thinking about solutions. In these chapters, we see that work organizations are likely to close, rather than open, space for developing positive interracial interactions among their employees. They do this in a variety of ways, including by constructing repertoires of emotion that place responsibility for satisfaction in work entirely on individuals and that favor get-along positivity without attention to the realities of interracial relations. Moreover, like with law, work organizations close racial emotion out of antidiscrimination concern in their diversity narratives and in their responses to complaints of discrimination on the job.

In this area, our sources are not legal cases but rather the work of historians and sociologists who have studied shifts in rhetoric and advice on work and emotion in the managerial literature. There is a wealth of material out there advising business and business leaders on how best to manage their employees, which many of these studies draw upon. In addition, sociologists have studied what organizations are doing in the area of diversity, including how they treat complaints about racial bias or discrimination. Often, these sociologists go inside organizations (sometimes undercover) to ask questions and to see how things are really operating.

5 Work Organizations: Constructing Emotion Repertoires

Commentators sometimes like to say that organizations in the industrial era sought to "cleanse" the workplace of emotion. As with many characterizations of history, however, the full story is more complicated—and more interesting—than that. Emotion has always played a role in work. How could it not? Humans experience emotion wherever they go, including in their work. This means that even if the goal were to cleanse the workplace of emotion, that goal would not be attainable. Moreover, historians and sociologists give us plenty of reason to believe that as organizations were undertaking to build repertoires of "efficiency" and "rationality" during the industrial era, they were simultaneously building repertoires of emotion, repertoires that tell workers what employers expect and value when it comes to emotion at work.

To tell a richer story of organizational approach to racial emotion, it helps to take a long view of how organizations have seen and see emotion generally. We do this here with an emphasis on three key, interrelated developments in the history of labor and the employer-employee relationship. First, emotional control, especially control over anger, rose in prominence as a skill or characteristic to be valued in employees in the industrial era. This is where we get the idea of "cleansing" work of emotion.

Second, work organizations have done more than ask for anger management. They have also shifted nearly full responsibility for work satisfaction, including positive emotions at work, to working individuals themselves. This shift has ties to neoliberalism, an ideology in which market freedom rules and individuals are expected to succeed without support, regardless of their circumstances, and also to an emphasis on psychology that grew from the industrial era. Third, organizations most recently have gone well beyond anger management to require that workers "be happy" at work. Together, these developments illustrate an organizational approach to emotion that is neither static nor passive. Organizations (and the gurus who guide them) are actively building repertoires about emotions, including which are desirable and which are not and how they should be conveyed and managed in and at work.

ANGER MANAGEMENT

The rise of the large-scale corporation, employing thousands, even tens of thousands of workers in a single organization, marked a pivotal moment in American labor history. The period from the 1880s to the 1920s, often dubbed the "golden age of capitalism," was more than an era of capitalism; it was an era of rapid change in how people worked and how they understood their work capacities.

Prior to the beginning of the twentieth century, work in the United States was largely dispersed across small and mid-sized enterprises with labor control a matter of the "foreman's empire."[1] As labor historian John Fabien Witt explains, "Although there was considerable variation among industries, foremen—usually skilled workers with little formal training who had risen through the ranks—generally utilized the 'driving' method of labor management, a method that combined 'authoritarian rule and physical compulsion.'"[2] One notable exception to this realm of labor, of course, was the massive plantation system founded on enslaved labor in the South. In each of these realms, however, managers and owners were often one and the same, and they were generally regarded as worthy of their position by nature of being in the position in the first place. The "merit" of the person in charge was not questioned. Those in lower positions were considered inherently lacking in physical, moral, and intellectual qualities required for higher positions.

Beginning in the late 1800s and early 1900s, the United States saw an explosion in railroads and manufacturing—and a rise in the large-scale corporation. By one account, 85 percent of all wage earners in the 1920s were employed in manufacturing.[3] With this increasing number of workers in large organizations came concern about "waste of human effort" (as workers decided how to carry out their tasks themselves) and, ultimately, the creation of a "managerial class," people who were neither owners nor workers on the lines. At the same time, extremely difficult working conditions, leading to regular injuries and deaths, made worker strife common.

We often hear of this era with its rise in attention to rationality and efficiency as an emotionless one. Workers were portrayed as the cogs that run the machine. This was the era of Fredrick Winslow Taylor's scientific management, which sought to "substitute . . . science for the individual judgment of the workman."[4] Huge companies developed intricate hierarchies and systematized work on the floors as well. As Max Weber famously described the virtue of bureaucracy: "Its specific nature . . . develops the more perfectly the bureaucracy is 'dehumanized,' the more completely it succeeds in eliminating from official business love, hatred, and all purely personal, irrational, and emotional elements which escape calculation. This is the specific nature of bureaucracy and it is appraised as its virtue."[5]

But to say that leaders of organizations during this time did not attend to emotion would be a mistake. Indeed, Taylor very much saw the emotions of workers. Taylor promised owners and leaders material wealth and social harmony by "removing the cause for antagonism" and demanding a "revolution in mental attitude" of workers.[6] Taylor translated what many would more accurately portray as worker agitation for fairer, safer working conditions into worker "anger" that could be managed in other ways.

And while Taylor was naming and taming emotions of workers, the new managerial class was also receiving key instructions on the role of emotion in their jobs. This new class of workers—the managers, neither owners nor line workers—were important players in the project of systematizing production and dampening strife. Taylor, in fact, saw managers as much a key to the success of scientific management as line workers themselves, and importantly he presented the case for why being in the position in the first place was not itself merit.

As sociologist Eva Illouz develops in *Saving the Modern Soul*, this was the beginning of organizational treatment of emotion through the influence of psychology.[7] In the wake of World War I, psychologists, who had been recently enlisted to aid with military morale, were called upon in the corporate sector to develop tests to identify workers with high productivity, including managers. And this brought emotions and relations to the fore. Elton Mayo, one of the most famous management theorists of the time, emphasized that attending to emotions in work was key to organizational success. Mayo and his theories later fell out of favor, but his teaching about the value of emotional control and especially control over one's anger stuck. Organizations began to train their personnel—managers and workers alike—in what today we might call anger management, including instructing them to resituate anger outside of work, to define it as "simply reenactments of . . . family conflicts."[8] Remaining "cool" thereby became an important attribute of competence, one that endures to this day.[9]

Of course, we all know that people "lose their cool" at work all the time, and there is reason to believe that anger is seen differently and used strategically by those in power. Anger is also a powerfully racialized emotion, as we have already seen. Moreover, we will see in the next chapter that rules around anger are likely to be racially stratified. My point here is merely that organizations have a long history of attending to emotions, anger among them.

IT'S ON YOU

A second development in the way organizations treat and construct emotion in work centers on our narratives about responsibility. We rarely talk these days of work conditions, tying workers and their work environments together; rather, we talk of things like professional development, self-fulfillment, worker flexibility, and resilience. Here are joined the increasing influence of the field of psychology, especially the rise of what is known as "therapy culture," and neoliberalism, both of which emphasize the individual self as the ultimate source of moral and ethical values and of one's destiny. This turn, like the ascendancy of a managerial class and the call for anger management, is a subtle and yet monumental shift in organizational approach to emotion and worker relations. Individuals, not organizations, now take center stage; individuals bear responsibility for making both the companies they work for and themselves successful.

In the 1980s, work organizations took a sharp turn from the Taylorist ride of the 1960s toward corporate culture as a tool of employee motivation and control. Growing out of a perceived management crisis in which American companies were thought to be losing competitive advantage over their Japanese counterparts, several influential books published in the early 1980s—such as *Theory Z* by William Ouchi, *Corporate Cultures* by Terrence Deal and Allen Kennedy, and *In Search of Excellence* by Thomas Peters and Robert Waterman—advocated in various ways that paying more attention to constructing values within organizations (and less attention to rigid systems of control) would lead to greater employee productivity and increased organizational performance.[10] As Deal and Kennedy put it, "We need to remember that people make businesses work. And we need to relearn old lessons about how culture ties people together and gives meaning and purpose to their day-to-day lives."[11]

One key thread of this call picked up on the themes of enterprise and individualism that were on the rise in the 1980s and remain dominant today. "Individual leaders, not organizations, create excellence," declared the authors of yet another management book from the 1980s, *Creating Excellence*.[12] The move to corporate culture over command-and-control systems promised to provide workers with greater autonomy and opportunity for self-fulfillment in an era in which employees expect their jobs to "mean" something.[13] Indeed, Ouchi may have borrowed the term "Theory Z," the title of his book, from the work of humanistic psychologist Abraham Maslow, who used it to refer to the highest levels of personal satisfaction that an individual can achieve.[14]

Together with the increased emphasis on organizational culture came interest in personality tests and hiring and promoting for "fit." By one account, most Fortune 1,000 companies were using personality tests or some form of psychological testing by the early 2000s.[15] According to the designer of IBM's preemployment test at the time, the test was designed to determine how well an applicant's character would mesh with the company's culture.[16]

Even outside of formal personality and culture-fit tests, workers today are expected to conform their attitudes and behaviors to that of the firm's culture, whether in the dorm-like atmosphere of a place like Google or the bar-oriented culture of Wall Street. Sociologist Lauren Rivera's research suggests that a substantial component to "fit" is often perceived as emotion based, even at hiring, framed as gut reactions revolving around "chemistry" and especially interpersonal "liking" and "excitement." Evaluators in Rivera's study, conducted in the 2000s, sought new hires with whom "they could envision themselves developing intimate relationships, on and off the job."[17] These evaluators were told to consider cultural fit by their HR departments, and they did so by looking for resume similarities between themselves and job candidates. One legal recruitment director explained, "It's like dating . . . You meet a lot of people and then sometimes there's just chemistry. You just know it in your gut. We try to make it 'objective' by having trainings to tell us what to ask and what not to ask and by having evaluations, but ultimately it's just something you *feel.*"[18]

By the time organizations started emphasizing culture and its benefits for workers (not just its capacity for worker control), a host of psychologists had already spurred what is now known as "therapy culture," an American phenomenon whereby we increasingly understand and talk about all facets of our lives in psychological terms.[19] Without delving too deeply into the fascinating story of how we got here, we can safely say that we have entered a world, at least in the United States, where we are expected to be perpetually bettering ourselves, psychologically and emotionally. And this reality surfaces in our workplaces as well as our private lives. Speakers and gurus are brought into our workplaces to help us make ourselves better people, to help us better mind ourselves and our relationships.

By the 1990s this emphasis on self-fulfillment and personal responsibility for emotions had expanded to include the idea of emotional intelligence (EI), often said to be measured by a person's "EQ," to be contrasted with their intelligence quotient or "IQ." According to one definition, EI is "a type of social intelligence that involves the ability to monitor one's own and others' emotions, to discriminate among them, and to use the information to guide one's thinking and actions."[20] In a service-oriented economy in which "communication" is heralded as king, individuals who are high in emotional intelligence are expected to be better employees. And here's where the responsibility comes in: If we make it our personal project, we can improve our EI, say Claude Steiner, author of *Achieving Emotional Literacy: A Personal Program to Improve Your Emotional Intelligence*, and Daniel Goleman, founding father of the term "emotional intelligence."[21]

BE HAPPY

Intimately intertwined with the call for anger management and the shift in responsibility for satisfaction to workers over organizations is an emotional requirement: that workers "be happy" in and at work. It's not just that individuals are deemed responsible for their own success or work satisfaction, or even their own happiness, or that they are expected to control their anger at work; it's that a "happy" worker is considered a better worker and a better person: "Happiness science insists on suffering and happiness as a matter of personal choice. Those who do not instrumentalize adversity into a means for personal growth are suspected of wanting and deserving their own misfortune."[22]

Again, the field of psychology—and popular psychology as well (who hasn't taken a personality test online or in a magazine?)—has played a central role, this time in the form of what's called "positive psychology." Psychologist Peter Seligman is known as the father of the positive psychology movement. In 2000, when he was president of the American Psychological Association, he declared that "positive psychology in this new century will allow psychologists to understand and build those factors that allow individuals, communities, and societies to flourish."[23] That alone sounds pretty good. And an industry built from there.

A number of critics challenge the positive psychology movement on a variety of grounds, including the alliance to neoliberalism mentioned earlier, which has pushed workers into more precarious jobs. Here, though, I want to focus on what the expectation that workers be "happy" might mean for organizations and emotion: specifically, this expectation that good workers are "happy" workers. Whereas once worker happiness may have been something to be derived from organizational conditions, over the past ten years or so happiness has been flipped. Like with EI, happiness is now understood by some to be "an important precursor or determinant of career success."[24] Happy workers are said to perform better, are more productive, and cope better with organizational changes and multitasking demands.[25] Shawn Achor, author of *The Happiness Advantage*, puts it this way: "Thanks to cutting-edge science, we now know that happiness is the precursor to success, not merely the result. And that happiness and optimism actually fuel performance and achievement."[26]

Happiness is not itself an emotion in the sense that we saw in chapter 1. It is usually described as a set of attributes, such as flexibility and resilience, and as a state of positivity generally toward the world. But the search for happy workers means that workers who want to be hired, promoted, and generally to "succeed" in work increasingly need to demonstrate the qualities of happiness and positivity to get ahead. And these qualities favor positive emotions portrayed in workers over negative ones. "A good 'team player' is by definition a 'positive person.' He or she smiles frequently, does not complain, is not overly critical, and gracefully submits to whatever the boss demands."[27]

Work organizations, in short, are playing a role in creating, supporting, and valuing emotions, including emotions in interactions and relations at work. They provide a blueprint of sorts of what it means to be a successful relational worker, increasingly someone who is themselves happy and can make others happy as well. What's more, they do this actively, not just as a passive conduit for broader social norms.

6 Work Organizations: Valuing Racial Emotion

Organizations are not just constructing repertoires for emotion generally, repertoires that have implications for racial emotion in work, as we will see; they are also constructing repertoires for racial emotion specifically. By this I mean that organizations cue race in various ways—by imposing different feeling rules along racial lines, for example, or by asking people of color to pose for diversity shows and to take on diversity management. At the same time, like their institutional counterpart the law, they close racial emotion, especially racial emotion of people of color, out of antidiscrimination concern, labeling complainants as overly emotional and "hypersensitive" to racial bias.

DUAL STANDARDS: ANGER AND TEARS

Almost forty years ago sociologist Arlie Hochschild brought the idea of "feeling rules" to the forefront of our thinking about emotions at work. In *The Managed Heart*, Hochschild described feeling rules as social expectations about the extent, direction, and duration of feelings called for in a situation or interaction. And work organizations, she showed, construct these feeling rules in the process of defining good workers, especially in the service industry, where workers who will satisfy customers and make sales serve the bottom line of the company. Much of the work reviewed in the previous chapter on work organizations and emotion builds at least in part on Hochschild's idea. Organizations, in short, play a role in shaping feeling rules, sometimes very consciously and expressly. For the flight attendant, for example, "the smiles are a *part of her work*, a part that requires her to coordinate self and feeling so that the work seems to be effortless."[1] The airlines that Hochschild studied held trainings for employees on how best to manage their emotions, created advertising to emphasize their employees' easygoing style, and hired and fired according to their employees' willingness and ability to adhere to the rules.

Since Hochschild's groundbreaking work in the 1980s, researchers have dug deeper. Feeling rules, it turns out, are not always neutral. Hochschild alluded to this reality. Many of her examples included sex-skewed work, jobs that were predominantly filled either by men or by women, and she devoted a chapter to exploring the topic.[2] It was hard to miss that the flight attendants whom she was studying were almost all women, each literally weighing in weekly on a scale and constrained not just in emotion but in what she wore, how long her hair was, and, yes, how many pounds she had gained in the last week. Too many pounds, and she would be asked to resign. Hochschild also noted that women, much more than men, are in jobs with higher emotional demands, and that the few male flight attendants were expected to step in with anger (something the female attendants were not allowed to do) when passengers overstepped the line of acceptable decorum.

A wealth of research today tells us that feeling rules can often be gendered, with different rules applied to men and women workers, even when those workers are performing the same job. Some of this research is in the legal field. In *Gender Trials*, sociologist Jennifer Pierce finds that male paralegals were discouraged from doing the deference and caretaking, emotion work that was expected from their women counterparts.[3] Pierce also finds that female litigators are penalized for displaying emotions such as anger and aggression, even when those emotion displays are regularly expected from male litigators. The famous legal case brought by Ann Hopkins against the accounting giant Price Waterhouse reinforces this point.[4] The case was brought by Hopkins after she was denied partnership. Of the 662 partners at the firm at the time that Hopkins was considered, 7 were women. Of the 88 candidates proposed for partnership in her year, Hopkins was the only woman. Her portfolio was stellar; she had landed some major clients and was uniformly lauded for her competence and drive. Where she went wrong was in the softer work, such as reportedly being too brusque in her dealings with staff members. Some of the partners who submitted comments for her promotion review mentioned that she should "take a course at charm school" and "wear more jewelry, makeup, and dress more femininely."

Feeling rules can also vary with status of job position. Pierce's study of the legal profession, for example, shows that male lawyers in law firms are permitted and even expected to show anger and frustration openly, but female attorneys are not, and neither are paralegals, who are mostly women.

It shouldn't surprise us to learn that feeling rules are also often racialized. We need simply recall our American history around slavery and Jim Crow. In his 1837 speech at the Annual Meeting of the Society for Advancement of Learning in South Carolina, lawyer and politician William Harper declared that the "African negro" had "blunter capacity" to feel than whites, "blunter capacity" for "enjoyment and suffering." He described them as having the "very limited . . . feelings" of an "animal."[5] Later in his speech, he went on to declare that people of African descent benefited from being enslaved because they could thereby be "protected" from one another's "revengeful passions."[6]

Beyond claims of diminished capacity for emotion, the justification for slavery leading up to the Civil War often included enslaved peoples' "happiness," even love, in the mix. Proslavery writer Thomas Roderick Dew, for example, claimed in his 1832 essay, *Abolition of Negro Slavery*, "We have no hesitation in affirming, that through the whole slave-holding country, the slaves of a good master are his warmest, most constant, and most devoted friends," going on to say that "everyone acquainted with southern slaves, knows that the slave rejoices in the elevation of prosperity of his master."[7] According to Dew, this happiness emerged from the state of complete dependence, leading enslaved people in Virginia to be "the happiest portion of our society."[8]

Of course, this is a descriptive account of emotion rather than a prescriptive one, but there is plenty of reason to believe that portrayal of happiness and satisfaction was required of Black enslaved people by their white owners. The slave was expected to be positive and docile, content with their status and conditions. And the feeling rules of slavery were no doubt well understood by enslaved people as well.[9] William Craft, for example, illustrates his keen awareness of the rules of slave emotion in his narrative of his life and escape from slavery. Craft recalls the day when he and his sister were separated at the auction block and he was denied his request to say goodbye: "[It] sent red-hot indignation darting like lightning through every vein. It quenched my tears and appeared to set my brain on fire, and made me crave for power to avenge our wrongs! But, alas! We were only slaves; and had no legal rights; consequently we were compelled to smother our wounded feelings, and crouch beneath the iron heel of despotism."[10]

Solomon Northup, a freed Black man who was stolen into slavery—and later featured in the movie *Twelve Years a Slave* (2013)—tells us another story about the price of expressed emotion in slavery. He recounts how a woman he was sold with, Eliza, expressed intense and ongoing pain at having been sold away from her children. According to Northup, Eliza later displeased their mistress by "being more occupied in brooding over her sorrows than in attending to her business," and as a result she was ordered "to work in the field" and ultimately was sold "for a trifle" to another man.[11]

Joy expressed by emancipated slaves was also a hazard, considered by some whites as disrespectful or somehow disloyal, as though delighting in the misery of the slaveholding whites. And while anger and hatred were permissible emotions for whites when Blacks stepped out of line, as evidenced by white-led massacres and public lynchings, Black people could not show affront in the face of daily insults. Historians document white former slaveholders as especially anxious over the possible loss of Black subservience and inferiority. Mississippi's Black Code, for example, prohibited "insulting gestures, languages or acts" toward whites, in addition to locking in labor contracts with the threat of vagrancy and sale to the highest bidder.[12]

As far as work was concerned, post-Reconstruction, while Black men were pushed into sharecropping, Black women were pushed primarily into domestic service. They were considered the ideal "servant" by white women seeking to avoid the drudgeries of housework.[13] According to one study in the Washington, DC, area in 1930, 80 percent of white employers of domestic workers said they preferred Black women as domestic servants. These women explained that in their view Black women were, among other things, "natural born servants," "obedient and respectful," "by reason of race, docile," and "good-natured and willing to serve." And Black women were expected to manage their emotions accordingly.[14]

Asian Americans were similarly segregated into service jobs during this time, especially into laundries and restaurants, where they sometimes catered to a white market. In the nineteenth century, Chinese Americans played a central role in a range of work sectors in the United States, from manufacturing to mining and agriculture, but by the early twentieth century they had been forced out of the general labor market by hostile labor unions, exclusionary legal policies (including the 1882 Chinese Exclusion Act, the first immigration law that banned a race from entering the United States), and stark and pervasive racial discrimination. Some of the anti-Asian hostility, including to Chinese-owned and -run restaurants, raged around fears of white women being lured into sexual relationships and marriages with Asian men.[15] Yet, at the same time, restaurants in Chinatowns across the country catered to a white, middle-class clientele.[16] As legal scholar and historian Samantha Barbas describes, "The image of Chinese Americans as restaurant servers or cooks posed little threat to most Americans—although they could not accept the presence of Chinese-Americans in mainstream social settings or business, they had little trouble envisioning them in subservient roles."[17]

This was neither a brief nor narrow slice of our racial history in the United States. Well into the 1960s and 1970s, businesses actively avoided hiring nonwhite people, especially Blacks, and especially in jobs that involved interaction with the public or that might provide them with status or respect. A number of the early cases brought after the Civil Rights Act was passed involved companies that had excluded Black people from certain jobs entirely up until the act's effective date, or had otherwise limited the numbers of Black people in public-facing jobs.[18]

This history of work segregation and discrimination in the United States is important not just as background for understanding how work organizations treat racial emotion today; it is important because it is part of each of our lived experiences. As we noted in chapter 2, in understanding the role of historical and other context in our experienced racial emotions at work, families and friends pass down their experiences through stories, attitudes, and warnings, among other things, and these experiences sit with us when we seek to make sense of ourselves and when we engage in interracial interactions at work.

We are more than half a century now from passage of the federal civil rights statutes aimed at dismantling Jim Crow, and even more from legally sanctioned slavery, and yet still today there is reason to believe that people of color are often expected to contain their anger and their tears, while whites can yell and cry. And this includes the workplace as much as it does society more broadly. Sociologist Adia Harvey Wingfield's recent interviews with Black health professionals reveal their sense that they are not allowed to show anger under any circumstances, while their white counterparts are allowed to do so. Much of this research is obtained through interviews with workers, so it tells us about how people perceive feeling rules. As Jay, a systems engineer, explains:

> One woman, management had a problem with her, with one of her presentations. The organization [of her presentation] wasn't tight, and she went off! "What is it now? You guys are really getting on my nerves!" And I'm like, "Wow, she's talking to managers like that?" She's still there, nothing's wrong. They met with her, I heard her threaten to quit, and they were like, "No, don't quit!" If it were me they'd probably be like, "All right!" You know? So they [whites] say what they want. If someone says, "Do this," they question it, or they get smart. If it was me, I'd be labeled as an angry black dude, can't get along with coworkers. Because it's them, it's all right.[19]

Treatment of "white women's tears" similarly calls up the racial differences in feeling rules in many workplaces. In her work on white fragility, Robin DiAngelo explores the racial (and racist) dynamics of white women's tears. One person of color whom DiAngelo spoke with described her objection to being subjected to white women's tears, revealing her understanding of how feeling rules apply to her as a woman of color:

> It's infuriating because of its audacity of disrespect to our experience. You are crying because you are uncomfortable with your feelings when we are

barely allowed to have any. You are ashamed or some such thing and cry, but we are not allowed to have any feelings because then we are being difficult. We are supposed to remain stoic and strong because otherwise we become the angry and scary people of color. We are only allowed to have feelings for the sake of your entertainment, as in the presentation of our funerals. And even then, there are expectations of what is allowed for us to express. We are abused daily, beaten, raped and killed but you are sad and that's what is important. That's why it is sooooo hard to take.[20]

DIVERSITY "MATTERS"

Organizations are also cuing race these days in ways that put people of color on the front line of "diversity management." Organizations increasingly claim that diversity "matters" to them, that it is good for business. The goal, they say, is one of managing diversity rather than merely achieving it. Consultant and former Harvard business professor R. Roosevelt Thomas coined the term "managing diversity" in the 1980s when he founded the American Institute for Managing Diversity. According to Thomas, managing diversity is a business imperative in an increasingly globalized world.[21]

Sociologists tie the rise in the business case for diversity and diversity management to Reagan-era deregulation and hostility toward affirmative action plans, as well as to a highly publicized report that projected increased diversity in workplaces by virtue of increased diversity in the country's workforce as a whole.[22] Much like with our understanding of the legal cases discussed in chapters 3 and 4, this move toward diversity management may itself be seen as the product of whites' desire to increase their own racial comfort, to "move past" racism and discrimination and the white resentment around affirmative action. While Thomas downplayed white resentment to affirmative action in his call for diversity management, that resentment was nonetheless provided as one reason why diversity management was a better path for work organizations. According to Thomas, affirmative action places what he called an "unnatural focus on one group," and in his view "what [affirmative action] means too often to too many employees is that someone is playing fast and loose with standards in order to favor that group."[23] This is a contested view of affirmative action, but one that has held considerable appeal, especially with whites.

Personnel managers and equal opportunity officers thereby turned their rhetoric in the 1990s to diversity management. In doing so, they also shifted organizational action to things like hiring diversity consultants and diversity officers and implementing diversity narratives and diversity trainings. And they sought to ramp up their images as "good" places for diverse people to work.

What these organizations mean by "diversity" is often unclear, and there remains substantial question as to whether the most common "diversity" measures, like mandatory bias trainings, are effective in increasing demographic diversity across levels of organizations.[24] What we do know is that organizations want to appear like they have happy people of color working for them, and they often ask people of color to provide that happy face.[25] At the same time, they expect people of color to serve as leaders internally on diversity issues. In the United States, diversity officers are often people of color, more so than in France, for example, where data suggests that white people dominate in those positions.[26]

Yet while organizations claim to value diversity and seek to manage diversity, they seem to be doing little to account for relations and racial emotion. Research on diversity narratives is one place where we see this. Diversity narratives are the messages that a work organization sends about why diversity matters in their workplace and how best to approach and experience it.[27] Firms often express their diversity narrative through human resources, training, and promotional materials. A diversity narrative serves as a framework for policies and practices and as a guiding ideology for how people should behave in diverse settings. Of course, an organization's express diversity narrative can morph in implementation, and even firms without express narratives will have an underlying one embedded into their work cultures that guides day-to-day behavior around race.

Studies suggest that the two most prevalent diversity narratives in organizations today are colorblindness and multiculturalism.[28] The colorblindness narrative is exemplified by the idea of the "melting pot" in American society. It emphasizes that people are at core the same, that racial categories should be ignored or avoided, and that differences should be assimilated into an overarching unifying category. Recognition of race and racial identities under this narrative is viewed as negative and to be avoided. The multiculturalism narrative, in contrast, explicitly acknowledges differences among groups, taking the position that interracial differences should be "accepted . . . and celebrated."[29]

Numerous studies suggest that a multiculturalism narrative can result in lower racial bias and greater acceptance of others than a colorblindness narrative, as well as an increase in perspective taking. Nonetheless, multicultural initiatives are often met with resistance by whites, who may feel excluded. Some research finds, moreover, that multiculturalism narratives can lead to increased stereotyping and normative expectations that racial minorities behave according to stereotypes. Indeed, one recent study suggested that people exposed to a multiculturalism narrative may be more likely to have essentialist beliefs about race, to conceive of racial groups as having inherent essences that are biologically based and immutable, and may be more likely to see racial inequality as less problematic than people not exposed to a multiculturalism narrative.[30] What's more, a multiculturalism narrative may lead to a false fairness effect whereby discrimination is concealed and racial bias concerns are delegitimized.[31]

Important when thinking about racial emotion, moreover, multiculturalism narratives tend to frame diversity as a matter of celebrating static identity states rather than of relational experience that requires attention to and understanding of others and their perspectives. A multiculturalism narrative does not acknowledge or address the reality that interracial interaction can involve negative racial emotions.

In her work studying race in the healthcare field, Wingfield identifies what she calls "racial outsourcing." Instead of improving structures and conditions to advance racial justice within the hospitals, including for patients as well as for employees, the hospitals expect their employees of color to do the racial justice work.[32] Moreover, even if the organizations do not formally demand such work of their employees of color, many of them feel an obligation to do the work in their position as a racial minority in a largely white field. Wingfield explains it this way:

> Black women physicians . . . find themselves in a contradictory position. They know that organizations rely on their commitment, dedication, and empathy in order to meet their patient populations' needs, and are attuned

to the ways this evokes gendered and racialized implications. Yet despite their status as doctors, being in the racial and gender minority means they still feel they have to work to hide their feelings of frustration and discontent at this arrangement. Hospitals do not establish specific guidelines for black women doctors' emotional performance, but the intersections of race, gender, and occupational status structure the sort of emotion work they do all the same.[33]

HANDLING INTERNAL COMPLAINTS

We also know something about how organizations treat internal complaints of bias and discrimination by people of color. There is reason to believe that organizations mirror law in this regard, labeling relational difficulties as personal and thereby nonracial and managing complaints as mere personnel problems rather than discrimination concerns. Over twenty years ago, sociologist Lauren Edelman identified the problem of "managerializing" antidiscrimination complaints within organizations.[34] By this she means that the people responsible for nondiscrimination within organizations often reframe nondiscrimination in terms of basic fairness with an organizational end goal of internalizing resolution of discrimination complaints and thereby managing away legal risk. This managerializing takes what might have been discrimination in violation of Title VII and turns it into personal conflict or misunderstanding.

Perceptions about the role of emotions are frequently in play in the ways that internal HR workers and defense counsel frame complaints about bias and discrimination. Sociologist Ellen Berrey and her colleagues interviewed in-house HR executives and defense attorneys as well as outside counsel for organizations about their perspectives on the discrimination claims brought by employees. The researchers note that "according to the ... attorneys and HR executives, the anger (while perhaps justified) blinds the plaintiffs to the 'facts' and makes them irrationally pursue litigation."[35] Emotion is considered personal and not racial (or involving other protected categories). As one attorney representing an employer organization stated, "I think this person, the plaintiff, was angry at her supervisor, and in her deposition she—although she was alleging ... discrimination—she admitted that she didn't get along with him."[36]

One attorney portrayed people who raise concerns of racial bias as "hypersensitive" and another explained his own role as one of re-sensitizing plaintiffs to more appropriately tolerate racially biased comments or actions. He explained that when it comes to racial epithets and racial jokes, sometimes he can make the complainant feel heard and redirect them for future interactions so that if they "hear just one or two remarks [they will] say, 'Oh, that's just old Clyde again,' instead of filing a complaint."[37] In short, said another, "The emotion is on the plaintiff's side of the equation in these cases," and the defense counsel's role is to diffuse that emotion away from concerns about bias or discrimination.[38]

People who complain are equally aware of this framing. One person interviewed by feminist scholar Sara Ahmed for *Complaint!* described how her complaint about a possible environment hostile to trans people on campus was turned into a "difference in opinion" and how she was framed as someone "having some kind of a tantrum for not getting my way rather than it being a fundamental issue about existence."[39] Ahmed describes complainers who were designated as individually motivated climbers, hypersensitive whiners, and even as neoliberals seeking to disrupt a progressive institutional agenda.

Korean poet and author Cathy Park Hong describes what she calls "minor feelings" perceived by some whites this way: "Minor feelings are the emotions we are accused of having when we decide to *be* difficult—in other words, when we decide to be honest. When minor feelings are externalized, they are interpreted as hostile, ungrateful, jealous, depressing, and belligerent, affects ascribed to racialized behavior that whites consider out of line. Our feelings are overreactions because our lived experiences of structural inequity are not commensurate with their deluded reality."[40] Similarly, a Black woman told me recently she was being "mined" by her institution in its response to the racial reckoning following the George Floyd murder, and yet she was nonetheless not allowed to be authentic. She felt she couldn't react negatively to the murder at work, that she had to control and calibrate her emotions, while at the same time she was being asked to celebrate the election of Kamala Harris as the new vice president of the United States at a public event held by the institution.

Whites, too, can experience this devaluing of their race concerns. Indeed, we might rightly imagine that when white people raise concerns about discrimination or bias against people of color, they will suffer similar treatment. They may be seen as illegitimate conveyors of those concerns because they are white (and thereby their emotions related to those concerns are deemed of little value) and also as race traitors because of their efforts to disrupt white silence or their refusal to perform what is sometimes called the "racial labor" of supporting white dominance.[41] It is important for us to keep in mind that racial emotion, after all, is not something that is attached to different races; it is experienced in various ways by people of all races.

This said, on the whole, our organizations' approach to racial emotion today goes something like this: Be careful of your emotion at work, especially as a person of color. Do our diversity work, but delicately and by putting whites at ease. Your negative racial emotion is not of antidiscrimination concern—indeed, it is on you, a sign of your weakness, your failure to fit in and "love" your work.

PART III Considering What's Wrong and
What to Do about It

7 What's Wrong with the Current Approach

Once we have some understanding of what our law and organizations are currently doing when it comes to racial emotion and interracial interactions at work—their "approach" to racial emotion, as I have been calling it—we can also begin to develop a deeper sense of why the current approach is problematic. We have seen glimpses of this already. Some of the cases that illustrate the law's approach to racial emotion are pretty extreme. But the discrimination that is being missed casts much more broadly than the few, specific individuals whose cases have been relayed here. What's more, the current approach is problematic not only because we are missing discrimination and putting people of color at a disadvantage—leaving people of color worse off in terms of work success—but also because we are missing a key opportunity for racial progress in our society.

There are at least three things wrong with the prevailing approach to racial emotion. First, we are missing discrimination. By this I mean claims of discrimination with merit are being dismissed because law and work organizations are closing racial emotion out of antidiscrimination concern. Second, and related to this, we are requiring people of color to bear the brunt of the negative consequences from racial emotion in the workplace. Our institutional repertoires for racial emotion are skewed to

protect whites from racial emotion and to punish people of color for raising racial justice concerns. This reality has implications beyond the specif-
ics of our civil rights laws. Third, we are missing an opportunity to advance
equality and justice by creating space for building interracial connections
in work. At a time when we are energized to make a difference, this is one
place where we can.

DISCRIMINATION IS BEING MISSED

The first problem with the prevailing approach to racial emotion in law
and work organizations has to do with our civil rights protections and
progress on racial justice. Congress passed the Civil Rights Act of 1964 to
make employment decisions based on a person's race, sex, color, religion,
or national origin unlawful. When an employee suspects that the act has
been violated, they have the right to sue. If an employer is found to have
violated the act by making an employment decision because of race, that
employer typically owes the suing plaintiff pay from the date of the judgment back to the date of the employment decision in question. Sometimes
the employer will be required to make specific changes going forward, for
example by giving the plaintiff a promotion or pay raise that was discrimi-
natorily denied.

The question in these cases, then, especially in cases brought by an
individual alleging discrimination in a specific employment decision, such
as a denial of a promotion or a pay raise, is whether the decision was based
at least in part on the plaintiff's race. In the words of the law, the question
is whether race was a "motivating factor" in the decision. Sometimes the
plaintiff will have evidence from the decision maker's mouth at the
moment in time of the decision, maybe something like "I am not promoting you because you are Black," but this evidence is rare in today's workplaces. This means that the statements reflecting bias—and here I mean
bias that includes emotion—are frequently more subtle and are made in
the context of an ongoing relationship leading up to the decision rather
than at the moment of decision itself.

If a judge narrows the legal inquiry to exclude the relationship between
Anthony Ash and his supervisor, Thomas Hatley, for example, a relation-

ship in which Hatley called Ash "boy" at least once in the course of their relationship, then that judge is less likely to find discrimination when in fact it may have been there. I do not mean by this that every interracial relationship that involves negative racial emotion and interactions should lead to a legal finding of discrimination. What I do mean is that closing out relations altogether will lead to missed cases of discrimination.

The same is true for cases involving nontargeted harassing behavior and harassing behavior behind closed doors. A racially hostile work environment can be created even when the behavior creating the environment is not directly targeted at a specific person who experiences it in that specific moment in time. In her work on "racetalk," defined as talk that demeans on the basis of race or ethnicity, sociologist Kristen Myers documents the talk that white people sometimes use when they perceive themselves to be in "private" spaces.[1] They sometimes tell racially offensive jokes, and make racially demeaning comments, when they would not do these things in more public or "mixed" spaces. Racetalk "delineates boundaries between whiteness, blackness, and brownness," says Myers; it "is a tool used in policing these boundaries." And, as such, the problem is not just that racetalk is demeaning of others. It is that racetalk "helps to normalize ... racist attitudes and practices."[2] Racetalk is contagious and often socially desirable behind closed doors. And each time someone expresses or tolerates a racially offensive comment or behavior, they are normalizing that behavior. The behavior is marking out a club: the "us" and the "not them." And it is teaching and reinforcing subordination: "Keeping old racial notions alive means that old structures will remain supported."[3]

Nolan Cabrera's *White Guys on Campus* relays similar reports about whites and racism behind closed doors. Cabrera interviewed white, male college students who reported that racially insensitive jokes were the most common form of discrimination that they had witnessed and also that those jokes took place in white spaces that were considered "private" and thereby safe from reprobation for bad behavior.[4] Heightened levels of racetalk and other expressions of biases and stereotypes can be a way of attaining emotional solidarity with the in-group, and it is harmful both within those "private" spaces and beyond.[5]

Closing racial emotion of people of color out of antidiscrimination concern by labeling it "personal," while favoring whites' racial emotion in being or perceiving themselves as being called racist, also prevents meritorious discrimination claims from going forward, as do narrow hostile work environment inquiries in which judges ratchet up reasonableness to the extreme. Requiring that an environment be *"permeated* with 'discriminatory intimidation, ridicule, and insult,'" as some courts have done, is an example of this. Ignoring relations also means that meritorious claims will be rejected because the plaintiff engaged in what is considered "inappropriate" or "insubordinate" behavior, including acting on anger arising out of a racially charged relationship.

By ignoring the reality that discrimination in a discrete decision is often the product of ongoing relations, moreover, organizations will miss an opportunity to address discrimination early on. Siphoning off cases involving racial emotion and difficult interracial relationships by declaring them merely "personal" or a matter of oversensitivity will prevent organizations from seeing, much less addressing, broader cultures and systems that may be resulting in discrimination.

PEOPLE OF COLOR ARE BEARING THE BRUNT OF NEGATIVE RACIAL EMOTION

But something else is going on that extends beyond specific employment decisions and individualized legal findings of discrimination: People of color are bearing the brunt of negative racial emotion at work. Because whites remain in positions of power in most workplaces, people of color are likely to suffer the consequences of weak relational ties. They will have fewer of the choice job opportunities and will miss out on the raise that is given to the candidate who is considered "connected" within the firm or with clients who are doled out by leaders. This alone is problematic. It is something of the flip side of giving special favors to members of one's own group, a phenomenon that already disadvantages people of color, and it is one reason why organizations should monitor for signs of discrimination at the workplace or organizational level and not just the individual or even relational level.

And there is more to the problem. While whites may continue to experience anxiety in interracial interaction out of fear of being perceived as biased or racist, their strategy of colorblindness (refusing to see race or to publicly acknowledge racial difference or disadvantage) can allow them to reduce their anxiety and, in many cases, to avoid more extreme racial emotions, like shame or embarrassment. It's hard to say something wrong when you don't say anything at all.

People of color then are left to raise race issues, whether delicately or indelicately, and to face the negative consequences of doing so, including antagonism when they are perceived as "playing the race card," causing trouble or raising false or exaggerated race concerns in an effort to get ahead or otherwise capitalize in some way on their race.[6] In *The Race Card*, legal scholar Richard Thompson Ford argues that a good number of the people who raise race concerns today are "play[ing] the race card," and thereby exhausting the good will of our country's citizens for civil rights causes.[7] In some ways, Ford's argument is a semantic one: It's about the language that we use rather than the claims that we make. Ford, contending that the terms "racist" and "racism" have been stretched too far, prefers a more narrow, person-focused use of the terms, more like the definitions used in the 1950s.

But there's something else going on around the "cards" that are played in race relations and conversations today. Beyond semantics, the card that is being played today is often the reverse of what Ford describes as the race card. Instead of a raising of race concerns, it is a card that is played to tamp down on those who raise those concerns.[8] To say that someone is playing the race card when they raise race concerns, in other words, is to discount the legitimacy of their account and of their race-related concern. This is arguably what is happening when judges are quick to label animosity in a relationship as personal and thereby not racial. The judges see the plaintiffs in these cases as reaching for race when really the judges think they were at most treated poorly by someone who was "mean" to them.

This is also what happens in organizations when HR executives and attorneys reframe complaints about racial bias as personal and seek to diffuse those concerns by adjusting expectations—"He'll know that next time when Clive uses a racial epithet, 'that's just Clive,' and not something that anyone should be complaining about." In this way, people who raise concerns about racial bias and discrimination are discounted and penalized, which may be one reason why research suggests that discrimination goes underreported.[9]

At the same time, we know that organizations define "good" workers as those who have a high emotional quotient and get along with others and who present themselves as possessing "happy" qualities of resiliency, positivity, and self-sufficiency around emotions. This puts people of color (and sometimes whites as well) at additional risk of being seen as bad workers when they raise concerns about bias and discrimination. Indeed, we see them labeled by our institutions as overly emotional, as taking things too personally. As Illouz puts it, emotions like "shame, anger, guilt, offended honor, admiration . . . have been progressively made into signs of emotional immaturity or dysfunction."[10]

This dynamic can be exacerbated by the increasing requests by organizations that people of color take on "diversity" work in response to Black Lives Matter and other efforts at racial justice. People of color in this era are expected to be heroes for racial justice and peacemakers at the same time, to advance racial progress and yet to raise race issues delicately and "safely" for whites, if they raise them at all. When the people who raise concerns about bias and discrimination are seen as the aggressors, and their racial emotions assigned little to no value, they are put in a double bind: not doing their job well if they don't raise issues they see, and not doing their job well if they do.

Indeed, research increasingly suggests that when organizations adopt "diversity" measures—even minimal ones like instituting a diversity narrative of multiculturalism—those organizations are perceived as more fair and more welcoming of people of color, especially among whites, and this can conceal discrimination and denigrate claims of racial concern.[11] This dovetails with a common response of whites, which is to argue away incidents of bias or discrimination (e.g., "Are you sure it was your race? He's really just a jerk to everybody.").

One Black woman who attended a mandatory diversity training at work relayed her experience of the bind in this way:

This was a sales job. One woman said point blank that she was afraid of dark skinned black people so she didn't really want to try to sell things to them. . . . I told them I didn't like what I was hearing, that it bothered me, and that I thought we needed to change the racial climate if we wanted to improve. Well, you can guess what happened. The next week they called me into the office, told me I was "too sensitive," and I got fired.[12]

A Black man in this same study expressed his concerns about raising issues of racial bias:

I work with a woman who is a complete racist and culturally clueless. And what do I do when she tells the biracial woman on our team that her hair looks like a poodle's? Or when she assumes that because I'm black I know people in [a predominantly black part of the city]? I stay calm, change the subject, get back to work. I have to do this, because how will it look if I curse her out, even when she deserves it? I'll be the one they fire, not her.[13]

And the law and organizations provide very little protection to those who raise race concerns. Neither of the people raising concerns about racial bias in these stories would likely be protected from retaliation because their complaints must be based on reasonable belief that the actions are "unlawful," and neither of the incidents relayed—either a comment in a diversity session that someone is fearful of selling to dark-skinned people or questions about hair or assumptions about community—are likely to rise to the level of a legal violation. This requirement that the complainant have a reasonable belief that they are objecting to action that is illegal is a high bar.

When law and organizations close racial emotion out of antidiscrimination concern, they are doing more than signaling the limits of legal rights and what the law requires of organizations; they are constructing racial emotion by assigning value within the antidiscrimination frame. It is not okay under this construction to feel anger and indignation at racialized slights and insults, while it is okay to feel anger and indignation at being perceived as biased or racist.

In this way, given our institutions' current approach to racial emotion, people of color are left to bear the brunt of negative racial emotion at work, leading to consequences that can affect not only their success in work but also take a toll on physical and mental health. The American Psychological Association, for example, has documented the stress effects of discrimination on people of color,[14] and a wealth of research buttresses this point: Experiencing discrimination and anxiety around race can lead not just to relational harms and less success in work but also to emotional, physical, and cognitive harms.[15]

WE ARE MISSING AN OPPORTUNITY FOR ADVANCING SOCIAL JUSTICE AND EQUALITY

Work has the potential to foster the type of contact—intimate, sustained, cooperative contact—that is thought to best facilitate improved interracial relations and to reduce prejudice. Work facilitates friendships both by bringing people together on a regular basis over a sustained period of time and by requiring that people work cooperatively to get jobs done. With work as a key place where positive interracial relations can develop, we are missing an opportunity for advancing social justice and stronger race relations.

When organizations tamp down on people of color (and white people) who raise race-related concerns, they are closing out the possibility of the learning and conversation needed for change. At the same time, when our institutions protect racetalk behavior that is conducted behind closed doors, they reinforce a safe space for denigration and subordinating behavior to flourish and to pass along to new generations. They exacerbate the discomfort of interracial interaction by buttressing the comfort of same-race interaction, especially when it is considered informal and "private." In much the same way, when our institutions ignore racial emotion at work, closing it out of antidiscrimination concern, they provide permission for whites to create white racialized work space and to define worker success, who "fits in" and also who "merits" trainings, raises, and promotions. Silence around race concerns and institutional unwillingness to disrupt work rules that are designed to advantage some over others may not only entrench that advantage but also generate feelings of entitlement on the part of those being advantaged. These feelings of entitlement may in turn heighten aversion to intergroup connection by reducing incentive to connect across difference.[16]

Instead of avoidance and antagonism, we need engagement. And that's not all. We need engagement that allows us to learn from each other. Some research suggests, for example, that talking to people about their experiences is generally better than "imagining yourself in their shoes" because it provides a more accurate understanding and is less mentally taxing.[17] But to do this we need space for those conversations. Indeed, what may ultimately be the most damaging aspect of our institutions' approach to racial emotion is that our institutions are creating and sustaining environments that close us out of productive engagement and conversation—and the stronger relations—we so desperately need.

8 What We Can Do

What can we do about the discrimination and inequality that flows from our institutions' current approach to racial emotion? In short, as leaders, workers, activists, advocates, and judges, we can change our institutions' approach. In this chapter, I focus on what our institutions can be doing, including some specific recommendations for change. It's important here to think not just about improving our institutions' approach to racial emotion for individuals by bringing racial emotion into antidiscrimination concern, but also about shifting our repertoires and demands around racial emotion more broadly, more evenly allocating the burden of negative consequences from racial emotion, and opening space for learning and positive relations in the long term. I then circle back to us as individuals and the power that we have to change not only our institutions and our repertoires of racial emotion but ourselves and our interactions, too.

ACKNOWLEDGING RELATIONS AND RACIAL EMOTION AS ANTIDISCRIMINATION CONCERN

There are a number of ways our institutions can better see and address racial emotion as a source of discrimination in the workplace. The most fundamental of these is a shift in conceptual frame. To the extent that some people, including judges and leaders in organizations, think that discrimination is a matter of static mind states or exclusively a matter of bias at discrete moments in time, such as a promotion decision, they will need to reorient their thinking. Discrimination is a problem not only of biases that operate in the minds of identifiable decision makers at such discrete moments; it is also a problem of relations that are capable of being derailed by biases and by emotions over time. Acknowledging relations as a root of discrimination and group-based disadvantage is an important first step in addressing racial emotion and in opening opportunities for developing positive racial emotion in the workplace. Acknowledging racial emotion, and not just cognitive biases, as a source of disadvantage and inequality within those relations is a second key step.

Following from this, our institutions should resist the temptation to assume (or presume) that an acrimonious workplace relationship is solely personal, and thereby nonracial. Racial emotion is personal *and* racial. It is experienced by people in interracial interaction and can result in relationships that exhibit emotionally laden, hostile behavior. This doesn't mean that interracial relations can't go sour for nonracial reasons. However, absent evidence that an acrimonious or otherwise emotionally laden relationship is nonracial, such as evidence that hostility developed after a specific, clearly nonracial incident, judges should permit an inference of discrimination to follow from animosity in interracial relations.

In addition, racialized behavior should not be protected from legal inquiry simply because it does not "target" a specific person of color or it is undertaken behind closed doors. Racialized behavior like that of the supervisor in *McCann v. Tillman* in chapter 3 who called the Black female plaintiff "girl" and Black male officers "boy" and of the sheriff in the department who referred to a former employee as a "n—— bitch" and remarked that "he had not received the 'n—— vote' and he didn't want it" should not be dismissed or downplayed as evidence of a hostile work environment merely because it was not always directed at or experienced firsthand by the plaintiff. The environment of work includes more than what we each experience individually and firsthand. In fact, given studies suggesting that racetalk and other racialized behavior is more prevalent in white spaces than in mixed-race spaces, we should be especially attuned to the overall work environment that these backstage behaviors create.

Nor should judges and employers be allowed to isolate behavior that is deemed "inappropriate" or "insubordinate" from the relations leading up to that behavior. As Judge Nelson pointed out in the *Clack* case detailed in chapter 3, organizations and law should consider relationships and racial animosity in those relationships as they consider whether a firing for insubordination was discriminatory. Testimony like in *Clack* that a supervisor "singl[ed] out . . . [the plaintiff] for his racially based rage" should be especially concerning, of course, as should racialized comments and insults, but evidence of less extremely racialized relations should also be considered.

Note that expanding the inquiry in this way does not require condoning violence. In existing law, in fact, we already allow plaintiffs to prove discrimination so long as bias (broadly understood and including relations) was a motivating factor for the challenged outcome decision. The Supreme Court has told us as much. The most recent case involved a woman who worked in a warehouse as a heavy equipment operator at Caesars Palace Hotel and Casino in Las Vegas, Nevada, in the late 1980s and early 1990s.[1] She was the only woman in the job (and in her unit of the Teamsters Union), and she brought suit after she was fired for being involved in a physical altercation in a warehouse elevator with a fellow worker.

Costa had worked most of her life in a male-dominated work environment, driving trucks and operating heavy equipment. After some time at Caesars, though, she began to notice that she was being singled out because she was a woman. When she complained, nothing was done. Indeed, as the court of appeals describes it, "Her concerns not only fell on deaf ears—'my word meant nothing'—but resulted in her being treated as an 'outcast.'"[2] The court goes on:

> In a series of escalating events that included informal rebukes, denial of privileges accorded her male co-workers, suspension, and finally discharge, Costa's efforts to solve problems were thwarted along the way. . . . [W]hen men came in late, they were often given overtime to make up the lost time; when Costa came in late—in one case, one minute late—she was issued a written reprimand. . . . [She] received harsher discipline than the men. For instance, she was frequently warned and even suspended for allegedly

hazardous use of equipment and for use of profanity, yet other [workers] engaged in this conduct with impunity.... Although her fellow [workers] frequently lost their tempers, swore at fellow employees, and sometimes had physical altercations, it was Costa, identified in one report as "the lady Teamster," who was called a "bitch," and told "you got more balls than the guys."... Supervisors frequently used or tolerated verbal slurs that were sex-based or tinged with sexual overtones. Most memorably, one co-worker called her a "f-ing cunt." When she wrote a letter to management expressing her concern with this epithet ... she received a three-day suspension in response. Although the other employee admitted using the epithet, Costa was faulted for "engaging in verbal confrontation with a co-worker in the warehouse resulting in use of profane and vulgar language by other employee."[3]

The final incident in the elevator involved a male coworker who was upset with Costa about a report she had filed indicating that he was taking unauthorized lunch breaks. He "trapped Costa in an elevator and shoved her against the wall, bruising her arm."[4] Following an investigation, which her supervisor determined was inconclusive, Costa was fired (the man was given a five-day suspension on the ground that his record was cleaner than Costa's).

The Supreme Court said that Costa could win her case if she could prove that her sex was a motivating factor in the decision to fire her.[5] She would then be entitled to damages unless the employer could show that it would have made the same decision anyway, regardless of her sex.[6] In this way, the law acknowledges that decisions often have multiple causes, and it provides the employer with a safeguard for cases in which the employee's behavior is so egregious that it would warrant firing on its own.

Judges and work organizations should also be careful not to favor racial emotions of whites over those of people of color. At first glance, this may seem easy enough, but it turns out that just telling ourselves to do better is not likely to be sufficient. Of course, education is a start, and for that reason a principal goal of this book has been to open our minds to the reality of our racial emotions in interactions at work and how our institutions (as well as we as individuals) construct and value them. But we should also think about more concrete ways to lead our law and organizations toward fairer treatment of racial emotion in work.

I present three such measures in this chapter, under the headings Seeing Discrimination, Shifting Repertoires, and Sharing Discomfort.

The first, Seeing Discrimination, involves bringing racial emotion into antidiscrimination concern through attention to individual behavior of racial assault, while otherwise consistently widening our lens to focus on systems and structures over individuals. The second, Shifting Repertoires, seeks to redefine the "good" worker and expand our language for racial emotion at work. The third, Sharing Discomfort, involves undertaking a vision of integration that requires sharing the burden of discomfort in difference. Together, these proposals seek to shift our institutional constructs around racial emotion and to open space for learning and engagement in our interracial interactions at work.

1

SEEING DISCRIMINATION: BRINGING RACIAL EMOTION INTO ANTIDISCRIMINATION CONCERN

We, especially white people, have a hard time seeing discrimination. Sometimes, as we have learned, this is because our racial emotions get in the way. Other times, it's because we have a hard time seeing past individuals and individual relationships to the broader sources of discrimination and inequality at work. This said, we can do better in bringing racial emotion into antidiscrimination concern. Here, I propose two ways that we might do better, one aimed at how we understand individual experiences and the other at widening the lens beyond individuals to the structures, cultures, and systems of the organizations in which we work.

Seeing Racial Emotion in Interpersonal Relations

To say that racial emotion should be understood as a source of workplace inequality and discrimination is not to say that racial emotion itself should be legally actionable in all circumstances, or even that every legal rule relied upon in the cases in chapter 3 should be abandoned. When an individual brings a claim of discrimination challenging a specific employment decision, for example, such as a promotion or pay decision, that individual is required to show causation, that their race was at least a motivating factor in the decision, even if not in the mind of the decision maker at the precise moment of decision. This legal requirement is likely to set a practical limit on many cases involving racial emotion. As I highlighted in the last chapter, racial emotion often won't surface in the form of racialized or other comments reflecting bias by decision makers, and it may be difficult for plaintiffs to track down comparators to show that they were treated differently than their peers. This is one reason why monitoring for patterns and turning to systemic theories (discussed later) is key. We can sometimes see in the aggregate what is difficult to discern by looking solely at an isolated decision or relationship.

Nonetheless, working at the level of individual claims, we can consider measures that would help shift the current institutional approach to bring racial emotion into antidiscrimination concern. One such measure would create a firm categorical legal recognition of the relational behaviors that are most likely to trigger negative racial emotion, acrimonious relationships, and workplace inequality. I call this category of behavior "racial assault."[7] We can expect racial assault behaviors to be the most disastrous to interracial relationships, possibly involving racial pleasure from domination in whites and often racial shame, anger, and indignation in people of color. The following proposed changes to law involve this category of racial assault. They are aimed at dislodging current blocks to fairly acknowledging and judging racial emotion.

What is behavior of racial assault? Behavior of racial assault is behavior that is expressively subordinating. Use of racially subordinating language, such as the N-word or "boy" to refer to someone who is Black, or "wetback" to refer to someone of Mexican descent, statements reflecting normative and/or descriptive race-based stereotypes about a person's ability to do a job, such as "black people should stay in their place"[8] or "that's a lot of money for a black to count,"[9] both of which have been downplayed by our courts, and other behavioral expressions of subordination and dominance, such as construction or display of nooses, would be considered behaviors of racial assault. Calls for Asian Americans and Latinx people to "go back to your country" would also likely fall in the category. The legal inquiry should not turn on the state of mind or emotions of the person exhibiting the behavior, or on the subjective perception of the person receiving it, but rather on the conduct and the expected impact on a work environment, the message of subordination that racial assault behavior sends generally and the racial emotion that is likely to result.[10]

The law should treat racial assault behavior as presumptively discriminatory and as constituting a hostile work environment.[11] Behaviors of racial assault are presumptively racial and the emotion experienced by people of color subjected to these behaviors is presumptively reasonable, as a matter of policy as much as a matter of fact. It is not merely a matter of personal offense but of onerous and unequal work conditions. Behavior of racial assault is conduct that creates a hostile work environment, altering conditions of employment. Judges should not be permitted to substitute their own judgment about what the actor "intended" for legal presumption in these cases. Most cases should go to a jury to determine whether the alleged racial assault behavior occurred, and, if a jury finds that it did, employer liability should flow from the fact of the occurrence.

Further, the law should presume that employment decisions made by someone who has exhibited racial assault behavior were motivated at least in part by race. The presumption should apply for a set period of time from when the behavior was exhibited.[12] This means that if someone uses the N-word to refer to Black employees, decisions by that person regarding Black employees will be presumptively discriminatory within the prescribed period. Only if the employer can show that it would have made the same decision anyway should the relief available to the plaintiff be limited, and even then discrimination should be legally established and only remedies altered.[13]

Notably, calling someone a racist should not be considered a racial assault. In this way, developing the concept of racial assault would draw up the stark difference between racial emotion tied to subordinating behavior and racial emotion associated with whites' perceptions of being called racist. While the emotions evoked may be similar if we construe them in an extremely narrow way, in that each may involve individualized feelings like indignation, their contexts are not at all similar, and neither then are the emotions as they are likely experienced in full. As we considered in chapter 3, the histories of the terms are drastically different. Being called a racist holds none of the deep pain of historical subordination over people of color that behaviors of racial assault hold. The racial emotion in response to perceptions of being called a racist is real, but it is of a different category than that of behaviors of racial assault and should be treated as such. What's more, raising race concerns (often perceived by whites as being called racist) is a calling out of potentially problematic behavior, unequal treatment based on race, while a white person calling a Black person the N-word is nothing but epithet.[14]

There may, of course, be some tough cases at the boundaries of the category of racial assault. Indeed, context will play a role in determining whether a behavior amounts to a racial assault. The N-word is a good example. The word has developed starkly different meanings and effects depending on context, who is using the word and how.[15] Instead of a firm category of language, therefore, the category of racial assault should be considered an inquiry with consideration of context that then has legal effects. Even the Supreme Court has acknowledged that context is important.[16]

Yet it will be key to keep the context inquiry from devolving into what the actor "intended," what they meant when they used the term or behavior. As we have seen, the law often allows for our preferences (and biases) to creep in. From what we know about law and racial emotion, judges will be inclined to protect whites from their racial emotions. This is why the inquiry should be firmly founded in considering the environment created, how conditions of employment are altered for others, rather than in what the actor intended.

These categorical legal presumptions around racial assault should help bring clarity to behavioral and emotional rules in work. Racial assault is racial behavior that is relationally divisive, inherently subordinating, and often disastrous to interracial relationships. People (especially whites) often complain about having to "walk around on eggshells" when it comes to race.[17] Clarity around racial assault behavior should help ease anxiety arising out of situational ambiguity and at the same time drive elimination of the most obvious forms of relational subordination from the workplace. Moreover, tamping down on racial assault can improve a work culture more broadly by firmly protecting workers for raising their concerns.

And yet a strong word of caution against overpolicing by work organizations is in order. Although this proposal identifies racial assault as individual behavior that should give rise to an organization's liability for discrimination—and urges tamping down on such behavior through cultures that condemn it—the proposed legal rule does not declare that every incident of racial assault must be punished with firing or other severe employment consequence. This is a common mistake in thinking about the law and its expectations of work organizations. Title VII of the Civil Rights Act regularly holds employers liable for the discriminatory actions of their employees. Some commentators and judges have understood this to mean that the only thing an employer can do to avoid liability for discriminatory behavior is to punish the people who engage in it.[18] But this misses that people can learn and grow from their mistakes and that work organizations can create new cultures and shift behaviors in multiple ways. Indeed, sometimes the right thing for a work organization to do will be to accept responsibility for an occurrence of racial assault and yet resist calls for a firing so that all employees can see that mistakes can be foundations for growth.[19]

Widening the Lens: Systems, Structures, and Cultures

Much racial emotion, as we know, is beneath the surface in the workplace; it is often the low-grade anxiety and discomfort around negative emotions that leads to avoidance and subtle antagonism over outright hostility. We also know that in the law, courts sometimes judge the racial emotion of people of color by declaring it unreasonable, and we know that in organizations, HR managers and others can be quick to label concerns about bias or discrimination as oversensitive, overly "emotional," and out of line, including a matter of "playing the race card."

At the same time, as we learned in chapter 2, research suggests that people of color are more attuned to biases and discrimination than their white counterparts. Social scientists have identified a range of behaviors that can be perceived (reasonably) by people of color as racist or discriminatory. In addition to behavior of racial assault, researchers also include racial insults and racial invalidations in this range of behaviors.[20] Together, these behaviors comprise the "microaggressions" that people of color (and people of other subordinated status) endure on a regular basis. Racial insults are behaviors that are insensitive to or inconsiderate of a person's racial identity, while not expressly hostile or subordinating. For example, asking Black people about their hair, asking Asian Americans where they are "from," telling a person of color that she "doesn't seem Black," mistaking a person of color for a service worker or other more subordinate employee, and mistaking one person of color for another all might be perceived reasonably as discriminatory. In addition, racial invalidations are behaviors that "minimize[] the psychological thoughts, feelings, or experiences of targets."[21] These behaviors might include suggestions that concerns expressed about perceived discrimination or bias are overblown or exaggerated.

Racial insults and invalidations can be powerful means of group-based subordination, especially when they add up over time and across space. Accordingly, the legal inquiry, even involving specific relationships, should be less one of whether a particular incident is perceived (subjectively or objectively) as hostile than whether the work environment more broadly is understood as subordinating or hostile. The inquiry should emphasize work conditions over personal offense, and if a reasonable person standard is used it should be understood as a reasonable person with the plaintiff's identity characteristics, across all dimensions such as sex and race and sexuality, to guard against bias.[22]

Importantly, organizations should be sure to consider each individual complaint as potentially part of a broader pattern at work. This is also true when thinking about hostile work environments. Hostile work environments often involve victims other than a single complainant as well as other contributors to the environment, other perpetrators, and also bystanders and organizational contributors, such as a work culture or physical features of the workplace.[23] Indeed, what may at first seem like an individual instance of harassment can often be linked to sex and race segregation and disparities in pay and promotion, unfettered decision-making by dominant groups, and notions of merit and other organizational practices that are stereotyped and inaccurate.

The case of *Vance v. Ball State* provides a simple reminder of how a narrow lens can keep us from seeing the problem of broader work environments.[24] Maetta Vance worked at Ball State University as a catering assistant from 1991 until 2007. For much of this time, she was the only Black person working in the division. In 2005, Saundra Davis, a white catering specialist, was given authority to direct Vance's work. Davis and another white employee, Connie McVicker, threatened Vance, and used epithets like "Buckwheat" and the N-word to refer to Vance and also to refer to Black students at the university. McVicker openly touted her family's connections to the Ku Klux Klan. Vance was also berated and yelled at by her immediate supervisor, a white man, Bill Kimes, who was known to "play favorites" and treat others terribly, but who nonetheless allegedly treated Vance worse than any of the non-Black employees. And she was "mean-mugged" by another white supervisor, Karen Adkins, who also stared intently at Vance when they were alone in the kitchen.

The trial judge in the case granted summary judgment for the defendant, treating each of the harassers and their behavior separately. As to Kimes and Adkins, both of whom were deemed supervisors of Vance, the judge determined a jury could not reasonably find their behavior to be racial harassment in violation of Title VII. Kimes's conduct was not racially motivated, the court said, and Adkins's behavior was not sufficiently severe or pervasive to be actionable.[25] As to McVickers and Davis, the judge held the employer was not liable because, as the court of appeals later put it, "Ball State satisfied its obligation under Title VII by promptly investigating each of Vance's complaints and taking disciplinary action where appropriate."[26]

By taking each of the incidents separately, the judge ignored that sometimes multiple incidents that may seem minor when considered in isolation can nonetheless add up to be sufficiently pervasive to violate Title VII when viewed together. What's more, if a story like this one is seen solely as a problem of several individuals and an employer's response to discrete incidents, we will miss the opportunity to ask some of the larger questions that can lead to institutional change, questions such as: What was the overall work environment experienced by Maetta Vance like? Why was Maetta Vance the only Black person working in the catering division of Ball State University? Why was Kimes allowed to play favorites and treat people terribly? And what was the race climate like for students at the university? These are structural questions that may be relevant to solutions as much as to understanding any problems regarding race at the university. To ask these questions doesn't mean that every legal case involving race discrimination must interrogate all aspects of an employee's working environment, but questions like these can and should be relevant in considering how best to advance racial justice, especially for those organizations that are sincerely committed to that end.

Importantly, along with this wider lens should come a de-emphasis on policing individuals for behavior other than racial assault. Recall that we want more learning and conversation, not less. Work organizations have a history of turning to policing in response to concerns about bias and discrimination. This move is consistent with a story of discrimination as an individualized problem, a story that portrays organizations as innocent.[27] It is arguably this story that drives diversity training and complaint processes (processes which often focus on individuals for punishment) as the most common antidiscrimination measures. And yet when organizations turn to heavy policing of individuals, they are likely to heighten anxieties around interracial interaction, leading to fewer relational ties.

Attending to broader sources of harassment and discrimination can get us past diversity training and individual policing as the sole or principal measures taken by organizations. Workers who understand themselves as working in a larger environment are also more likely to identify patterns of discrimination and to seek more innovative solutions.

Conveniently, our law already has a legal theory that can be used to monitor organizations for patterns of discriminatory outcomes. We call it systemic disparate treatment theory. Under this theory, plaintiffs can allege that their employer engaged in or is currently engaging in a pattern or practice of discrimination.[28] It's enough to see the outlines of this theory, without getting mired in the details. In short, to prove a pattern or practice, plaintiffs must prove that discrimination is the regular rather than the unusual occurrence within the organization. This is usually done with a combination of anecdotal evidence involving instances of discrimination or bias by decision makers and evidence about structures and work cultures that can lead to biased decisions, together with statistical analyses of the difference between what we see within the employer's workplace— the observed outcome—and what we would expect to see, given the relevant labor pool. For example, in one famous case, the government (as the plaintiff) compared the number of Black teachers hired in the Hazelwood School District outside of St. Louis with what one would expect to see in terms of hiring, taking the geographical area and number of credentialed, experienced Black teachers into account.[29] This was an early case involving statistical analyses, and since then the statistical techniques have gotten more sophisticated. But the idea remains the same: If outcomes are starkly off from expectations, given the relevant labor pool, we should be concerned that discrimination is operating within the organization.

Of course, identifying patterns of discriminatory outcomes will not tell us exactly what is causing an observed disparity, or even whether negative interracial relationships are among the causes of the disparity. It can tell us, however, whether discrimination is likely to be operating within an organization and can put pressure on the organization to assess and make changes to the structures and cultures that shape the conditions for interaction as a means of improving outcomes.

And work organizations *should* be focusing on their systems, structures, and cultures, including the ways that they can shift relations toward learning and engagement. What we need is not just fair, transparent HR systems and diversity training, not just better "listening" or therapy sessions, but concrete, structural measures that can be taken to improve conditions for interracial interactions. These measures often include things like improving demographics. Yes, numbers matter. Segregation and skewed numbers lead to fewer interracial interactions. They also lead to more biased perceptions and more negative racial emotion in interactions when those interactions occur.[30] Tokenization—being one among few of your group rather than one among many—puts workers in a position where their emotional performance is more carefully scrutinized. Demographics and hierarchies can also affect people's expectations about whether interactions within a workplace are likely to be threatening, such as involving stereotyping and discrimination.[31]

Structural measures also include ways of organizing work. Research suggests, for example, that women and people of color have better career outcomes in organizations where work is arranged in network rather than hierarchical structures.[32] One recent nationwide study across nine industries found that women and people of color were more likely to be promoted into managerial ranks in firms that adopted cross-boundary work teams—work teams that bring together workers from different jobs on a regular basis to share information and participate in decision making—than in firms that did not adopt those types of team-based work.[33] Further research suggests that self-managed work teams, "which allow people in different roles and functions to work together on projects as equals," lead to greater success for women and people of color.[34] Together, this research tells us relations are working better when people are crossing boundaries and learning from each other along the way.

Diversity narratives should also be shifted away from colorblindness or multiculturalism and toward learning and integration. Most organizations implement diversity narratives through human resources materials, training, and promotional materials, both internal and external. These narratives should match up to practices within the organization, and should be used not just as a formal commitment to individual workers but also as a framework for policies and practices and as a guiding ideology about how people should behave in diverse settings. As we saw in chapter 2, research in this area increasingly suggests that a diversity narrative of learning and integration—valuing diversity as an avenue for thinking about how to organize and carry out work together—is more likely to enhance group functioning and to reduce stereotype threat than either of the more commonly adopted narratives. In an integration and learning environment, biases in interactions are more likely to be called out and addressed than ignored or reinforced, and the racial emotions that go along with those conversations are understood as part of that process.[35]

This idea of instilling a learning mindset comes out of work done by psychologist Carol Dweck in the area of education.[36] Her work over several decades now shows that when people understand their intelligence as expandable and not set in stone, they perform better academically, asking more questions and digging into learning rather than merely performing (or avoiding performing for fear of failure). The research on a learning frame in interracial interactions builds on this idea by asking whether people's racial emotions—their fears and anxieties, at least—can be dampened by an emphasis on learning from others. Claude Steele and colleagues found in their studies that assuring people they wouldn't be judged in an interracial interaction or telling them that differences in perspectives were valued (a multiculturalism narrative) did not lead to increased willingness to engage. What did work was telling their white participants prior to an expected conversation with a Black person about racial profiling that tension is natural in these conversations and that "they should treat the conversation as a learning experience—that is, try to learn what they could about the issue and, more generally, about how to talk about charged issues with people who might have different perspectives."[37]

Work cultures more broadly[38] as well as spatial features[39]—physical features such as meeting spaces and office organization, offerings like coffee stations and gyms (where they are located and when), and even contract terms—are key organizational levers for developing better interracial relations at work. Work cultures can be explicitly racialized, as when hostile behavior is prevalent, and also more implicitly racialized, as when "fit" involves expectations of "excitement" and "liking" that introduce racial emotion directly into notions of merit and success. As organizations pour money into strengthening their work cultures and into restructuring their workplaces to get more out of their workers, they should also consider how those cultures and spatial features of work affect the frequency and quality of relations and thereby contribute to or reduce discrimination.[40]

This may sound abstract—changing the conditions for interracial interactions at work—but it's really not. What it requires is that organizations put nondiscrimination, including fair treatment of racial emotion, squarely on the table as strategic initiative. Take, for example, strategy around what I call "spatial features."[41] Much like with corporate culture, organizations already are taking seriously the ways that spatial features of work affect interactions and relations. They are gathering data on everything from office temperature and layout to schedules, including measuring how often people interact and with whom (using electronic badges that can assess not just physical location but how often someone speaks and with whom).

They are using this data to decide everything from the size of cafeteria tables to how many coffee stations to provide and where. Zappos, for example, uses a metric called "collisionable hours" to assess a space's effectiveness.[42] And at the Google headquarters in Silicon Valley, says Laszlo Bock, senior vice president of people operations, workers are never supposed to be more than 200 feet from food. The reason for this, according to Bock, is innovation: It's a spatial way of nudging people to interact and collaborate by creating a space and reason for employees to leave their desk and interact with others whose desks may not be near their own.[43] We are entering a new, more virtual world of work, and this means that apps and virtual meeting room structures and processes will also be important for interactions.

The list goes on. Organizations already are paying attention to systems, cultures, and spatial features of their workplaces—and they are also paying attention to emotions and relations; they should acknowledge that relations and discrimination are inextricably intertwined and that organizations have power over how those relations are structured. We don't need to ignore or excuse individuals as agents in their own interactions, but solutions to discrimination in work organizations are often best undertaken at the organizational level. Organizations, after all, create the conditions for relations—and all of the biases and emotions that go along with them.

2
SHIFTING REPERTOIRES: RACIAL EMOTION AND DIVERSITY IN WORK

Beyond structural changes designed to reduce discrimination and thereby strengthen relations, there are also ways that our institutions can shift their repertoires of racial emotion to more fairly balance the burdens of those emotions. The most obvious of these is to equalize feeling rules so people of color are not penalized for expressing emotions that their white counterparts are permitted to express. If anger and outbursts are allowed for whites at work, then they should also be allowed for people of color. Organizations need not tolerate angry outbursts, but they should be expected to treat anger in Blacks and other people of color similarly as they would treat anger in whites.

Reassessing the "Good" Worker

Law and organizations can also more fairly value the emotional labor that is expected of people of color. Specifically, our institutions will need to shift emotion repertoires to allow complaints involving racial bias and discrimination to fall within the "good" worker purview. Workers must be permitted to raise race concerns when they arise, as a matter of practice as well as of policy. Indeed, this is true regardless of the race of the person seeking to raise racial justice concerns. Those who raise concerns should be valued as facilitators of conversation and possibly needed change, not as troublemakers.

For similar reason, retaliation law also should protect individuals who complain about bias or discrimination, even if they may not have a reasonable belief that what they are complaining about amounts to a legal violation. To require a reasonable belief of legal violation is too onerous. It allows organizations to punish people for raising legitimate racial concerns and thereby closes rather than opens space for conversation and learning. The law already builds in sufficient constraints, such as requiring the retaliatory conduct be such that it would dissuade a reasonable person from objecting to discriminatory conduct, and requiring plaintiffs to establish a causal connection between their complaint—opposition conduct—and the retaliation.

We know that many organizations today claim to value diversity and to be committed to racial justice. Part of this commitment must be investing in systems and practices that foster diversity narratives of learning and conversation and importantly this requires openness to people raising racial concerns, not just in formal complaint systems but in diversity trainings and other settings.[44] It also means guarding against the "white fragility" that comes with professed public (and private) commitment to racial justice.[45] Lashing out and emotion-laden behaviors of whites when racial concerns are raised need to be understood as they operate in a context of white superiority and feelings of entitlement, and our institutions must put measures in place to consistently value, assess, and act on those concerns, whether they are about broad cultures or practices, systems or structures, or bias or discrimination in relations with coworkers, supervisors, or high-level leadership.

Developing Language to Expand Our Repertoires for Racial Emotion

Drawing on our understanding of emotion and of how concepts and language affect our experience of emotion, another way that our institutions might more fairly allocate burdens of racial emotion is to build a language that more appropriately acknowledges differences in racial emotions.[46] The idea of racial assault is one step in this direction. But we could go further.

Indeed, most of the recommendations provided so far work within our existing racial emotion concepts. In other words, they use our familiar emotion language, much as I have throughout the book. This is because there is a lot to be done to equalize our institutions' approach to racial emotion even within our current emotion language. But we can push further to better capture the variations in our racial emotions—to create new space for thinking about our interracial interactions in ways that improve those interactions and relations in the long term.

It is common for kids to learn in school that some languages have more than fifty words for snow. By one recent report, the Inuit dialect spoken in Canada's Nunavik region really does have fifty-three words for snow, with some northern dialects having even more for ice than snow.[47] A linguist in Norway says that the Sami people who live on the northern tip of Scandinavia and Russia have 180 words related to snow and ice. The precise count is less important than the idea. This can be the first time that some of us realize the words we use to think and talk about things can be constraining—and also liberating. Words shape how we think. The idea makes perfect sense: If snow and ice are important to us—indeed, our lives may depend on whether the snow we walk on is dense and can carry our weight or loose and will lead to avalanches or whether the ice is filled with crystals—then we will develop more ways to talk about snow and ice.[48]

Research on emotions today goes even further to suggest that everything that we experience and attribute to our emotions has also been shaped by the words and concepts our cultures use to acknowledge or describe emotions. You may recall from chapter 1: Concepts shape not just how we think but how we feel. The German word "Schadenfreude" has been seeping into American culture for some time now. It is used in German cultures to describe the feeling of "pleasure from someone else's misfortune." The German language also has three distinct "angers"; Mandarin has five. Often, people learning new languages will misuse emotion words because they have not built up experiences to easily classify them. Russian, for example, has two concepts of "anger," one involving anger at a person and another anger for more abstract reasons. American English speakers tend to default to the latter because anger in the United States is often directed at events or situations. Russians, though, tend to use the former anger more frequently, which means that Americans are often misunderstood when they talk about their anger.[49] The same is true for other emotion words, like "guilt" or "sadness."

Once someone explains a new emotion concept, you can begin to experience it. Before that, it tends to get overlooked or lumped in with your existing concepts. You may feel something without it ("I feel generally good or not so good about this"), but it won't be an emotion that can be easily communicated or discussed with others.[50] Psychologist Lisa Feldman Barrett tells the story of visiting a friend in Belgium. When she and her friend were cozied up in her living room sharing wine and chocolates, her friend told her they were experiencing the emotion *gezellig*, a concept that means "comfort, coziness, and togetherness of being at home, with friends and loved ones."[51] Once her friend described it, Barrett says she immediately experienced it. That said, her ability to describe it was probably still limited because the emotion concepts that we draw on in the United States, "comfort," "well-being," and "happiness," are more focused on internal states than on specific situations.

This may be going a bit far. It seems likely that we can experience an emotion even if we don't have a precise word to describe it. Moreover, we should be careful in what we're saying. This isn't about English versus other languages and experience of emotion across cultures, as if some cultures are better at experiencing emotion than others. The idea that language determines ideas and thereby cabins our thinking has been questioned for this reason. But the larger point is an interesting one: that we might be able to advance our institutions' approach to racial emotions by expanding emotion repertoires, not just by policing those repertoires or trying to calibrate them to more fairly value emotion. In this sense, language and emotions are a system, not a one-way determinant, and on this, linguists seem much more comfortable. Language, as sociologist Eva Illouz puts it, "defines categories of emotions, establishes what an 'emotional problem' is, provides causal frameworks and metaphors to make sense of these problems, and constrains the ways emotions are expressed, made sense of, and managed."[52]

I bring this up here because it may be helpful in thinking about solutions to the current approach to racial emotion. What if we could expand our conceptual repertoire of racial emotion in the United States? Barrett calls this "emotional granularity," and she emphasizes how we as individuals can develop more emotion concepts to help us manage the world around us.[53]

We might develop concepts that are specifically attuned to the feelings we experience in interracial interaction, concepts that tell us something about the context for the emotion, even something about where the emotion sits within our current historical moment. We don't have to fully subscribe to a "language-cabins-thinking" hypothesis to decide that this is a good idea. Whether it is our culture driving the language or the language driving our culture, developing language around emotion concepts that matter to us can help us better articulate, consider, and value racial emotion in ways that advance racial justice rather than hinder it.

We could, for example, rightly differentiate racial emotion concepts like racial pleasure and racial humiliation, or types of racial anxiety. Indeed, we might constructively acknowledge that the racial anxiety that a person of color experiences at the prospect of being judged according to subordinating stereotypes—what we might call an emotion of "honor," borne out of desire to be judged on equal terms in the present moment with knowledge of deeply subordinating history—is different from the racial anxiety or even "shame" that a white person experiences at the prospect of being judged according to normative expectations of nonracism. As we have seen, the indignation in each—"how dare you judge me according to a stereotype rather than seeing my 'true' self and qualities"—may be similar, but their contexts and even meanings or value in the present moment differ substantially. One also often involves concern about the tangible effects of being unfairly treated differently on the basis of race, such as receiving less pay or fewer job opportunities, while the other usually involves a psychological concern about being uncomfortable or embarrassed. We can use language to capture these differences and to construct or shift old repertoires to more appropriately value the emotions that we feel as well as how we manage them.

As another example, we might develop a concept that encompasses the mixed feeling of discomfort and yet satisfaction of pursuing rather than avoiding a difficult interaction with someone different from us in a way that leads to learning and connection, perhaps something like an emotion of "perseverance." We may not all experience this emotion in the same way; indeed, we probably won't. But with language we can begin to talk about it, our experiences, what it feels like to each of us and why. And from there, we can begin to develop a feeling of "racial equality," as legal scholar Janine Young Kim has written, defined as "the positive emotions we feel when we believe we enjoy equal status in relation to others."[54]

These repertoires may also include behaviors. Just as smiling is built into our repertoire for affection or admiration, for example, so putting a hand over our heart or raising our eyebrows might become a racial emotion behavior when we realize that we have made a racial misstep, having said something that causes racial humiliation or a racial honor response in our interactional partner.

We should not be afraid of labeling, of using words and language to express and develop a range of racial emotion concepts. Our concepts will not be set in stone—they can and will change as we grow, leading us to new ways of thinking and communicating and, yes, even feeling. Moreover, developing racial emotion concepts through language to describe our experiences and their places in context does not require that we create a rigid value hierarchy. The goal is not to say that one emotion is more legitimate than another; only that how we understand emotions should calibrate with our histories and our collective goals for justice.

3

SHARING DISCOMFORT: BUILDING A NEW VISION OF INTEGRATION

> We have all been programmed to respond to the human
> differences between us with fear and loathing and to handle
> that difference in one of three ways: ignore it, and if that is
> not possible, copy it if we think it is dominant, or destroy it if
> we think it is subordinate. But we have no patterns for
> relating across our human differences as equals.
> Audre Lorde

What if we also endeavored to create patterns for relating across our human differences as equals? For individuals, a better understanding of our emotions in interracial interaction can open our eyes to ways we cope with those emotions and importantly how we place burdens on others in doing so. But there is more to consider here both at the individual level and at the level of our institutions. Specifically, we should consider the choices we make about who bears the brunt of negative emotion, including anxiety or discomfort around race.

We know that people of color and whites alike can experience negative racial emotion, often experienced as discomfort and anxiety, in interracial interactions, and that avoidance is a common coping mechanism. We also know that whites, who still hold the positions of power in most organizations, are likely to have more success in avoidance. While whites can avoid conversations about race and keep interactions short, people of color are required to push on, to bear their discomfort in the interest of making headway in the workplace. One way that people of color ease the discomfort of whites is by assimilating their appearance and behaviors to dominant white norms.

Devon Carbado and Mitu Gulati deftly illustrate this reality in *Acting White?*[55] They describe the "extra identity work" that outsiders must perform to send the message that they fit in. Whether it's "whitening" a resume so it doesn't appear "too Black," laughing at a racial joke, or logging in extra hours to overcome the stereotype of someone from your group being lazy or slow on the uptake, "acting white" is a means of getting ahead in a white world. The time, money, and energy devoted to this extra work, they argue, is itself problematic, as it is also time, money, and energy that is not being devoted to performance tasks and accordingly can lead to less success. Others have emphasized the personal, identity costs of dominant group assimilation demands, including legal scholar Kenji Yoshino, who so beautifully describes his personal journey that has involved passing and covering—or downplaying—his "true" self to make others (and sometimes himself) more comfortable.[56]

At the very least, the costs that Carbado and Gulati identify will have to be taken into account by law and organizations if those institutions are to equalize the burdens of racial emotion in work. One way to do this, as I mentioned earlier, would be to identify work cultures that may be detrimental to people of color, cultures that value "fit," as almost all cultures do, and yet exclude through chosen social norms and subjective judgments. A story relayed by sociologist Jennifer Pierce comes to mind of Randall Kingsley, a Black male lawyer working in the legal department of a large corporation.[57] Kingsley describes his experience in the legal department, staffed mostly by white men, as involving jokes about his style of dress, lukewarm reception when he asked for help as a new associate, and lunch appointments that were "forgotten" by white colleagues. His colleagues, on the other hand, mentioned that he was "too flashy" and "too demand-ing," noting that he just didn't "fit in."

There are additional implications for social equality in this vision of integration that have gone largely unexplored. By this I mean that even as organizations increasingly claim to "value diversity," they may be simulta-neously ramping up their demands for homogeneity. Why? Because "valu-ing diversity" can seem threatening to whites, who may increase their calls for good "fit," by which they mean lowering their discomfort with differ-ence (and reducing the risk that their dominance will be disrupted).

Take the case of English-only rules. As legal scholar Cristina Rodríguez points out, while we often think of English-only rules in terms of balanc-ing individual and employer rights (e.g., should someone who speaks Spanish have the right to speak that language at work?; should employers have the right to limit the languages spoken?), we can consider the English-only workplace rule as an effort to "control the social dynamics of the workplace."[58] By "English-only rule" I mean a rule where only English is allowed to be spoken in the workplace. This is different from a rule requiring an employee be able to speak English; it is a demand that no language can be spoken other than English. Even more than an effort to control social dynamics, an English-only rule can be seen as an effort to relieve English-only speakers of the discomfort of working in a place where multiple languages are spoken, languages that this English-only speaker does not understand. English-only rules understood in this way are about discomfort and who is expected to bear discomfort with difference.

Another language-oriented example involves interactions between native English speakers and nonnative English speakers. We often hear complaints by the former that the latter's English is not good enough because it is difficult for native English speakers to understand. Not impossible, but difficult; it may require slowing down, looking directly at the person to whom we are speaking, asking for repetition and clarifica-tion, etc. An expectation that each encounter with others will be entirely smooth and easy for native English speakers is a demand that someone else bear the full cost of our discomfort with difference. We are not willing to meet halfway, to slow down, and to consider each other's efforts as equal participants with equal burdens in the project of a multicultural society.

Race-related assimilation demands can operate more broadly in much the same way. Appearance is a common demand, though there are also many behavioral assimilation demands in most workplaces. Many of these demands revolve around comfort and so-called "professionalism" that adheres to white norms. An employer may require "nonbraided" hair, whether informally or formally, for example, because it makes white coworkers and clients more comfortable. These hair rules effectively require that many Black women straighten their hair rather than wearing it naturally, resulting, as legal scholar Wendy Greene puts it, in "hyper-regulation of Black women's bodies via their hair."[59] Seeing this, some states have begun to adopt what have been called CROWN (Creating a Respectful and Open World for Natural hair) acts, laws that expressly recognize that race discrimination includes discrimination encountered by African descendants "based on their natural and protective hairstyles, such as afros, twists, locs, and braids." This is an example of a movement that presses for more racially equalized assimilation demands and thereby greater sharing of discomfort in interracial interactions.

Moreover, we should keep in mind that research suggests that interracial relations are more likely to lead to prejudice reduction in whites, and thereby to stronger interracial relations in the long term, if people of color are allowed to express their racial identities rather than to cover or hide them. This is because people tend to exceptionalize those who do not seem typical of the out-group. "We don't really think of you as Black" is an example of this exceptionalism, and it thwarts disruption of stereotypes, while putting pressure on people of color to conform. What's more, research suggests that greater comfort in interracial interactions—*feeling* better about race in our interactions—can actually conceal discrimination and delegitimize race-related concerns when they are raised.[60]

From this I do not make an individual-rights argument—although there may be good basis for that as well—but a social equality one: Easing assimilation demands can increase social equality and advance racial justice. Together, individuals can bear the discomfort of difference and open space for engagement and learning over antagonism and avoidance. This is a fundamentally different vision of integration than the one that is touted in most workplaces today. It is a vision of integration in which discomfort with difference is experienced instead of avoided, shared instead of hoisted on others.

SOME SPECIFIC CALLS FOR LAW, WORK ORGANIZATIONS, AND INDIVIDUALS

One way of dodging the hard work of reform is to insist on specific measures—a bullet-point checklist of sorts: Tell me exactly what we should do so that we will make no mistakes and can "move on" as quickly as possible (e.g., "What should I say?"; "What trainings should we provide?"; "What should I do when someone gets upset?"). In a world with how-to videos showing precisely which piece to place where, we find ourselves seeking the same when it comes to our institutions, relationships, and race. This, of course, is not possible, and it would be a mistake to suggest otherwise. Instead of quick relational fixes and merely admirable statements supporting diversity on workplace websites, we will need to do the hard work of changing our institutions—our law and work organizations alike—to more equally value racial emotion as well as open ourselves to more difficult truths and conversations about our own racial emotions. This chapter has set out a rough roadmap for this work by presenting three broad proposals. In my view, this overarching roadmap—and the story that leads up to it—is the ultimate contribution of this book.

Some readers may nonetheless have noticed that within the three broad proposals detailed in this chapter—Seeing Discrimination, Shifting Repertoires, and Sharing Discomfort—emerge a number of specific, concrete recommendations for law, work organizations, and individuals. Here are just a few.

Law

Acknowledge our history. Law, as we saw in chapters 3 and 4, is itself the product of racial emotion and also shapes and values (and devalues) racial emotion in various ways.

Accept that racial emotion is personal and *racial.* Judges should resist the temptation to conclude that an acrimonious workplace relationship is somehow solely personal and thereby nonracial. Racial emotion is personal *and* racial.

Expand antidiscrimination inquiries to relations, not just specific decision moments or incidents. Judges should not close out racial emotion that occurs outside of the immediate time frame of a specific employment decision; nor should they isolate behavior that is deemed "inappropriate" or "insubordinate" from the relations leading up to the behavior.

Attend to racial assault behavior. The law should treat racial assault behavior as presumptively discriminatory and as constituting a hostile work environment. Judges should not (and should not be permitted to) substitute their own judgment about what the actor "intended" for a legal presumption in these cases. The law should further presume that any adverse employment decisions (such as a pay or promotion decision) made by someone who has exhibited racial assault behavior as to any individuals against whom the behavior was exhibited within a specific time period was motivated at least in part by race.

Allow raising race concerns as part of being a "good" worker. The law should protect workers who raise concerns about racial bias and discrimination regardless of whether the actions complained of amount to or could be reasonably understood to amount to legally actionable conduct.

Facilitate a systemic lens. The law should support efforts that focus on systemic discrimination, including hostile work environments involving behavior across work areas, and the law should facilitate class-based litigation, assessment, and solutions to this end.

Work Organizations

Acknowledge our history. Work organizations generally, as well as specific work organizations, have history involving race and racial emotion, as we saw in chapters 5 and 6, and this history leads to the valuing of some racial emotions over others. Work organizations cannot "rid" the workplace of racial emotion, and they cannot "move past" race and racial emotion and the discomfort that comes along with it; instead, they can work to create work environments that treat

workers fairly and that facilitate engagement and create space for
positive interracial interactions at work.

Attend to worker concerns. Work organizations should encourage all
workers to raise race issues and concerns and should undertake to
evaluate those concerns not just as "personal" or "personnel" matters
but also as race matters; they should not isolate behavior that is
deemed "inappropriate" or "insubordinate" from the relations leading
up to the behavior; and they should monitor race concerns raised in
interpersonal relations for ties to broader patterns, practices, systems,
and work cultures.

Assess and modify job expectations and emotion rules. Work organizations
should assess their job expectations and emotion rules for inequalities
and shift expectations toward equality. This can mean taking a variety
of measures, such as: formalizing hiring and promotion expectations
and processes to guide decisions and interrogate explanations of lack
of "fit" or "professionalism"; calibrating institutional response to white
women's tears and anger in people of color as well as other racialized
emotions; and adopting diversity narratives that emphasize learning
over colorblindness or multiculturalism. It also includes addressing
racial assault behavior with attention to broader work environments
and acknowledging that whites perceiving themselves as being called
"racist" (or even being called "racist") is not racial assault.

Take a systemic approach to assessment and change. Work organizations
should assess their workplaces for systemic patterns of inequality and
make changes to structures, practices, systems, and cultures that will
foster more space for equal-power interracial interactions, thought,
and conversations about race concerns, including shared discomfort.
Measures at the organizational level include not just changes aimed
at softer, sometimes inchoate expectations, but those aimed at
improving demographics, HR systems and practices, spatial features,
and how work and time are organized.

Be wary of diversity and antiracism training. Organizations should be
careful not to focus their efforts too closely on individuals, including
through diversity or antiracism training. Diversity training done well
can be useful, but it is neither sufficient nor typically nonproblem-
atic.[61] In some cases, diversity trainings urge individuals to reveal

their racial emotions and yet they enforce strict, often unstated rules for how to experience or navigate those emotions and, not surprisingly, value some racial emotions over others. Diversity training can build and value anger, fear, and resentment among some whites and at the same time minimize the anger, fear, and resentment of some people of color.[62] Moreover, turning to the training and even punishment of individuals can distract from the structural problems—organizational systems, practices, and cultures, among other things—that most need attention and change.[63]

Individuals

As advocates, leaders, and workers, we can seek change in our institutions, pressing for fairer treatment of racial emotion in law and work organizations in the ways discussed above. We can also open our own eyes to the ways we tend to cope with racial emotions and importantly how we place burdens on others in doing so. Even if our emphasis has been on institutions in this book, we have also learned that as individuals we can help shape our own interracial interactions and our racial emotions within them. The research discussed earlier in this chapter and also in chapter 2 is helpful here, suggesting, for example, that individuals will benefit from

being internally motivated to be and act nonprejudiced;

cultivating belief in self-efficacy in interaction;

adopting a learning over performance approach to interracial interaction; and

understanding that anxiety (and prejudice) can be reduced over time.

At the very least, as individuals who engage in interracial (and intraracial) interaction every day, we should:

Acknowledge our history and our racial emotions. Individuals should seek space for thought and conversation about race rather than avoiding it. They, especially whites, should seek to experience their discomfort rather than hoisting it on others, to be, as one author puts it, "more intentional about navigating" race, privilege, and racial experiences, including racial emotions.[64]

Admit missteps and mistakes. Individuals should be open to admitting mistakes and learning from interracial experiences. Admitting that we may have been racially biased in an interaction—or that we otherwise behaved in a way that we are not proud of—is not the same as labeling ourselves a bad person.[65] Nor does being self-conscious about white identity mean that white identity is under threat.[66]

Speak up and value others' speaking up. Individuals should speak up about bias and discrimination when they see it, should welcome and learn from others' racial concerns when they are raised, and should be alert to bias and racial emotions in intraracial and closed door as well as interracial and open door settings.[67] Expressing emotion through language may also help us develop new words and concepts to explore our experiences and set us on a more solid path toward justice.

Advocate for institutional change. Individuals should seek broad assessments of racial inequality and justice concerns, question seemingly "neutral" practices, and demand the type of action in organizations and law described above.

Conclusion

There is a lot we haven't done in this book. We haven't worked on our interpersonal skills, for example, nor have we developed a guide for how work organizations might mediate difficult interracial interactional moments when they arise. In fact, I expect that some readers, especially those who have been following the business press over the past few years, will wonder why I haven't said more about empathy—and how we can go about getting more of it.[1] The project in this book, however, has not been to identify the best emotions for progress or to delineate self-help measures for our relational difficulties, as key as those projects surely are,[2] but rather to open our eyes to the importance of racial emotion in our interactions and to the ways that our institutions are treating racial emotion and closing space for learning and conversation. There may be some promise in the idea of emotional intelligence and the capacity of empathy to generate inclusive workplaces and success in working with others, and we should continue working to bring about research-driven training and insights about interpersonal interactions, interracial as well as intraracial, just as we should encourage and support work in a variety of fields aimed at techniques for improving our interracial interactions.[3]

But we will need to be extremely cautious about efforts to make ourselves *feel* good about race before we have taken on the structural change required to treat it fairly in our workplaces. Among other things, we will need to be careful not to turn our newfound understanding of racial emotion into a call for a consciousness-raising model of diversity under which workshops and trainings provide space for whites to "work out feelings" about racism, to share their guilt and fear. As Canadian sociologist Sarita Srivastava notes, under a "let's talk" approach: "Racism is interpreted and softened through therapeutic discourse: racism becomes 'old hurts' that are only remembered because they are the 'only power' marginalized women of colour might have. At the same time, women of colour are counselled that they 'need to let go,' they need to forget their disappointments with previous failures of anti-racist efforts because they are holding the organization back."[4]

Related to this is the haunting trouble with optimism. I see this book's premise as an optimistic one: As we learn about racial emotion in interracial interactions at work and about our institutions' approach to racial emotion, we are better situated to push for meaningful change, including pushing our institutions to better see and more fairly judge racial emotion and to create space for developing positive emotions in interracial relations in the long run. This said, any optimist must grapple with the realities of racial history and subordination in our country. This book is about racial emotion in interracial interactions at work and our institutions' approach to that racial emotion, but we can't help but also see—as we should—that racial emotion itself pushes our institutions (through the humans who create and sustain those institutions) to neglect racial emotion in some and to rush to protect racial emotion in others, thereby building spaces and stories that skew our experiences in troubling ways and undermine our efforts at change.

Even the simple prospect of fairly valuing racial emotion or of expanding language and concepts to distinguish emotion repertoires may feel like a threat to some, a way of restructuring the world to lessen the advantage of the dominant group. In one recent study, merely making whites aware of the majority-minority shift in population in the United States resulted in greater expectation by them of discrimination against whites.[5] Yet when the study participants were told that the majority-minority people of color will "appreciate and conform to the mainstream culture," they no longer predicted greater antiwhite discrimination.

This reality brings us full circle to remind us that our project for equality and racial justice will have to include racial emotion as it operates well beyond our interpersonal interactions at work. In this book, we have undertaken study of interpersonal, especially interracial interactions at work, which represent only a slice of racial emotion in our broader lives, in our resistance or embrace, for example, of various key social policies having to do with welfare, immigration, family, housing, education, and criminality, among others.[6] And even our emotions involving race in interactions at work will necessarily take place within a broader cultural context, not just a context influenced by law and work organizations. In themselves, our bodies do not carry with them affective or emotional value.[7] It is the cultures and the stories that we tell about those bodies that provide them with emotional values, that make our bodies to be feared, hated, or loved. Our feelings are not individual, in other words; they are cultural and political. We have known this all along. To acknowledge all of this beyond our interactions at work is to acknowledge the complexity of our project for racial progress, not to defeat it.

Indeed, some argue that racial emotion can have as much to do with vantage as advantage; fear and resentment are borne of stories of prosperity as zero-sum, especially when it comes to race.[8] Yet emotion has never been zero-sum. When we increase the spread of our positive emotions, even if realistically to include ambivalence and confusion as well as joy, dignity, and love, why should we expect losers and winners? We can expand our repertoires of racial emotion and our relations in ways that benefit all.

This said, shifting our institutions' approach to racial emotion (and our own) at work is admittedly an uncomfortable and for many of us even a frightening project. If we agree that racial equality and justice are our goals, then our solutions will have to include easing stark hierarchy and subordination. We have a long history in this country of prioritizing white harmony and comfort over structural racial change. Understanding the role of racial emotion in our relations, and specifically our institutions' approach to racial emotion, opens opportunity for structural change rather than closing it down. Remaining in silence must be the worse alternative.

Notes

INTRODUCTION

1. I capitalize "Black" in this book out of respect for shared culture and experience of the Black community. I do not capitalize "white" because, while I realize there is room for disagreement on this, in my view it has a different set of meanings and history such that capitalizing "white" in this moment risks following the lead of white supremacists.

2. I use the term "equality" broadly to encompass systemic fairness in treatment of people of all races; in this way, I use the term "equality" interchangeably with "equity" aimed at "racial justice."

3. I use the singular "racial emotion" when referring to the broad category of racial emotion and the plural "racial emotions" when talking about the range of emotions a person experiences in any moment.

4. "The pain is in our DNA at this point," one Black woman told a reporter in Buffalo after the racially motivated mass shooting at a supermarket. Troy Closson, "'Nobody Cares about Us Here': Anguish and Anger on Buffalo's East Side," *New York Times*, May 15, 2022, https://www.nytimes.com/2022/05/15/nyregion/east-side-buffalo-neighborhood.html. For discussion of group pain and cultural trauma, including through exposure to public and reinforced "routine" harm, see Angela Onwuachi-Willig, "The Trauma of the Routine: Lessons on Cultural Trauma from the Emmett Till Verdict," *Sociological Theory* 34, no. 4 (2010): 335–57, https://doi.org:10.1177/0735275116679864.

5. It is important for us to expressly acknowledge that these calls are not new. Current voices are joining with those who have been making these claims for generations. For a description of one example at one of my own teaching institutions, the University of San Francisco, see Rhonda V. Magee, "Legal Education and the Formation of Professional Identity: A Critical Spirituo-Humanistic—'Humanity Consciousness'—Perspective," *New York University Review of Law and Social Change* 31 (2007): 467. Indeed, the fact that our institutions—including our law and work organizations and also the academy and others—have refused to see and fairly value racial emotion is arguably a result of white dominance in these institutions and itself the product of whites' desires for racial comfort, to "move past" racism and the realities of race in our lives.

6. The idea here is that understanding implicit bias and implementing change based on that knowledge is not the same thing as providing a list of behavioral dos and don'ts in diversity trainings. For a short review of some of the recent research on diversity programs, including what doesn't work and what might, see Frank Dobbin and Alexandra Kalev, "Why Diversity Programs Fail: And What Works Better," *Harvard Business Review*, July–August 2016, https://hbr .org/2016/07/why-diversity-programs-fail. For a deeper and broader look at structural measures that empirical research suggests will improve outcomes for women and people of color at work, see Frank Dobbin and Alexandra Kalev, *Getting to Diversity: What Works and What Doesn't* (Cambridge, MA: Harvard University Press, 2022). On the industry that has built up around diversity efforts—and its largely dismal effects—see Pamela Newkirk, *Diversity Inc.: The Failed Promise of a Billion-Dollar Business* (New York: Bold Type Books, 2020).

CHAPTER 1. WHAT IS RACIAL EMOTION?

1. Winthrop D. Jordan, *White over Black: American Attitudes toward the Negro, 1550-1812* (Chapel Hill: University of North Carolina Press, 1968), 3–43 (detailing early accounts of the English coming into contact with Africans). Jordan includes an account of the emotionality of the words "black" and white" for the English during this time (7–8).

2. Scientific race was also key to Black Codes and later Jim Crow laws that enforced segregation. In the famous *Dred Scott v. Sanford* case in which the Supreme Court held that neither enslaved African Americans nor their descendants—whether free or enslaved—were citizens under the U.S. Constitution, and therefore were not entitled to the rights that it confers, the Court observed in support of its conclusion: "[Black people] had for more than a century before been regarded as beings of an inferior order, and altogether unfit to associate with the white race, either in social or political relations; and so far inferior that they had no rights which the white man was bound to respect; and

that the negro might justly and lawfully be reduced to slavery for his benefit."
Dred Scott v. Sanford, 60 U.S. 393, 407 (1857).

For more on the use of scientific claims of race and inferiority to bolster pro-slavery and other similar positions, see Laura E. Gómez, "Off-White in an Age of White Supremacy: Mexican Elites and the Rights of Indians and Blacks in Nineteenth-Century New Mexico," *Chicano-Latina Law Review* 25 (2005): 9; Dorothy E. Roberts, *Fatal Invention: How Science, Politics, and Big Business Re-create Race in the Twenty-First Century* (New York: New Press, 2012); Ann Morning, *The Nature of Race: How Scientists Think and Teach about Human Difference* (Berkeley: University of California Press, 2011).

3. Roberts, *Fatal Invention*, 36 (quoting English scientist Sir Francis Galton, who coined the word "eugenics" in 1833) and 36–42 (on eugenics); Morning, *Nature of Race*, 30.

4. Although losing ground, the essentialist view arguably never really went away. See Roberts, *Fatal Invention*, 43–49 (describing continued reliance on "scientific race" and eugenics even as fields shifted publicly toward the view that science shows one human race rather than multiple races).

5. Michael Omi and Howard Winant, *Racial Formation in the United States: From the 1960s to the 1980s* (New York: Routledge, 2nd ed., 1994), 55. Legal scholar Ian Haney López provides a similar definition of race in his influential *White by Law: The Legal Construction of Race* (New York: NYU Press, 2nd ed., 2006). He defines race there as "the historically contingent social systems of meaning that attach to elements of morphology and ancestry" (xvi; restating and elaborating on this definition). Race is constantly evolving and even today is tied inextricably to dominance, power, and ideology.

6. Trina Jones and Jessica Roberts, "Genetic Race? DNA Ancestry Tests, Racial Identity, and the Law," *Columbia Law Review* 120 (2020): 1929; Roberts, *Fatal Invention* (including also government approval of race-specific drugs and law enforcement use of DNA databases to seek racial identification of suspects).

7. Rene Almeling, "Selling Genes, Selling Gender: Egg Agencies, Sperm Banks, and the Medical Market in Genetic Material," *American Sociological Review* 72, no. 3 (2007): 319, 326, https://www.jstor.org/stable/25472466 ("In Creative Beginnings' office, there is a cabinet for 'active donor' files. The top two drawers are labeled 'Caucasian,' and the bottom drawer is labeled 'Black, Asian, Hispanic.' During a tour of Cryo-Corp, the founder lifted sperm samples out of the storage tank filled with liquid nitrogen, explaining that the vials are capped with white tops for Caucasian donors, black tops for African American donors, yellow tops for Asian donors, and red tops for donors with 'mixed ancestry.'").

For more on race and genetics, see Patricia J. Williams, "The Elusive Variability of Race," in *Race and the Genetic Revolution: Science, Myth, and Culture*, ed. Sheldon Krimsky and Kathleen Sloan (New York: Columbia University Press, 2011), 241. For more on race in ART, see Camille Gear Rich, "Contracting Our

Way to Inequality: Race, Reproductive Freedom, and the Quest for the Perfect Child," *Minnesota Law Review* 104 (2020): 2375.

8. Morning, *Nature of Race*.

9. Ann Morning, Hannah Brückner, and Alondra Nelson, "Socially Desirable Reporting and the Expression of Biological Concepts of Race," *Du Bois Review: Social Science Research on Race* 16, no. 2 (2019): 439–55, https://doi.org:10.1017/S1742058X19000195.

10. "The answer: there are no biological races in the human species. Period. That conclusion was confirmed by the most ambitious research project on human biology yet undertaken, the Human Genome Project. A mountain of evidence assembled by historians, anthropologists, and biologists proves that race is not and cannot possibly be a natural division of human beings." Roberts, *Fatal Invention*, 77, and chap. 3 (on the Human Genome Project).

11. For thinking on the idea of "marginal whiteness," see Camille Gear Rich, "Marginal Whiteness," *California Law Review* 98 (2010): 1497; and on intraracial distinctions, see Devon W. Carbado and Mitu Gulati, *Acting White?: Rethinking Race in "Post-Racial" America* (New York: Oxford University Press, 2013).

12. Camille Gear Rich, "Elective Race: Recognizing Race Discrimination in the Era of Racial Self-Identification," *Georgetown Law Journal* 102 (2014): 1501.

13. Aliya Saperstein and Andrew M. Penner, "Racial Fluidity and Inequality in the United States," *American Journal of Sociology* 118, no. 3 (2012): 676–727, https://doi.org/10.1086/667722.

14. Devon W. Carbado and Mitu Gulati, "The Fifth Black Woman," *Journal of Contemporary Legal Issues* 11 (2001): 701. Carbado and Gulati call this "working identity" in *Acting White?* This idea that we perform race and racial identity builds on the work of sociologist Erving Goffman exploring the importance of how we present ourselves in our daily lives. Erving Goffman, *The Presentation of Self in Everyday Life* (New York: Doubleday, 1959 [1956]).

15. Devon W. Carbado, "Critical What What?," *Connecticut Law Review* 43 (2011): 1593, 1609–10.

16. Gary Peller, "History, Identity, and Alienation," *Connecticut Law Review* 43 (2011): 1479, 1501.

17. Khiara M. Bridges, *Critical Race Theory: A Primer* (St. Paul, MN: West, 2019), 129.

18. Dacher Keltner and Jennifer S. Learner, "Emotion," in *Handbook of Social Psychology, Vol. 1*, ed. Susan T. Fiske, Daniel T. Gilbert, and Gardner Lindzey (Hoboken, NJ: John Wiley & Sons, 5th ed., 2010).

19. Keltner and Lerner, "Emotion," 312 (describing Western constructions of emotions as being guided by a "Romanticism thesis").

20. Charles Darwin, *The Expression of the Emotions in Man and Animals* (London: John Murray, 1872). For argument that Darwin may have been less

universalistic than commonly stated, see Jan Plamper, *The History of Emotions: An Introduction* (New York: Oxford University Press, 2015), 167–72.

21. Paul Ekman, E. Richard Sorenson, and Wallace W. Friesen, "Pan-Cultural Elements in Facial Displays of Emotion," *Science* 164 (1969). For a summary of Ekman's work and the influence of universalism, including critique, see Plamper, *History of Emotions*, chap. 3.

22. Paul Ekman consulted on *Inside Out* (2015) and was also retained as a consultant by the Dalai Lama to create an "atlas of emotions," an interactive website that "builds your vocabulary of emotions and illuminates your emotional world." The site does acknowledge that "triggers" of emotions occur "in a context," which includes "our worldview, which is influenced by our prior experiences, personal history and inherited universal scripts about important events" (http://atlasofemotions.org/#triggers/).

23. Arlie Russell Hochschild, *The Managed Heart: Commercialization of Human Feeling* (Berkeley: University of California Press, 2nd ed., 2003), 213.

24. The universal versus constructed debate about emotion has been ongoing in the field of social psychology for some time. One effort to reconcile the two views situates them as different perspectives, one emphasizing "potential" and the other "practice." See Keltner and Lerner, "Emotion," 327, stating: "Evolutionists are right in arguing that in the abstract across cultures emotions arise in response to similar events and serve similar functions; constructivists are right in concluding that in practice the specific events that trigger emotion often vary dramatically in different cultures." These same authors propose that emotions may show greater universality in some features than in others, citing findings that they argue "dovetail with constructivists' claims that . . . cultures select and arrange the elements of emotional expression in culturally specific ways" (328). See also generally Plamper, *History of Emotions*, on the long-standing debate.

25. Lisa Feldman Barrett, *How Emotions Are Made: The Secret Life of the Brain* (New York: Houghton Mifflin, 2017).

26. Barrett, *How Emotions Are Made*, xii.

27. Barrett, *How Emotions Are Made*, xii.

28. This idea of construction goes further to include workings in the brain: psychological construction and neuroconstruction. See Barrett, *How Emotions Are Made*, 35. For a description of recent work in linguistic anthropology and related fields that situates emotion and language together as "collaboratively co-constructed," see Sonya E. Pritzker, "Language, Emotion, and the Politics of Vulnerability," *Annual Review of Anthropology* 49, no. 1 (2020): 241–56, https://www.annualreviews.org/doi/10.1146/annurev-anthro-010220-074429.

29. Eva Illouz, *Saving the Modern Soul: Therapy, Emotions, and the Culture of Self-Help* (Berkeley: University of California Press, 2008), 11.

30. Illouz, *Saving the Modern Soul*, 11.

31. That is, intellectually, as philosopher Martha Nussbaum would remind us. Martha Nussbaum, *Upheavals of Thought: The Intelligence of Emotions* (New York: Cambridge University Press, 2001). Nussbaum argues that emotions are "appraisals or value judgments, which ascribe to things and persons outside the person's own control great importance for that person's own flourishing" (4).

32. Sara Ahmed, *The Cultural Politics of Emotion* (Edinburgh: Edinburgh University Press, 2nd ed., 2014).

33. Daniel Dukes et al., "Comment: The Rise of Affectivism," *Nature Human Behavior* 5 (2021): 816–20, https://doi.org/10.1038/s41562-021-01130-8.

34. Lisa Feldman Barrett and Ajay B. Satpute, "Historical Pitfalls and New Directions in the Neuroscience of Emotion," *Neuroscience Letters* 693, no. 6 (2019): 9–18, https://doi.org/10.1016/j.neulet.2017.07.045 (proposing a multi-level constructivist theory of emotion for neuroscientific study). For argument that expecting a one-to-one connection is unduly narrow and that there may indeed be neurobiological evidence of basic emotions, see Alessia Celeghin et al., "Basic Emotions in Human Neuroscience: Neuroimaging and Beyond," *Frontiers in Psychology* 8 (2017): 1432, https://doi.org/10.3389/fpsyg.2017.01432.

35. See Jan Plamper, "The History of Emotions: An Interview with William Reddy, Barbara Rosenwein, and Peter Stearns," *History and Theory* 49, no. 2 (2010): 237–65, https://doi.org:10.1111/j.1468-2303.2010.00541.x.

36. Jennifer L. Eberhardt, *Biased: Uncovering the Hidden Prejudice That Shapes What We See, Think, and Do* (New York: Viking Press, 2019).

37. Malcolm Gladwell, *Blink: The Power of Thinking without Thinking* (New York: Little Brown, 2005).

38. Eberhardt, *Biased*, 5.

39. Eberhardt, *Biased*, 6. Although, as Eberhardt's story conveys, race stereotypes can operate in all of us, they are not equivalent (studies show that cross-race facial recognition is lower for whites than for Blacks, for example); moreover, they necessarily operate in a broader context of power distribution and white supremacy that we cannot ignore. See Charles Lawrence III, "Unconscious Racism Revisited: Reflections on the Impact and Origins of the 'Id, the Ego, and Equal Protection,'" *Connecticut Law Review* 40 (2008): 931. For a book review of *Biased* expanding on this point, see Osamudia James, "The 'Innocence' of Bias," *Michigan Law Review* 119 (2021): 1345.

40. Eberhardt, *Biased*, 36. As this latter study suggests, some stereotypes involving race are themselves about emotions, the emotions that we expect in others. Jefferson as far back as 1781 claimed that skin color is tied to emotion. Among other things, he asserted that Black people's "griefs are transient." Thomas Jefferson, *Notes on the State of Virginia* (1785). On whites' racial framing of African Americans and Native Americans, see Joe R. Feagin, *The White Racial Frame: Centuries of Framing and Counter-Framing* (New York: Routledge, 3rd ed., 2020).

41. Darren Lenard Hutchinson, "Ignoring the Sexualization of Race: Heteronormativity, Critical Race Theory and Anti-Racist Politics," *Buffalo Law Review* 47 (1990): 83.

42. K. Sue Jewell, *From Mammy to Miss America and Beyond: Cultural Images and the Shaping of US Social Policy* (New York: Routledge, 1993).

43. Morning, *Nature of Race*, 26 (although noting controversy over whether there existed a "pre-racial" world prior to the fifteenth and sixteenth centuries).

44. Judith Warner, "Psychiatry Confronts Its Racist Past, and Tries to Make Amends," *New York Times*, May 1, 2021, https://www.nytimes.com/2021/04/30/health/psychiatry-racism-black-americans.html.

45. For discussions of white women's tears, including firsthand stories involving interracial interaction, see Robin DiAngelo, *White Fragility: Why It's So Hard for White People to Talk about Racism* (Boston: Beacon Press, 2018), 132–36; Sarita Srivastava, "Tears, Fears and Careers: Racism and Emotion in Social Movement Organizations," *Canadian Journal of Sociology* 31, no. 1 (2006): 55. For more on the treatment of race concerns raised by people of color and the idea of using the "race card," see chapter 4.

46. Lisa Feldman Barrett and E. Bliss-Moreau, "She's Emotional. He's Having a Bad Day: Attributional Explanations for Emotion Stereotypes," *Emotion* 9, no. 5 (2009): 649–58, https://doi.org/10.1037/a0016821.

47. Social psychologists have developed intergroup emotions theory to better understand and study these group-level emotions. See Diane M. Mackie, Angela T. Maitner, and Eliot R. Smith, "Intergroup Emotions Theory," in *Handbook of Prejudice, Stereotyping, and Discrimination*, ed. Todd D. Nelson (New York: Routledge, 2009), 285. For a recent call for attention to anger or "Lordean rage" as a positive force for change, see Myisha Cherry, *The Case for Rage: Why Anger Is Essential to Anti-Racist Struggle* (New York: Oxford University Press, 2021). For more on emotion cultures in organizations, see Kathryn Abrams, *Open Hand, Closed Fist: Practices of Undocumented Organizing in a Hostile State* (Oakland: University of California Press, 2022), 62–73.

48. Ian Haney López, *Dog Whistle Politics: How Coded Racial Appeals Have Reinvented Racism and Wrecked the Middle Class* (New York: Oxford University Press, 2013).

49. Birgitte Bargetz, "The Distribution of Emotions: Affective Politics of Emancipation," *Hypatia* 30, no. 3 (2015): 582, https://www.jstor.org/stable/24542144 (describing how the study of "affective mechanisms of exclusion" is not only about study of something an individual possesses but also of something "deeply imbricated in the political and the social").

50. Eduardo Bonilla-Silva, "Feeling Race: Theorizing the Racial Economy of Emotions," *American Sociological Review* 84, no. 1 (2019): 1–25, https://www.jstor.org/stable/48588887. Bonilla-Silva provides a rich portrait of racial emotion broadly in our lives and surveys some of the important research in the area.

On racial emotion as it is embedded in our histories and our hope for better future relations, see Janine Young Kim, "On Race and Persuasion," *CUNY Law Review* 20 (2017): 505, 511: "The story of race in America is a story of dire inequality. Racial hatred, anger, grief and fear dominate our understanding of race. It is no wonder that racial discourse is so fraught and demands an inordinate amount of courage to engage."

51. Richard Rothstein, *The Color of Law: A Forgotten History of How Our Government Segregated America* (New York: Liveright, 2017); Sheryll Cashin, *White Space, Black Hood: Opportunity Hoarding and Segregation in the Age of Inequality* (New York: Random House, 2021).

52. Bonilla-Silva, "Feeling Race."

CHAPTER 2. RACIAL EMOTION AND OUR RELATIONS AT WORK

1. Christopher Leslie Brown, "Foreword," in Winthrop D. Jordan, *White over Black: American Attitudes toward the Negro* (Chapel Hill: University of North Carolina Press, 2nd ed., 2012), 1550–812, vii, x–xi.

2. This refusal to see racial emotion by whites is beginning to change as concepts like "white fragility" gain a foothold. See DiAngelo, *White Fragility*. The widespread sharing of "Karen" videos showing white women in emotional states about Black people around them is another sign of change, with more open conversation about whites, race, and racial emotion.

3. See Jeff Larson, "Introduction to the Special Section on Mixed Emotions," *Emotion Review* 9, no. 2 (2017): 97–98, https://doi.org/10.1177/1754073916672523.

4. Ariela Gross, *What Blood Won't Tell: A History of Race on Trial in America* (Boston: Harvard University Press, 2008), 10.

5. Thomas F. Pettigrew and Linda R. Tropp, "A Meta-Analytic Test of Intergroup Contact Theory," *Journal of Personality and Social Psychology* 90, no. 5 (2006): 751–83, https://doi.org/10.1037/0022-3514.90.5.751 (finding that intergroup contact does reduce prejudice even when all of Allport's conditions are not attained).

6. For recent analysis of residential segregation in the United States, see Jacob S. Rugh and Douglas S. Massey, "Segregation in Post–Civil Rights America: Stalled Integration or End of the Segregated Century?," *Du Bois Review: Social Science Research on Race* 11, no. 2 (2014): 205, doi:10.1017/S1742058X13000180; and of segregation in schools in the United States, see Carl Kaestle, "Federalism and Inequality in Education: What Can History Tell Us?," in *The Dynamics of Opportunity in America: Evidence and Perspectives*, ed. Irwin Kirsch and Henry Braun (Princeton, NJ: Educational Testing Service, 2016). Racial and gender segregation

in work decreased substantially in the 1970s, mostly stalled in the 1980s, and has seen a resurgence since then. Keven Stainback and Donald Tomaskovic-Devey, *Documenting Desegregation: Racial and Gender Segregation in Private-Sector Employment since the Civil Rights Act* (New York: Russell Sage Foundation Press, 2012). According to recent longitudinal research on segregation in work establishments across forty years: "For white workers, exposure to non-white co-workers has steadily increased for 40 years . . . . During the same time period, exposure tended to fall for non-white workers—fitfully for blacks, more steadily for Hispanics, Asians, and others." John-Paul Ferguson and Rembrand Koning, "Firm Runover and the Return of Racial Establishment Segregation," *American Sociological Review* 83, no. 3 (2018): 445, 466, https://www.jstor.org/stable/48588667.

7. Mahzarin R. Banaji and Anthony G. Greenwald, *Blindspot: Hidden Biases of Good People* (New York: Random House, 2013).

8. Barbara F. Reskin, "Including Mechanisms in Our Models of Ascriptive Inequality: 2002 Presidential Address," *American Sociological Review* 68, no. 1 (2003): 1–21, 10, citing Carl O. Word et al., "The Nonverbal Mediation of Self-Fulfilling Prophecies in Interracial Interactions," *Journal of Experimental Social Psychology* 10 (1974): 109, https://doi.org/10.2307/3088900. See also J. Nicole Shelton and Jennifer A. Richeson, "Interacting across Racial Lines," in *Handbook of Personality and Social Psychology: Vol. 2* (Washington, DC: American Psychological Association, 2015), 395 (reviewing research on interracial interactions).

9. Eberhardt, *Biased*.

10. Audre Lorde, *Sister Outsider: Essays and Speeches* (New York: Random House, 1984), 34.

11. Shelton and Richeson, "Interacting across Racial Lines."

12. Gordon Allport, *The Nature of Prejudice* (Cambridge, MA: Addison-Wesley, 1954), 281.

13. Shelton and Richeson, "Interacting across Racial Lines," 397.

14. Shelton and Richeson, "Interacting across Racial Lines."

15. Another meta-study conducted by Pettigrew and Tropp suggests that emotion-related, affective ties with out-group members contribute to more positive feelings that can generalize to the out-group as a whole, even if the relationship between intergroup contact and cognitive prejudice (e.g., stereotypes) is less clear. See Linda R. Tropp and Thomas F. Pettigrew, "Differential Relationships between Intergroup Contact and Affective and Cognitive Dimensions of Prejudice," *Personality and Social Psychology Bulletin* 31, no. 8 (2005): 1145–58, https://doi.org:10.1177/0146167205274854.

16. Recent research on the contact hypothesis buttresses Allport's point that interracial interactions are most likely to be positive when interactions are sustained (continue to occur over time). One study found that individuals engaging in interracial interaction that involved discussing intimate aspects of their lives

and cooperating on activities over a three-day period resulted in closer feelings to their out-group partner at the end of the third day compared with the first and also less stress over time in the interaction, as assessed by self-report and physiological (i.e., levels of cortisol) measures. Elizabeth Page-Gould, Rodolfo Mendoza-Denton, and Linda R. Tropp, "With a Little Help from My Cross-Group Friend: Reducing Anxiety in Intergroup Contexts through Cross-Group Friendship," *Journal of Personality and Social Psychology* 95, no. 5 (2008): 1080–94, https://doi.org/10.1037/0022-3514.95.5.1080. Moreover, the study suggests that feelings of closeness to an interracial partner can influence the quantity and also the quality of individuals' interracial interactions beyond that partner. Another study suggests that negative emotions that participants experience in interracial interactions tend to decrease across multiple interactions. Negin R. Toosi, Laura G. Babbitt, Nalini Ambady, and Samuel R. Sommers, "Dyadic Interracial Interactions: A Meta-Analysis," *Psychological Bulletin* 138, no. 1 (2012): 1–27, https://doi.org/10.1037/a0025767.

For a brief and general overview of some of the research in the area of intergroup contact, including from extended contact (rather than direct contact) and consideration of future avenues for research, see John F. Dovidio, Angelika Love, Fabian M. H. Schellhaas, and Miles Hewstone, "Reducing Intergroup Bias through Intergroup Contact: Twenty Years of Progress and Future Directions," *Group Processes and Intergroup Relations* 20, no. 5 (2017): 606–20, https://doi.org/10.1177/1368430217712052.

17. See Natalia Molina, Daniel Martinez HoSang, and Ramón A. Gutiérrez, *Relational Formations of Race: Theory, Method, and Practice* (Oakland: University of California Press, 2019). See also Claire Jean Kim, "The Racial Triangulation of Asian Americans," *Politics and Society* 27, no. 1 (1999): 156, https://journals.sagepub.com/doi/10.1177/0032329299027001005 ("Asian Americans have not been racialized in a vacuum, isolated from other groups; to the contrary, Asian Americans have been racialized relative to and through interaction with Whites and Blacks.").

18. Russell K. Robinson, "Perceptual Segregation," *Columbia Law Review* 108 (2008): 1093. See also Leonard Steinhorn and Barbara Diggs-Brown, *By the Color of Our Skin: The Illusion of Integration and the Reality of Race* (New York: Penguin Group, 1999).

19. For example, in answer to the questions "Just your impression, are Black people in your community treated less fairly than White people in the following situations? How about—on the job or at work?" in a 2021 Gallup poll, 26% of white respondents said that Black people were treated less fairly, while 63% of Black respondents said that Black people were treated less fairly. Gallup, "Race Relations," https://news.gallup.com/poll/1687/Race-Relations.aspx.

Although there is some reason to believe that whites, especially white Democrats, may have shifted their views in some ways in recent years—see Pew

Research Center, "The Partisan Divide on Political Values Grows Even Wider," October 5, 2017, https://www.pewresearch.org/politics/2017/10/05/4-race-immigration-and-discrimination/ (noting that "in recent years the share of Hispanics and whites saying the country needs to continue making changes to give blacks equal rights with whites have grown significantly, narrowing the opinion gap with blacks")—I am unaware of studies indicating that the perceptual gap in day-to-day perceptions of discrimination has diminished.

20. Robinson, "Perceptual Segregation."

21. As legal scholar Barbara J. Flagg once stated, "White people tend to view intent as an essential element of racial harm; nonwhites do not.... The white perspective can be, and frequently is, expressed succinctly and without any apparent perceived need for justification.... For black people, however, the fact of racial oppression exists largely independent of the motives or intentions of its perpetrators." Barbara Flagg, "'Was Blind, but Now I See': White Race Consciousness and the Requirement of Discriminatory Intent," *Michigan Law Review* 91 (1993): 953, 968.

22. Robinson, "Perceptual Segregation," 1118. Some research suggests that people of color are reluctant to attribute specific decisions to discrimination, even if they may see bias and discrimination as prevalent. See Katie Eyer, "That's Not Discrimination: American Beliefs and the Limits of Anti-Discrimination Law," *Minnesota Law Review* 96 (2012): 1275 (surveying some of this research).

23. There is research to suggest that perceptions of discrimination by people of color are unlikely to be exaggerated. See Robinson, "Perceptual Segregation," 1139–51 (reviewing studies).

24. J. Nicole Shelton, Jennifer A. Richeson, and Jacquie D. Vorauer, "Threatened Identities and Interethnic Interactions," *European Review of Social Psychology* 17, no. 1 (2006): 327–28, https://doi.org/10.1080/10463280601095240.

25. Shelton, Richeson, and Vorauer, "Threatened Identities and Interethnic Interactions," 327 (citing studies showing awareness of stereotypes about groups). See Vinay Harpalani, "Asian Americans, Racial Stereotypes, and Elite University Admissions," *Boston University Law Review* 102 (2021): 233 (describing common Asian American stereotypes); Kara Harris, Angel D. Armenta, Christina Reyna, and Michale A. Zárate, "Latinx Stereotypes: Myths and Realities in the Twenty-First Century," in *Stereotypes: The Incidence and Impacts of Bias*, ed. Joel T. Nadler and Elora C. Voyles (Santa Barbara: Praeger, 2020), 128 (describing common Latinx stereotypes). Stereotypes facing people of color, whether Black, Indian, Asian, Latino, Native American, or otherwise, are complex and may overlap substantially and interact with other identity status, such as sex and immigrant status. I do not mean to suggest that stereotypes facing one race are universally applicable to all of that race, or to suggest that even those generally identified stereotypes are static or simple.

26. Claude M. Steele, *Whistling Vivaldi: How Stereotypes Affect Us and What We Can Do* (New York: W. W. Norton, 2010).

27. Celeste Doerr, E. Ashby Plant, Jonathan W. Kuntsman, and David Buck, "Interactions in Black and White: Racial Differences and Similarities in Response to Interracial Interactions," *Group Processes and Intergroup Relations* 14, no. 1 (2011): 31–43 (finding Blacks higher in self-efficacy but also having heightened concerns about being the target of bias), https://doi.org/10.1177/1368430210375250. J. Nicole Shelton, Jennifer A. Richeson, and Jessica Salvatore, "Expecting to Be the Target of Prejudice: Implications for Interethnic Interactions," *Personality and Social Psychology Bulletin* 31, no. 9 (2005): 1189–202, https://doi.org:10.1177/0146167205274894.

28. Shelton, Richeson, and Salvatore, "Expecting to Be the Target of Prejudice."

29. Richard Fry, Jesse Bennett, and Amanda Barroso, "Racial and Ethnic Gaps in the U.S. Persist on Key Demographic Indicators," *Pew Research Center*, January 12, 2021, https://www.pewresearch.org/interactives/racial-and-ethnic-gaps-in-the-u-s-persist-on-key-demographic-indicators/, noting that 41% of white Americans ages 25 years or older hold a bachelor's degree or higher, as compared to only 28% of Black Americans; the median household income for white Americans, adjusted for household size and scaled to reflect a three-person household, was $91,000, as compared to $57,100 for Black Americans; and 19% of Black Americans live in poverty, as compared to only 7% of white Americans.

30. Field experiments in hiring are one form of research that suggest continued discrimination against people of color. Field experiments are experimental studies in which fictionalized matched candidates (e.g., candidates with identical resumes) from different racial groups apply for jobs. A recent meta-analysis of published studies since 1989 found no changes in the levels of discrimination against African Americans, with some indication of declining discrimination against Latinos. Since 1989, whites receive on average 36% more callbacks than Blacks and 24% more callbacks than Latinos. See Lincoln Quillian, Devah Pager, Ole Hexel, and Arnfinn H. Midtboen, "Meta-Analysis of Field Experiments Shows No Change in Racial Discrimination in Hiring over Time," *Proceedings of the National Academy of Sciences of the United States of America* 114, no. 41 (2017), 10870–75, https://doi.org/10.1073/pnas.1706255114. Another meta-analysis suggests that "racial discrimination in hiring is substantially more severe than an analysis of solely callback outcomes would suggest," finding that "majority applicants in our sample receive 53% more callbacks than comparable minority candidates, but they receive 145% more job offers than comparable minority candidates." Lincoln Quillian, John J. Lee, and Mariana Oliver, "Evidence from Field Experiments in Hiring Shows Substantial Additional Racial Discrimination after Callback," *Social Forces* 99, no. 2 (2020): 752, https://doi.org.10.1093/sf/soaa026.

31. In addition, because whites are often socialized to be colorblind, they can react with strong emotion when race issues are raised. Robin DiAngelo addresses some of this racial emotion in *White Fragility*.

32. On intergroup threat theory, see Walter G. Stephan and Cookie White Stephan, "Intergroup Threats," in *The Cambridge Handbook of the Psychology of Prejudice*, ed. Chris G. Sibley and Fiona Kate Barlow (Cambridge: Cambridge University Press, 2016).

33. Allport, *Nature of Prejudice*, 371.

34. Maureen A. Craig and Jennifer A. Richeson, "Majority No More? The Influence of Neighborhood Racial Diversity and Salient National Population Changes on Whites' Perceptions of Racial Discrimination," *Russell Sage Foundation Journal of Social Science* 4, no. 5 (2018): 141, https://doi.org/10.7758/RSF.2018.4.5.07.

35. For discussion of social closure generally see Raymond Murphy, "The Structure of Closure: A Critique and Development of the Theories of Weber, Collins, and Parkin," *British Journal of Sociology* 35, no. 4 (1984): 547–67, https://doi.org/10.2307/590434.

36. Bonilla-Silva, "Feeling Race," 10.

37. John F. Dovidio and Samuel L. Gaertner, "Aversive Racism," *Advances in Experimental Social Psychology* 36 (2004): 1–52, https://doi.org/10.1016/S0065-2601(04)36001-6.

38. Toosi et al., "Dyadic Interracial Interactions," 1, 4.

39. Toosi et al., "Dyadic Interracial Interactions."

40. David A. Butz and E. Ashby Plant, "Perceiving Outgroup Members as Unresponsive: Implications for Approach-Related Emotions, Intentions, and Behavior," *Journal of Personality and Social Psychology* 91, no. 6 (2006): 1066–79, https://doi.org/10.1037/0022-3514.91.6.1066; see also Lydia E. Hayward, Linda R. Tropp, Matthew J. Hornsey, and Fiona Kate Barlow, "Toward a Comprehensive Understanding of Intergroup Contact: Descriptions and Mediators of Positive and Negative Contact among Majority and Minority Groups," *Personality and Social Psychology Bulletin* 43, no. 3 (2017): 347–64, https://doi.org/10.1177/0146167216685291, on anger and antagonism as well as avoidance.

41. Shelton, Richeson, and Vorauer, "Threatened Identities and Interethnic Interactions," 321 (describing studies suggesting that individuals will resort to "defensive derogation" to protect a threatened identity, and that individuals are especially likely to disparage a person who they believe is the source of their identity threat if the person is from a low-status group); see also Walter G. Stephan, Oscar Ybarra, and Kimberly Rios Morrison, "Intergroup Threat Theory," in *Handbook of Prejudice, Stereotyping, and Discrimination*, ed. Todd D. Nelson (New York: Psychology Press, 2009), 43.

42. E. Ashby Plant and Patricia G. Devine, "The Antecedents and Implications of Interracial Anxiety," *Personality and Social Psychology Bulletin* 29, no. 6 (2003): 790–801, https://doi.org/10.1177/0146167203252880.

43. Sheryll Cashin, *The Failures of Integration: How Race and Class are Undermining the American Dream* (New York: Hachette Book Group, 2004).

44. Cashin, *Failures of Integration*, 13.

45. Phillip Atiba Goff, Claude M. Steele, and Paul G. Davies, "The Space between Us: Stereotype Threat and Distance in Interracial Contexts," *Journal of Personality and Social Psychology* 94, no. 1 (2008): 91–107, https://doi.org/10.1037/0022-3514.94.1.91.

46. Adia Harvey Wingfield, *Flatlining: Race, Work, and Health Care in the New Economy* (Berkeley: University of California Press, 2019), 154.

47. Jessica Sullivan, Leigh Wilton, and Evan P. Apfelbaum, "Adults Delay Conversations about Race Because They Underestimate Children's Processing of Race," *Journal of Experimental Psychology: General* 150, no. 2 (2021): 395–400; Evan P. Apfelbaum et al., "Learning (Not) to Talk about Race: When Older Children Underperform in Social Categorization," *Developmental Psychology* 44, no. 5 (2008): 1513–18, https://doi.org/10.1037/a0012835.

48. This microstrategy of not acknowledging race is different from larger ideological frames of colorblindness, although the two can overlap. In some of the research by social psychologists, whites are understood to avoid talking about race in an effort to avoid the appearance of bias. See Evan P. Apfelbaum and Samuel Sommers, "Seeing Race and Seeming Racist? Evaluating Strategic Colorblindness in Social Interaction," *Journal of Personality and Social Psychology* 95, no. 4 (2008): 918–32, https://doi.org/10.1037/a0011990. For discussion of the various ways that colorblindness is used, see Laura Babbitt, Negin Toosi, and Samuel R. Sommers, "A Broad and Insidious Appeal: Unpacking the Reasons for Endorsing Racial Color Blindness," in *The Myth of Racial Colorblindness: Manifestations, Dynamics, and Impact*, ed. Helen A. Neville, Miguel E. Gallardo, and Derald Wing Sue (Washington, DC: American Psychological Association, 2016), 53 ("Racial colorblindness is a malleable ideology that appeals to people across a spectrum of motivations and perspectives."); Eduardo Bonilla-Silva, *Racism without Racists: Color-Blind Racism and Racial Inequality in Contemporary America* (Lanham, MD: Rowman & Littlefield, 2010).

49. E. Ashby Plant and David A. Butz, "The Causes and Consequences of an Avoidance-Focus for Interracial Interactions," *Personality and Social Psychology Bulletin* 32, no. 6 (2006): 833–46, https://doi.org/10.1177/0146167206287182; Hayward et al., "Toward a Comprehensive Understanding of Intergroup Contact," 347, 361 (noting that intergroup anxiety across three studies was influential in predicting avoidance and that the studies therefore added to "mounting evidence that intergroup anxiety significantly reduces the likelihood of engaging in future contact").

50. Shelton and Richeson, "Interacting across Racial Lines."

51. Jennifer Crocker and Julia A. Garcia, "Downward and Upward Spirals in Intergroup Interactions: The Role of Egosystem and Ecosystem Goals," in *Handbook of Prejudice, Stereotyping and Discrimination*, ed. Todd D. Nelson, 229–46 (New York: Psychology Press, 2009).

52. Shelton and Richeson, "Interacting across Racial Lines."

53. Beverly Daniel Tatum, *Why Are All the Black Kids Sitting Together in the Cafeteria?* (New York: Hachette Book Group, 2017), 56 ("Those who identify with the alt-right are characterized by their heavy use of social media and online memes, their rejection of traditional conservatives as weak, and their embrace of White supremacist nationalism as a fundamental value. Much of their rhetoric is 'explicitly racist, anti-immigrant, anti-Semitic and anti-feminist.'").

54. One study found that the more internally motivated white people were, the more details they remembered about what their partner was saying and doing. Jennifer LaCosse and E. Ashby Plant, "Internal Motivation to Respond without Prejudice Fosters Respectful Responses in Interracial Interactions," *Journal of Personality and Social Psychology* 119, no. 5 (2020): 1049, https://doi.org/10.1037/pspi0000219.

55. Hillary B. Bergsieker, J. Nicole Shelton, and Jennifer A. Richeson, "To Be Liked Versus Respected: Divergent Goals in Interracial Interactions," *Journal of Personality and Social Psychology* 99, no. 2 (2010): 248, https://doi.org/10.1037/a0018474.

56. Doerr et al., "Interactions in Black and White," 31. See also Kristen Pauker, Evan P. Apfelbaum, Carol S. Dweck, and Jennifer L. Eberhardt, "Believing That Prejudice Can Change Increases Children's Interest in Interracial Interactions," *Developmental Science* 25, no. 4 (2022): 1–14, https://doi.org/10.1111/desc.13233.

57. For a classic on this point, see Rosabeth Moss Kanter, *Men and Women of the Corporation* (New York: Basic Books, 1977).

58. Tristin K. Green, "'I'll See You at Work': Spatial Features and Discrimination," *UC Davis Law Review* 55 (2021): 141.

59. Crocker and Garcia, "Downward and Upward Spirals in Intergroup Interactions."

60. Katya Migacheva, Linda R. Tropp, and Jennifer Crocker, "Focusing beyond the Self: Goal Orientations in Intergroup Relations," in *Moving beyond Prejudice Reduction: Pathways to Positive Intergroup Relations*, ed. Linda L. Tropp and Robin K. Mallett (Washington, DC: American Psychological Association, 2011), 99, 105. See also Goff, Steele, and Davies, "The Space Between Us: Stereotype Threat and Distance in Interracial Contexts," 91; Katya Migacheva and Linda R. Tropp, "Learning Orientation as a Predictor of Positive Intergroup Contact," *Group Processes and Intergroup Relations* 16 (2012): 426 (studying the effect of learning goals on comfort and interest in intergroup contact).

61. Shelton and Richeson, "Interacting across Racial Lines," 399 (discussing the "common in-group identity" research of Samuel Gaertner and Frank Dovidio).

62. Eileen O'Brien, "The Political Is Personal: The Influence of White Supremacy on White Antiracists' Personal Relationships," in *White Out: The Continuing Significance of Racism*, ed. Ashley "Woody" Doane and Eduardo Bonilla-Silva (New York: Routledge, 2003), 259.

CHAPTER 3. LAW: CLOSING RACIAL EMOTION OUT OF ANTIDISCRIMINATION CONCERN

1. For a sampling of some of the influential work on emotion in law, including its construction through law and in legal proceedings, see Susan A. Bandes, ed., *The Passion of Law* (New York: NYU Press, 1999); Martha C. Nussbaum, *Hiding from Humanity: Disgust, Shame, and the Law* (Princeton, NJ: Princeton University Press, 2004); Kathryn Abrams and Hila Keren, "Who's Afraid of Law and the Emotions?," *Minnesota Law Review* 94 (2010): 1997; Susan A. Bandes and Jeremy A. Blumenthal, "Emotion and the Law," *Annual Review of Law and Social Science* 8 (2012): 161; Erin Ann O'Hara and Sara Sun Beale, "Victims, 'Closure,' and the Sociology of Emotion," *Law and Contemporary Problems* 72 (2009): 1.

2. Title VII is part of the larger Civil Rights Act of 1964, which outlawed segregation in public spaces as well as prohibiting employers and federal agencies from discriminating on the basis of race, color, religion, sex, and national origin. For some of the history leading up to the act's passage, see Clay Risen, *The Bill of the Century: The Epic Battle for the Civil Rights Act* (New York: Bloomsbury Press, 2014); Charles and Barbara Walen, *The Longest Debate: A Legislative History of the 1964 Civil Rights Act* (Cabin John, MD: Seven Locks Press, 1985).

3. Title VII of the Civil Rights Act declares it an "unlawful employment practice" for an employer

(1) to fail or refuse to hire or to discharge any individual, or otherwise to discriminate against any individual with respect to his compensation, terms, conditions, or privileges of employment, because of such individual's race, color, religion, sex, or national origin; or

(2) to limit, segregate, or classify his employees or applicants for employment in any way which would deprive or tend to deprive any individual of employment opportunities or otherwise adversely affect his status as an employee, because of such individual's race, religion, sex, or national origin.

42 U.S.C. §2000e2(a).

4. Although the Court frequently uses language of intent or purpose, it has consistently described the "because of" inquiry in terms of treating people differently

on the basis of a protected characteristic and not in terms of a required state of mind. See Furnco Constr. Corp. v. Waters, 438 U.S. 567, 577, 579–80 (1978) (noting that "the central focus of the inquiry in a case such as this is always whether the employer is treating 'some people less favorably than others because of their race, color, religion, sex, or national origin'"); U.S. Postal Service v. Aikens, 460 U.S. 711, 715 (1983) (stating that the relevant inquiry is whether "the employer [is] treating 'some people less favorably than others because of their race, color, religion, sex, or national origin'"); Price Waterhouse v. Hopkins, 490 U.S. 228 (1989) (justices differing on the proper causation standard but all emphasizing causation, not state of mind); Los Angeles Dept. of Water & Power v. Manhart, 435 U.S. 702 (1978) (employer's motivation is irrelevant if employer treats women different from men); Int'l Bthd. of Teamsters v. United States, 431 U.S. 324 (1977) (describing disparate treatment as "the employer simply treats some people less favorably than others because of their race, color, religion, sex or national origin"). For a recent case emphasizing "because of" as requiring a causation inquiry and not a specific state of mind, see Bostock v. Clayton County, 140 S. Ct. 1731 (2020) (relying on "because of" language to decide that discrimination against LGBTQ employees is prohibited under Title VII).

5. Ash v. Tyson Foods, Inc., 546 U.S. 454 (2006) (per curiam).

6. Ash v. Tyson Foods, Inc., 664 F.3d 883, 896 (11th Cir. 2011) (internal quotation marks omitted) (describing Ash's wife's testimony that Hatley "just looked at [her] with a smirk on his face like it was funny and then he walked off").

7. Ash v. Tyson, 664 F.3d 883, 896.

8. Amici Curiae Brief in Support of Plaintiff-Appellant's Petition for Rehearing En Banc of Civil Rights Leaders Hon. U. W. Clemon; Ms. Dorothy Cotton; Rev. Robert S. Graetz, Jr.; Dr. Bernard LaFayette, Jr.; Rev. Joseph E. Lowery; Mrs. Amelia Boynton Robinson; Hon. Solomon Seay, Jr.; Rev. Fred L. Shuttlesworth; Rev. C. T. Vivian; Dr. Wyatt Tee Walker; Hon. Andrew Young, Hithon v. Tyson Foods, Inc., Eleventh Circuit On Appeal from the United States District Court for the Northern District of Alabama No. CV96-RRA-03257-M.

9. Amici Curiae Brief in Support, 10, quoting Martin Luther King, Jr., *Why We Can't Wait* (1964), 69.

10. See Ash v. Tyson Foods Inc., No. 96-RRA-3257, 2004 WL 5138005 (N.D. Ala. 2004).

11. Ash v. Tyson, No. 96-RRA-3257, *6.

12. Ash v. Tyson Foods, Inc., 129 F. App'x 529, 533 (11th Cir. 2005).

13. Ash v. Tyson Foods, Inc., 546 U.S. 454, 456 (2006) (per curiam).

14. Ash v. Tyson Foods, Inc., 129 F. App'x 924, 926 (11th Cir. 2006).

15. Ash v. Tyson Foods, Inc., 664 F.3d 883 (11th Cir. 2011) (reconsidering and reversing an earlier appellate panel decision).

16. In another case, a supervisor called the plaintiff "black motherfucker" and an "ugly black man" and said that Black people "can be a lot of trouble." The

Court of Appeals for the Fourth Circuit in affirming summary judgment for the defendant mentioned only that "McNeal [claims] Tignor made several racist and harassing comments about him" and held that this did not constitute evidence of bias in the plaintiff's employment ratings because the plaintiff did not show that the comments were "temporally connected" to the ratings decisions and because two coworkers, in addition to the supervisor, were responsible for the ratings. Brief of Appellant at 4, McNeal v. Montgomery Cty., 307 F. App'x 766 (4th Cir. 2009) (Mem.) (No. 07-1323).

On the "stray remarks doctrine," including a recent database search that yielded 2,943 cases referring to "stray remarks," see Jessica A. Clarke, "Explicit Bias," *Northwestern University Law Review* 113 (2018): 505, 540–42, and 540n240; see also Sandra F. Sperino and Suja A. Thomas, *Unequal: How America's Courts Undermine Discrimination Law* (New York: Oxford University Press, 2017), 59–66; Kerri Lynn Stone, "Taking in Strays: A Critique of the Stray Comment Doctrine in Employment Discrimination Law," *Missouri Law Review* 77 (2012): 149, 153–73.

17. Bolden v. PRC Inc., 43 F.3d 545, 548 (10th Cir. 1994).

18. Bolden v. PRC, 551.

19. Bolden v. PRC, 551.

20. McCann v. Tillman, 526 F.3d 1370, 1379 (11th Cir. 2008).

21. McCann v. Tillman, 1379. See also Cain v. Elgin, Joliet E. Ry. Co., 04-CV-0347, 2006 U.S. Dist. LEXIS 4373, at *12 (N.D. Ind. 2006) (noting that a statement made outside the presence of plaintiff that he was a "dumb ass n——" was not sufficient to establish an objectively hostile work environment); EEOC v. A. Sam & Sons Produce Co., 872 F. Supp. 29, 36 (W.D. N.Y. 1994) ("Less compelling are Titus's claims that she was subjected to hostile environment sexual harassment. Although she, on three occasions, overheard Charles through the walls of his office refer to the women in the office as 'whores,' Titus herself stated that Charles never called her a whore."); EEOC v. RJB Properties, Inc., 857 F. Supp. 2d 727, 752 (N.D. Ill. 2012) (holding that one incident in which the term "wetback" was used in the plaintiff's presence was not sufficiently severe or pervasive despite testimony that the term, as well as "spic" and "beaneaters," was used regularly together with demeaning and derogatory statements about work ethic).

22. Lawrence v. Chemprene, Inc., No. 18-CV-2537, 2019 WL 5449844 (S.D. N.Y. 2019).

23. Lawrence v. Chemprene, 14. This reasoning is consistent with the view that "backstage" use of slurs, etc., are not problematic if not said directly to people of color. In fact, however, backstage racialized behavior, including jokes and epithets, sets the foundation for continued discrimination on the front stage. See chapter 7 for more discussion.

24. Edwards v. Foucar, Ray & Simon, Inc., No. C-79-0313, 1980 U.S. Dist. LEXIS 13748 (N.D. Cal. 1980).

25. Civil Rights Act of 1964, §704, 42 U.S.C. §2000e-3.

26. See, e.g., Niswander v. Cincinnati Ins. Co, 529 F.3d 714, 721 (6th Cir. 2008). Some courts frame the inquiry in terms of balancing the employee's interest against the employer's interest. See, e.g., Laughlin v. Metropolitan Washington Airports Authority, 149 F.3d 253, 259–60 (4th Cir. 1998). In "Everyday Indignities," legal scholar Terry Smith argues that Donald Edwards would have had a better chance of succeeding in his discrimination suit had he framed his claim in terms of retaliation instead of disparate treatment; *Columbia Human Rights Law Review* 34 (2003): 529. Although Smith rightly emphasizes the frequently overlooked importance of retaliation claims for many plaintiffs (and rightly points out the potential of retaliation law to better capture relations as they play out in the workplace), I think it is unlikely that Edwards would have fared better on a retaliation claim.

27. Clack v. Rock-Tenn Co., 304 F. App'x 399 (6th Cir. 2008).

28. Clack v. Rock-Tenn, 403n2 (quoting from Bonine's affidavit).

29. Clack v. Rock-Tenn, 403n2.

30. Clack v. Rock-Tenn, 409 (Moore, C.J., dissenting).

31. Natasha Martin, "Pretext in Peril," *Missouri Law Review* 75 (2010): 313; Catherine A. Lanctot, "Secrets and Lies: The Need for a Definitive Rule of Law in Pretext Cases," *Louisiana Law Review* 61 (2001): 539.

32. See Sperino and Thomas, *Unequal* (describing a variety of ways in which courts have pushed back against Title VII claims through use of legal rules and frameworks narrowing the meaning of discrimination under Title VII); Eyer, "That's Not Discrimination," 1275 (describing research suggesting under-attribution of discrimination and arguing that this may explain, at least in part, the low likelihood of success for plaintiffs in employment discrimination cases).

33. St. Mary's Honor Ctr. v. Hicks, 509 U.S. 502 (1993).

34. St. Mary's Honor Ctr. v. Hicks, 508.

35. Chad Darum and Karen Engle, "The Rise of the Personal Animosity Presumption in Title VII and the Return to 'No Cause' Employment," *Texas Law Review* 81 (2003): 1117.

36. Reeves v. Sanderson Plumbing Products, Inc., 530 U.S. 133 (2000).

37. Sweezer v. Mich. Dep't of Corr., 229 F.3d 1154 (table), 2000 WL 1175644 (5th Cir. 2000).

38. Sweezer v. Mich. Dep't of Corr., *15–16. According to the court, "Sweezer's . . . confrontations with Allen . . . bespeak an acrimonious relationship and not racial tension" (*16).

39. Taylor v. Potter, No. 99-CV-4941, 2004 WL 1811423, *16, aff'd Taylor v. Potter, 148 F. App'x 33 (2nd Cir. 2005).

40. Roberts v. Potter, 378 F. App'x 913, 914–15 (11th Cir. 2010).

41. Meritor Savings Bank v. Vinson, 477 U.S. 57 (1986), citing to Rogers v. EEOC, 454 F.2d 234 (5th Cir. 1971).

42. Rogers v. EEOC, 454 F.2d 234 (5th Cir. 1971).

43. Meritor Savings Bank v. Vinson.

44. Meritor Savings Bank v. Vinson, 67 (internal quotations omitted).

45. Harris v. Forklift Syst., Inc., 510 U.S. 17 (1993).

46. Pratt v. Austal, USA, 2011 WL 3203740 (S.D. Ala. Jul. 27, 2011).

47. Barrow v. Georgia Pacific Corp., 144 F. App'x 54, 57 (11th Cir. 2005). See also Abdel-Ghani v. Target Corp., 686 F. App'x 377, 379 (8th Cir. 2017) (holding evidence that the plaintiff's supervisor, during an argument, told him he should "go back home, go back to your country," coworkers "called him names like camel jockey, Muslim, Arab, terrorist, and sand n——," and another employee said, "You should be rounded up in one place and nuke[d]" was insufficient to meet the "demanding standard" of an objectively hostile work environment and therefore summary judgment was warranted for the defendant); Colenburg v. Starcon Int'l, Inc., 619 F.3d 986, 990, 995 (8th Cir. 2010) (affirming district court holding that evidence of supervisor analogizing pace of plaintiff's work to speed at which a Black man was killed in a dragging death in Texas; comment by the same supervisor to plaintiff, "You black guys up North; you guys speak boldly, but down South you don't act that way; down South, it's differently [sic]," and the same supervisor's response to plaintiff's question about why he and another Black employee were not receiving raises and promotions, "Do you know any, you know, black leadmen?" was insufficient to meet the standard for an objectively hostile work environment and therefore warranted summary judgment for the defendant).

48. Barrow v. Georgia Pacific, 57.

49. See, e.g., Lounds v. Lincare, Inc., 812 F.3d 1208 (10th Cir. 2015); Blue v. City of Hartford, No. 3:18-CV-974, 2019 WL 7882565 (D. Conn. 2019) ("In the instant case, Plaintiff's allegations do not 'go[] beyond a few uses of the n word by a single co-worker,' which, although offensive, fail to state a claim of hostile work environment."). See also Nichols v. Mich. City Plant Planning Dep't, 755 F.3d 594, 601 (7th Cir. 2014) (holding that use of the N-word to refer to the plaintiff, together with six other alleged incidents of harassment in a two-and-a-half week period, was not sufficient and warranted summary judgment for the employer).

Judges have done the same in cases involving epithets involving national origin. See EEOC v. Rotary Corp., 297 F. Supp. 2d 643, 661 (N.D. N.Y. 2003) (holding that two occasions of being called "wetback" was not sufficiently severe or pervasive to amount to a hostile work environment); Arroyo v. West LB Admin, Inc., 54 F. Supp. 2d 224 (S.D. N.Y. 1999) (granting summary judgment for employer in part because a coworker called the plaintiff a "f-g spick," a "wetback," and an "asshole" on only three occasions). Some judges do say otherwise. See, e.g., Henao v. Wyndham Vacation Resorts, Inc., 927 F. Supp. 978 (D. Ha. 2013) (permitting a case involving allegations that the plaintiff was called "wetback" and "Pancho Villa" to go to a jury on the hostile work environment claim).

50. Nat'l RR Passenger Co. v. Morgan, 526 U.S. 101, 115 (2002).

51. Yelling v. St. Vincent's Health System, No. 2:17-CV-01607, 2020 WL 7059450 (N.D. Ala. 2020).

52. Collier v. Dallas Cnty Hosp. Dist., 827 F. App'x 373 (5th Cir. 2020). In *Collier*, the panel cited to three other cases where the court had found racial epithets and graffiti insufficient. According to the court, these cases meant that "the two instances of racial graffiti and being called 'boy'—are insufficient to establish a hostile work environment under our precedent":

> We have found that the oral utterance of the N-word and other racially derogatory terms, even in the presence of the plaintiff, may be insufficient to establish a hostile work environment. See, e.g., Dailey v. Shintech, Inc., 629 F. App'x 638, 640, 644 (5th Cir. 2015) (no hostile work environment where a coworker called plaintiff a "black little mother-r" and threatened to "kick his black a-s"); Frazier v. Sabine River Auth., 509 F. App'x 370, 374 (5th Cir. 2013) (finding that use of the N-word, the word "Negreet," and a noose gesture "were isolated and not severe or pervasive enough to create a hostile work environment); Vaughn v. Pool Offshore Co., 683 F.2d 922, 924–25 (5th Cir. 1982) (use of the N-word, "coon," and "black boy"). (378)

The parties sought certiorari, but the Supreme Court declined to hear the case; 827 F. App'x 232 (2021).

53. Lawrence v. Chemprene, Inc., No. 18-CV-2537, 2019 WL 5449844 (S.D. N.Y. 2019); see also Alexander v. Opelika City Sch., No. 3:06-CV-0498, 2008 WL 401353, *1 (M.D. Ala. 2008) (detailing at least five instances in which the plaintiff was called "boy"; in each, a white man told him to do something, laughed at him, cursed at him, or questioned him, and in one his supervisor called him "boy" while "talking about 'how you tie a noose around somebody's neck'"). The district court held that these facts were insufficient to rise to the level of "severe or pervasive," and the court of appeals affirmed. The court of appeals noted that eight incidents in two years was not "frequent," that the plaintiff had testified that he did not know whether the explanation of a noose "referred to black people," and that "none of the alleged racial comments contained threats of physical violence"; 352 F. App'x 390, 393 (11th Cir. 2009).

54. Blue v. City of Hartford, 3:18-CV-974, 2019 WL 7882565 (D. Conn. 2019).

55. White v. Gov't Emps. Ins., 457 F. App'x 374, 376, 381 (5th Cir. 2012) (Mem.) (citation omitted).

56. White v. Gov't Emps., 381n35.

CHAPTER 4. LAW: THE RACIST CALL AND CARING FOR RACIAL EMOTION OF WHITES

1. Executive Order on Combating Race and Sex Stereotyping, September 22, 2020.

2. Executive Order, 2.

3. Executive Order, 3. The order followed a memorandum earlier in the month put out by Russell Vaught, director of the Office of Management and Budget, calling on federal agencies to "cease and desist from using taxpayer dollars to fund ... divisive, un-American propaganda training sessions" and directing all agencies "to begin to identify all contracts or other agency spending related to any training on 'critical race theory,' 'white privilege,' or any other training or propaganda effort that teaches or suggests either (1) that the United States is an inherently racist or evil country or (2) that any race or ethnicity is inherently racist or evil." Memorandum for the Heads of Executive Departments and Agencies, September 4, 2020.

4. Some of what is going on here is a matter of storytelling, especially the building of a story of white innocence in which talking about race and racism is seen as a source of racial division. This may sound harmless enough, but the deep stories we tell about racial inequality, much like those of racial emotion and race, substantially impact our laws and our lives. For further discussion of this storytelling and what legal scholar Jonathan Feingold urges us to call "Backlash Bills," see Jonathan P. Feingold, "Reclaiming CRT: How Regressive Laws Can Advance Progressive Ends," *South Carolina Law Review* 73 (2022): 723. The story presented by Trump and these bills is part of a larger one that has surfaced throughout history and that seeks to explain continued material inequality along racial lines as the product of individual or cultural differences. See also Sam Adler Bell, "Behind the CRT Crackdown," *The Forum*, January 13, 2022, https://www.aapf.org/theforum-critical-race -theory-crackdown. Indeed, one project of this book is to tell a story of racial emotion, discrimination, and inequality, with strong empirical foundation, that includes institutions and not merely individuals or even interpersonal interactions.

5. 2021-H State of Rhode Island. In April 2023, Florida extended the state's civil rights act's definition of an "unlawful employment practice" to include any mandatory employer training "based on race, color, sex, or national origin," prohibiting any training that "espouses, promotes, advances, inculcates, or compels" any of eight specified concepts, including that "an individual, by virtue of his or her race, color, or national origin, bears personal responsibility and must feel guilt, anguish, or other forms of psychological distress because of actions, in which the individual played no part, committed in the past by other members of the same race, color, sex, or national origin" (H.B. 7 [2022]). For a count of bills introduced between January and September 2021, see Pen America Index of Educational Gag Orders, https://pen.org/report/educational-gag-orders/. For discussion and categorization of the various bills, see Feingold, "Reclaiming CRT." For more on some of the recent lawsuits challenging antiracist education and their construction of identity and white innocence, see Osamudia James, "White Injury and Innocence: On the Legal Future of Antiracism Education," *Virginia Law Review* 108, 1689 (2022).

6. Kim Shayo Buchanan and Phillip Atiba Goff, "Racist Stereotype Threat in Civil Rights Law," *UCLA Law Review* 67 (2020): 316, 319.

7. Ladelle McWhorter, *Racism and Sexual Oppression in Anglo-America: A Genealogy* (Bloomington: Indiana University Press, 2009), 36–41, quoting Robert Miles, *Racism* (London: Routledge, 1989).

8. Justin D. Hatch, "Disassociating Power and Racism: Stokely Carmichael at Berkeley," *Advances in the History of Rhetoric* 22, no. 3 (2019), 303–25, https://doi.org/10.1080/15362426.2019.1671705.

9. Bonilla-Silva, *Racism without Racists*.

10. Omi and Winant, *Racial Formation in the United States*, 134, and last chapter generally. See also Haney López, *Dog Whistle Politics*.

11. Ibram X. Kendi, *How to Be an Antiracist* (New York: One World Press, 2019), 13.

12. Kendi, *How to Be an Antiracist*, 9.

13. Buchanan and Goff, "Racist Stereotype Threat in Civil Rights Law," 316n4 (relaying this story).

14. Jim Waterson, "Were Trump's Racist Tweets Racist? Some News Outlets Won't Say," *The Guardian*, July 16, 2019, https://www.theguardian.com/media/2019/jul/16/were-trumps-racist-tweets-racist-some-news-outlets-wont-say (noting Trump's tweet: "I don't have a Racist bone in my body!").

15. Kendi, *How to Be an Antiracist*, 10.

16. Debra Walker King, "The Not-So-Harmless Social Function of a Word That Wounds," in *Handbook of the Sociology of Racial and Ethnic Relations*, ed. Hernán Vera and Joe R. Feagin (New York: Springer, 2007), 104. See also Richard Delgado and Jean Stefancic, *Understanding Words That Wound* (New York: Routledge, 2004); Randall Kennedy, *Nigger: The Strange Career of a Troublesome Word* (New York: Random House, 2002).

17. Joe R. Feagin and Karyn D. McKinney, *The Many Costs of Racism* (New York: Rowman & Littlefield, 2005), 48.

18. Buchanan and Goff, "Racist Stereotype Threat in Civil Rights Law."

19. Buchanan and Goff, "Racist Stereotype Threat in Civil Rights Law," 341.

20. Buchanan and Goff, "Racist Stereotype Threat in Civil Rights Law," 343–44.

21. Regents of University of California Davis v. Bakke, 438 U.S. 265, 292 (1976); see also 298 (describing concern about "a measure of inequity in forcing innocent persons in respondent's position to bear the burdens of redressing grievances not of their making" even without evidence that the plaintiff in the case would have been admitted had the school not had an affirmative action policy).

22. City of Richmond v. J.A. Croson Co., 488 U.S. 469, 495–96 (1989).

23. Ricci v. DeStefano, 557 U.S. 557, 598–605 (2005).

24. Meredith v. Jefferson Cnty Bd of Educ. 548 U.S. 938 (2006), oral argument at 26:03 (available at www.oyez.org).

25. Wilcoxon v. Ramsey Action Programs, Inc., No. 04-CV-92, 2005 WL 2216289 (D. Minn. 2005).

26. Wilcoxon v. Ramsey, *5.

27. Washington v. Cnty of Onandaga, No. 04-CV-0997,2009 WL 3171787 (N.D. N.Y. 2009).

28. Ceus v. City of Tampa, 803 F. App'x 235 (11th Cir. 2020); see also Gress v. Temple Univ. Health Sys., 784 F. App'x 100, 106 (3d Cir. 2019) (describing requirement of specificity).

29. Felder-Ward v. Flexible Staffing Services Inc., No. 14-C-9246, 2018 WL 1235013 (N.D. Ill. 2018).

30. Vance v. Ball State Univ., No. 06-CV-1452, 2008 WL 4247836,*13 (S.D. Ind. 2008). The Supreme Court focused closely on Vance's interactions with a "fellow BSU employee" and not with her supervisor mentioned earlier, deciding the question of how to define "supervisor" for purposes of the standard to be applied for employer liability. See Vance v. Ball State Univ., 570 U.S. 421, 450 (2013) (defining "supervisor" narrowly to include only those who are "empowered by the employer to take tangible employment actions against the victim").

31. Tademy v. Union Pacific Corp., 614 F.3d 1132, 1140–41 (10th Cir. 2011) (reversing a district court award of summary judgment for defendant).

32. Ash v. Tyson Foods Inc., 392 F. App'x 817, 833 (11th Cir. 2010) (stating that "the only evidence presented at the retrial was Ash's and Hithon's testimony about how and why the use of the term 'boy' is offensive to them, but the issue is not what was in their mind when they heard the term but what was in Hatley's mind when he used it, and there was no new evidence about that"). This decision was later overturned on grant of rehearing at the appellate court, but the opinion reversing made no mention of the court's earlier reasoning. Ash v. Tyson Foods Inc., 664 F.3d 883, 897–98 (11th Cir. 2011).

33. A report by the Center for American Progress using data from 2019 determined that 27% of active federal judges (those who serve on the courts full time) in the federal trial and circuit or appellate courts are people of color; 13% are African American; 9% are Hispanic; 2.5% are Asian American; and less than 1% are American Indian. See The Democracy and Government Reform Team, "Examining the Demographic Composition of U.S. and Circuit and District Courts," *Center for American Progress*, February 13, 2020, https://www.americanprogress.org/article/examining-demographic-compositions-u-s-circuit-district-courts/.

34. We might see the law's approach to racial emotion as an example of what historian Carol Anderson calls "white rage." See Carol Anderson, *White Rage: The Unspoken Truth of Our Racial Divide* (New York: Bloomsbury, 2016), 3 (noting that "white rage is not about visible violence, but rather it works its way through the courts, the legislatures, and a range of government bureaucracies").

CHAPTER 5. WORK ORGANIZATIONS:
CONSTRUCTING EMOTION REPERTOIRES

1. See John Fabien Witt, *The Accidental Republic: Crippled Workingmen, Destitute Women, and the Remaking of American Law* (Cambridge, MA: Harvard University Press, 2004), 104–7 (describing the "foreman's empire"); 107 ("So long as the scale of production remained relatively small, Alfred Chandler has argued, there was little call for systemic attention to the rational organization of the workplace itself."). See also Illouz, *Saving the Modern Soul*, 63–66 (describing this period).

2. Witt, *The Accidental Republic*, 104–5.

3. Illouz, *Saving the Modern Soul*, 66, relying on Reinhard Bendix, *Work and Authority in Industry: Ideologies of Management in the Course of Industrialization* (1956).

4. Witt, *The Accidental Republic*, 108–10.

5. Max Weber, "Bureaucracy," in *From Max Weber: Essays in Sociology*, ed. and trans. H. H. Gerth and C. Wright Mills (New York: Routledge, 1991), 215–16.

6. Illouz, *Saving the Modern Soul*, 65.

7. Illouz, *Saving the Modern Soul*.

8. Illouz, *Saving the Modern Soul*, 76. See also Peter N. Stearns, *American Cool: Constructing a Twentieth-Century Emotional Style* (New York: NYU Press, 1994).

9. Studies of organizations "have consistently found that the twentieth-century American workplace demanded a much stricter control of emotions than its predecessors, the nineteenth-century shop floor or factory." Illouz, *Saving the Modern Soul*, 61.

10. William Ouchi, *Theory Z: How American Business Can Meet the Japanese Challenge* (Reading, MA: Addison-Wesley, 1981); Terrence E. Deal and Allen A. Kennedy, *Corporate Cultures: The Rites and Rituals of Corporate Life* (New York: Basic Books, 1982): Thomas J. Peters and Robert H. Waterman, Jr., *In Search of Excellence: Lessons from America's Best-Run Companies* (New York: Harper & Row, 1982). For more on this shift in what is sometimes called the "psychological contract" between companies and workers, see Katherine V. W. Stone, *From Widgets to Digits: Employment Regulation for the Changing Workplace* (New York: Cambridge University Press, 2004), 88–96.

11. Deal and Kennedy, *Corporate Cultures*, 5.

12. Craig R. Hickman and Michael A. Silva, *Creating Excellence: Managing Corporate Culture, Strategy, and Change in the New Age* (New York: Routledge, 1984), 25.

13. Paul Du Gay, *Consumption and Identity at Work* (London: SAGE, 1996), 71.

14. For more on the emergence of organizational culture as managerial practice, see Martin Parker, *Organizational Culture and Identity: Unity and Division at Work* (London: SAGE, 2000).

15. Harry Wessel, "Attracting the Best: Can Standardized Tests Really Predict How Well You'll Do on the Job?," *Chicago Tribune*, February 5, 2003, https://www.chicagotribune.com/news/ct-xpm-2003-02-05-0302080309-story.html.

16. Carla D-Nan Bass, "Personality Tests Increasingly Popular among Employers," *Dallas Morning News*, December 13, 1999.

17. Lauren Rivera, "Go with Your Gut: Emotion and Evaluation in Job Interviews," *American Journal of Sociology* 120, no. 5 (2015): 1339–89, https://www-journals-uchicago-edu.eu1.proxy.openathens.net/doi/10.1086/681214.

18. Rivera, "Go with Your Gut," 1352.

19. For a critique of therapy culture from the perspective of feminism, see Angela P. Harris, "Care and Danger: Feminism and Therapy Culture," *Studies in Law, Politics, and Society* 69 (2016): 113.

20. Illouz, *Saving the Modern Soul*, 203–4.

21. Daniel Goleman, *Working with Emotional Intelligence* (New York: Bantam Books, 1998), 7 (emphasizing that EQ, unlike IQ, "seems to be largely learned" and providing advice throughout on how to improve one's EQ).

22. Edgar Cabanas and Eva Illouz, *Manufacturing Happy Citizens: How the Science and Industry of Happiness Control Our Lives* (Cambridge: Polity Press, 2019), 10.

23. Martin E.P. Seligman and Mihaly Csikszentmihalyi, "Positive Psychology, An Introduction," *American Psychologist* 35, no. 1 (2000): 13, https://doi.org/10.103710003-0665x.55.1.5.

24. Cabanas and Illouz, *Manufacturing Happy Citizens*, 93.

25. Edgar Cabanas and Eva Illouz, "The Making of a 'Happy Worker': Positive Psychology in Neoliberal Organizations," in *Beyond the Cubicle: Job Insecurity, Intimacy, and the Flexible Self,* ed. Allison J. Pugh, 34 (New York: Oxford University Press, 2017).

26. Shawn Achor, *The Happiness Advantage: The Seven Principles of Positive Psychology That Fuel Success and Performance at Work* (New York: Random House, 2010), 4. This is also seen in literature urging attention to organizational culture. See Jerry Want, "Corporate Culture: Illuminating a Black Hole," *Journal of Business Strategy* 24, no. 4 (2003), 14–21, https://doi.org/10.1108/02756660310698542 ("The culture is about behaviors. Politics as usual, punishment, projection of blame, persistently negative attitudes and obsessive compulsive behaviors must be replaced by positive behaviors or the people who exhibit them.").

27. Barbara Ehrenreich, *Bright-Sided: How the Relentless Promotion of Positive Thinking Has Undermined America* (New York: Metropolitan Books, 2009). And this ties back to responsibility: "This notion of happiness combines the

modern romantic ideal of the emotional and affective inner life as a space that has to be cultivated and expanded, with the rational and utilitarian demand of self-control as the ability to discipline and be responsible for channeling emotions in terms of one's interests." Cabanas and Illouz, "The Making of a 'Happy Worker,'" 30.

CHAPTER 6. WORK ORGANIZATIONS: VALUING RACIAL EMOTION

1. Hochschild, *Managed Heart*, 8.

2. Hochschild, *Managed Heart*, chap. 8, "Gender, Status, and Feeling."

3. Jennifer L. Pierce, *Gender Trials: Emotional Lives in Contemporary Law Firms* (Berkeley: University of California Press, 1996).

4. Price Waterhouse v. Hopkins, 490 U.S. 228 (1989).

5. Drew Gilpin Faust, ed., *The Ideology of Slavery: Post-Slavery Thought in the Antebellum South, 1830-1866* (New York: LSU Press, 1981), 90 (selections from the works of proslavery apologists).

6. Faust, *Ideology of Slavery*, 97.

7. Faust, *Ideology of Slavery*, 65.

8. Faust, *Ideology of Slavery*, 65–66.

9. For an account of emotional power dynamics between enslaved people and slaveholders, see Erin Austin Dwyer, *Mastering Emotions: Feelings, Power, and Slavery in the United States* (Philadelphia: University of Pennsylvania Press, 2021).

10. William Craft and Ellen Craft, *Running a Thousand Miles for Freedom, Introduction by Barbara McCaskill* (Georgia: Brown Thrasher, 1999), 10.

11. Solomon Northup, *Twelve Years a Slave: Narrative of Solomon Northup, A Citizen of New York, Kidnapped in Washington City in 1841, and Rescued in 1853, From a Cotton Plantation Near the Red River in Louisiana*, ed. David Wilson (Minnesota: Lerner, 2014), 65–66, 80, 121.

12. Dwyer, *Mastering Emotions*, 191; Anderson, *White Rage*, 18–19 (describing the Black Codes of Mississippi and other confederate states requiring Black workers to sign labor contracts with plantation, mill, or mine owners).

13. Enobong Hannah Branch, *Opportunity Denied: Limiting Black Women to Devalued Work* (New Brunswick, NJ: Rutgers University Press, 2011) (describing how whites worked to keep them in those positions). The time from emancipation through to the Civil Rights Act spanned a century, and work patterns differed in rural versus urban areas, yet Black women were systematically confined throughout to domestic and other menial work, including field work and dangerous, grueling factory jobs. For an account of Black women and work and family across these years, see Jacqueline Jones, *Labor of Love, Labor of Sorrow: Black Women, Work, and the Family, from Slavery to Present* (New York:

Basic Books, 2009) (detailing work patterns of Black women and providing narratives and quotations from some of the women).

14. Jones, *Labor of Love, Labor of Sorrow* (describing some of the ways Black women resisted this expectation).

15. Chinese women were barred from coming to the United States by the Page Act from 1875 until World War II; this, among other things, led to a disproportionate number of Chinese men in the United States and concerns on the part of whites that Chinese men would take their white women. See Ronald Takaki, *Strangers from a Different Shore: A History of Asian Americans* (Boston: Little, Brown, 1989). For a similar history involving fear, sex, and Black Americans, see Jane Dailey, *White Fright: The Sexual Panic at the Heart of America's Racist History* (New York: Basic Books, 2020).

16. Samantha Barbas, "'I'll Take Chop Suey': Restaurants as Agents of Culinary and Cultural Change," *Journal Popular Culture* 36, no. 4 (2003): 682, https://doi.org/10.1111/1540-5931.00040; Joan S. Wang, "Race, Gender, and Laundry Work: The Roles of Chinese Laundrymen and American Women in the United States, 1850–1950," *Journal of American Ethnic History* 58, no. 1 (2004): 60, https://www.jstor.org/stable/2750153 (describing the drive of Chinese Americans out of most industries and into femininized areas of domestic service and laundry work).

17. Barbas, "'I'll Take Chop Suey,'" 682. For more on ways the law was used to fight against Chinese restaurants and for white dominance, see Gabriel J. Chin and John Ormonde, "The War against Chinese Restaurants," *Duke Law Journal* 67 (2018): 681–741.

18. See, e.g., Griggs v. Duke Power, 401 U.S. 424 (1971) (prior to the effective date of the Civil Rights Act, Duke Power openly excluded Black applicants from any department other than the labor department; on the effective date of the act, the company instituted a test requirement and high school diploma requirement for nonlabor positions); Watson v. Forth Worth Bank and Trust, 798 F.2d 791, 808 (5th Cir. 1986) (Goldberg, J., dissenting) (noting that when the plaintiff began her career at the bank as a teller in 1973, there were four Black people in the fifty-member workforce at the bank: "Two printed checks in the basement, one was a kitchen attendant, and the last was a porter."). For an account of civil rights advocates' attempt to use the concept of disparate impact to combat an employer turn toward "neutral" practices of exclusion after the effective date of the 1964 act, see Robert Belton, *The Crusade for Equality in the Workplace* (Lawrence: University Press of Kansas, 2014).

19. Adia Harvey Wingfield, "Are Some Emotions Marked 'Whites Only'? Racialized Feeling Rules in Professional Workplaces," *Social Problems* 57, no. 2 (2010): 259, https://doi.org/10.1525/sp.2010.57.2.251.

20. DiAngelo, *White Fragility*, 136.

21. R. Roosevelt Thomas, Jr., "From Affirmative Action to Affirming Diversity," *Harvard Business Review*, March–April 1990, https://hbr.org/1990/03/from-affirmative-action-to-affirming-diversity.

22. Frank Dobbin, *Inventing Equal Opportunity* (Princeton, NJ: Princeton University Press, 2009). It is worth noting that much of the hostility to affirmative action in the Reagan era was rooted in a framing of affirmative action as harming "innocent whites," thus provoking intense emotions in whites. This framing continues to dominate today, even though affirmative action historically and presently can often be better understood as an antidiscrimination measure that reduces the relevance of race, not as a measure that makes race relevant on a neutral background.

23. Thomas, "From Affirmative Action to Affirming Diversity."

24. Ellen Berrey, *The Enigma of Diversity: The Language of Race and the Limits of Racial Justice* (Chicago: University of Chicago Press, 2015) (exploring the varied meanings of "diversity" in three contexts). For more on the empirical research suggesting what works and what doesn't, see Dobbin and Kalev, "Why Diversity Programs Fail"; Dobbin and Kalev, *Getting to Diversity*.

25. For more on the ways that insiders (usually whites and organizations dominated by whites) capitalize on identities of nonwhite people, see Nancy Leong, *Identity Capitalists: The Powerful Insiders Who Exploit Diversity to Maintain Inequality* (Stanford: Stanford University Press, 2021).

26. Laure Bereni, manuscript on file with author; see also Laure Bereni and Camille Noûs, "La Valeur Professionnelle de L'Identité: Racialization, Genre, et Légitimité Managériale à New York et à Paris," *Sociétés Contemporaine* 117 (2020): 99.

27. Flannery G. Stevens, Victoria C. Plaut, and Jeffrey Sanchez-Burks, "Unlocking the Benefits of Diversity: All-Inclusive Multiculturalism and Positive Organizational Change," *Applied Behavioral Science* 44, no. 1 (2008): 116–34, https://doi.org/10.1177/0021886308314460.

28. Suval Gündemir and Adam D. Galinsky, "Multicultural Blindfolds: How Organizational Multiculturalism Can Conceal Discrimination and Delegitimize Discrimination Claims," *Social Psychological and Personality Science* 9, no. 7 (2018): 825–34, https://doi.org/10.1177/1948550617726830 (citing some of these studies).

29. Gündemir and Galinsky, "Multicultural Blindfolds," 825. For a review of the approaches, see Victoria C. Plaut, Sapna Cheryan, and Flannery G. Stephens, "New Frontiers in Diversity Research: Conceptions of Diversity and Their Theoretical and Practical Implications," in *Handbook of Personality and Social Psychology: Attitudes and Social Cognition*, ed. Mario Mikulincer et al. (Washington, DC: American Psychological Association, 2015), 593–619, https://doi.org/10.1037/14341-019.

30. Leigh S. Wilton, Evan P. Apfelbaum, and Jessica J. Good, "Valuing Differences and Reinforcing Them: Multiculturalism Increases Race Essentialism," *Social Psychological and Personality Science* 10, no. 5 (2019), 681–89, https://doi.org/10.1177/1948550618780728.

31. Gündemir and Galinsky, "Multiculturalism Blindfolds." See also Cheryl R. Kaiser et al., "Presumed Fair: Ironic Effects of Organizational Diversity Structures," *Journal of Personality and Social Psychology* 104, no. 3 (2013): 504–19, https://doi.org/10.1037/a0030838.

32. Wingfield, *Flatlining*, 37–38.

33. Wingfield, *Flatlining*, 154.

34. Lauren B. Edelman, *Working Law: Courts, Corporations, and Symbolic Civil Rights* (Chicago: University of Chicago Press, 2016) (describing earlier work on managerializing antidiscrimination complaints).

35. Ellen Berrey, Robert L. Nelson, and Laura Beth Nielsen, *Rights on Trial: How Workplace Discrimination Law Perpetuates Inequality* (Chicago: University of Chicago Press, 2017), 192.

36. Berrey, Nelson, and Nielsen, *Rights on Trial*, 192–93.

37. Berrey, Nelson, and Nielsen, *Rights on Trial*, 195.

38. Berrey, Nelson, and Nielsen, *Rights on Trial*, 94.

39. Sara Ahmed, *Complaint!* (Durham, NC: Duke University Press, 2021), 169–70.

40. Cathy Park Hong, *Minor Feelings: An Asian American Reckoning* (New York: One World, 2020), 57.

41. See Joe R. Feagin, Hernán Vera, and Pinar Batur, *White Racism: The Basics* (New York: Routledge, 2nd ed., 2001), 240–42 (describing "talking back" to racism as "an act of courage, an act of risk" that requires one to defy cultural norms and sometimes speak up about racism in seemingly ambiguous and subtle situations). For discussion of how we might begin to better conceptualize whites' interests in raising race concerns, including discussion of the concept of "racial labor," see Rich, "Marginal Whiteness," 1497. For a positive spin on the idea of a "race traitors" as whites who proactively seek to disrupt white privilege, see Noel Ignatiev and John Garvey, eds., *Race Traitor* (New York: Routledge, 1996).

CHAPTER 7. WHAT'S WRONG WITH THE CURRENT APPROACH

1. Kristen Myers, *Racetalk: Racism Hiding in Plain Sight* (Lanham, MD: Rowman & Littlefield, 2005).

2. Meyers, *Racetalk*, 23.

3. Meyers, *Racetalk*, 4.

4. Nolan Cabrera, *White Guys on Campus: Racism, White Immunity, and the Myth of "Post-Racial" Higher Education (The American Campus)* (New Brunswick, NJ: Rutgers University Press, 2018). See also Leslie Houts Picca and Joe R. Feagin, *Two-Faced Racism: Whites in the Backstage and Frontstage* (New York: Routledge, 2007).

5. See Lu-In Wang and Zachary Brewster, "Dignity Transacted: Emotional Labor and the Racialized Workplace," *University of Michigan Journal of Legal Reform* 53 (2020): 531 (discussing the way that backstage racetalk translates to stereotyping in the front stage and results in negative interactions between wait staff and clients).

6. See Cheryl R. Kaiser and Carol T. Miller, "Derogating the Victim: The Interpersonal Consequences of Blaming Events on Discrimination," *Group Processes and Intergroup Relations* 6, no. 3 (2003): 228, https://doi.org/10.1177/13684302030063001 (discussing prior research showing that women and African Americans were less likely to publicly claim that they had suffered discrimination in the presence of a racial or gender out-group member). Kaiser and Miller's subsequent experiments showed that this seeming reluctance or fear about reporting was in part justified as out-group members, specifically whites or male coworkers, judged persons who claimed race or gender discrimination more harshly than noncomplaining persons. These out-group members continued to disfavor persons who complained about discrimination even when exposed to evidence showing that the complaints lodged had some basis, such as that the complainant was being forced to work for someone with discriminatory attitudes. Kaiser and Miller, "Derogating the Victim," 234.

7. Richard Thompson Ford, *The Race Card: How Bluffing about Bias Makes Race Relations Worse* (Stanford: Stanford University Press, 2008).

8. Legal scholar Julie Suk calls this the "race card card." Julie Suk, "Race without Cards?," *Stanford Journal of Civil Rights and Civil Liberties* 5 (2009): 111.

9. Statistics of reported and unreported discrimination are difficult to obtain, but research does suggest individuals might be reluctant to report discrimination, even when they perceive it. See Kaiser and Miller, "Derogating the Victim"; Cheryl L. Kaiser and Carol T. Miller, "Stop Complaining! The Social Costs of Making Attributions to Discrimination," *Personality and Social Psychology Bulletin* 27, no. 2 (2001): 254–63, https://journals.sagepub.com/doi/pdf/10.1177/0146167201272010; see generally Cheryl R. Kaiser and Brenda Major, "A Social Psychological Perspective on Perceiving and Reporting Discrimination," *Law and Social Inquiry* 31 (2003): 80.

In addition, the culture and system push for individuals to identify specific bad actor discriminators in their stories of discrimination may lead to underreporting of broader problems involving race and racial bias at work. See Tristin K. Green,

Discrimination Laundering: The Rise of Organizational Innocence and the Crisis of Equal Opportunity Law (New York: Cambridge University Press, 2017).

10. Illouz, *Saving the Modern Soul*, 103.

11. Gündemir and Galinsky, "Multicultural Blindfolds."

12. Wingfield, "Are Some Emotions Marked 'Whites Only'?," 264–65.

13. Wingfield, "Are Some Emotions Marked 'Whites Only'?," 261.

14. American Psychological Association, *Stress in America: The Impact of Discrimination* (Washington, DC: APA, 2016).

15. Elizabeth A. Pascoe and Laura Smart Richman, "Perceived Discrimination and Health: A Meta-Analytic Review," *Psychological Bulletin* 135, no. 4 (2009): 531–54, https://doi.org/10.1037/a0016059. See also Derald Wing Sue et al., "Disarming Racial Microaggressions: Microintervention Strategies for Targets, White Allies, and Bystanders," *American Psychologist* 74, no. 1 (2019): 130, https://doi.org/10.1037/amp0000296 (gathering sources on the impact of microaggressions on health and well-being of people of color).

16. Tristin K. Green, "Rethinking Racial Entitlements: From Epithet to Theory," *Southern California Law Review* 93 (2020): 217.

17. Adam Waytz, "Spotlight on the Emotional Organization: The Limits of Empathy," *Harvard Business Review*, February 2016, https://hbr.org/2016/01/the-limits-of-empathy.

CHAPTER 8. WHAT WE CAN DO

Section epigraph: Lorde, *Sister Outsider*, 115.

1. Desert Palace, Inc. v. Costa, 539 U.S. 90 (2003).

2. Costa v. Desert Palace, Inc., 299 F.3d 838, 844 (9th Cir. 2002).

3. Costa v. Desert Palace, 844–46.

4. Costa v. Desert Palace, 846.

5. Desert Palace v. Costa, 101 (interpreting the 1991 Civil Rights Act, codified in Title VII at 42 U.S.C. § 2000e-2(m)).

6. 42 U.S.C. § 2000e-2(g)(2)(B).

7. This legal category of "racial assault" builds on the important work of Derald Wing Sue and colleagues. It nonetheless differs from the category of "microassault" defined by them in that they require that microassault behavior be "meant to hurt." See Derald Wing Sue et al., *Microintervention Strategies: What You Can Do to Disarm and Dismantle Individual and Systemic Racism and Bias* (New York: Wiley, 2021), 7. Sue and colleagues place microassaults within a broader category of microaggressions, defined as "brief and commonplace daily verbal and behavioral interpersonal indignities, whether intentional or unintentional, which communicate hostile, derogatory, or negative slights, invalidations, and insults to an individual because of their marginalized status in society" (7). See also Derald

Wing Sue et al., "Racial Microaggressions in Everyday Life: Implications for Clinical Practice," *American Psychology* 62, no. 4 (2007): 271–86, https://doi .org/10.1037/0003-066X.62.4.271. Theorists have explored similar ideas in the area of constitutional law, arguing in favor of law that asks, for example, about cultural meaning of language and acts rather than actor intent as a particular state of mind. See Charles R. Lawrence III, "The Id, the Ego, and Equal Protection: Reckoning with Unconscious Racism," *Stanford Law Review* 39 (1987): 317.

8. Slack v. Havens, 552 F.2d 1091 (1975).

9. Watson v. Fort Worth Bank & Trust, 487 U.S. 977 (1988).

10. Judith Butler, *Excitable Speech: The Politics of the Performative* (New York: Routledge, 2021), 52, noting: "If a performative [speech act] provisionally succeeds . . . then it is not because an intention successfully governs the action of speech, but only because that action echoes prior actions, and accumulates the force of authority through the repetition or citation of a prior authoritative set of practices." With respect to derogatory slurs in particular, Butler adds, "The speaker who utters the racial slur is thus citing that slur, making linguistic community with a history of speakers."

11. Recovery on an individual's hostile work environment claim will be limited in part by the statute of limitations period, which under Title VII is quite short. Title VII administrative rules require initiation of a complaint with the state or federal administrative agency within 300 days in most cases. Recovery on an individual claim will also be limited by the individual plaintiff's showing of harm.

12. The set period of time allows someone who engages in racial assault behavior to learn and progress and eases the risk that employers will overpenalize out of concerns about long-term liability. Although it is true that a bright line may allow strategic behavior, such as holding off on an employment decision until after the period has passed, given relational realities, that behavior is likely to be minimal. Moreover, a plaintiff could still prove discrimination based on all of the circumstances, including racial assault behavior outside of the specified time period; they simply would not benefit from the bright-line legal presumption of racial assault.

13. As explained earlier, this is how the law works under Title VII. It is an unlawful employment practice under the act for an employer to take employment action in which race is the "motivating factor." In this scenario, racial assault would satisfy this requirement (§ 703(m)). If the employer shows that it would have made the same decision anyway, absent any racial reason, then the plaintiff's remedies are altered (§ 706(g)(2)(B)).

14. See Matias, "'And Our Feelings Just Don't Feel It Anymore," 135.

15. Kennedy, *Nigger*.

16. In *Ash v. Tyson*, the Court noted that meaning of the term "boy" "may depend on various factors, including context, inflection, tone of voice, local custom, and historical usage." Ash v. Tyson, 456. Note: This "inflection, tone of

voice," may suggest a search for what the person "intended," which is contrary to what I propose here.

17. Jennifer L. Pierce, *Racing for Innocence: Whiteness, Gender, and the Backlash against Affirmative Action* (Stanford: Stanford University Press, 2012), 67.

18. See Richard Thompson Ford, "Bias in the Air: Rethinking Employment Discrimination Law," *Stanford Law Review* 66 (2014): 1381, 1411 (arguing that employers should be liable only for discrimination they can prevent "without overly draconian policing of the expression of their employees" as if the only tool employers have to combat discrimination is that of policing employees); Jansen v. Packaging Corp. of America, 123 F.3d 490, 511–13 (7th Cir. 1997) (Posner, C.J., concurring and dissenting, stating his view that "courts know, more or less, what is reasonable for the employer to do about hostile-environment harassment—institute a tough policy, disseminate it, establish a procedure by which a worker can complain without fear of retaliation . . . [and] respond promptly and effectively to any report of possible harassment").

19. As the next section details, work organizations should keep in mind that sources of discrimination are often located structurally at the level of systems, practices, and cultures rather than merely at the level of an individual's bad action. Tending too closely to feelings at the individual level—through calls for town halls and diversity trainings—can derail progress at the structural level, where long-standing change might better be achieved. Even when it comes to racial assault, work organizations need to calibrate and strategize response so that it is not lost in the minutiae of bettering discrete relationships.

20. Eden B. King et al., "Discrimination in the 21st Century: Are Science and the Law Aligned?," *Psychology Public Policy and the Law* 17, no. 1 (2010): 56, https://doi.org/10.1037/a0021673. See also Sue et al., "Racial Microaggressions in Everyday Life."

21. King et al., "Discrimination in the 21st Century," 56.

22. Angela Onwuachi-Willig, "What about #UsToo? The Invisibility of Race in the #MeToo Movement," *Yale Law Journal Forum* 128 (2018): 105.

23. Tristin K. Green, "Was Sexual Harassment a Mistake?: The Stories We Tell," *Yale Law Journal Forum* 128 (2018): 152 (showing ways the judges and justices in cases decided by the Supreme Court have narrowed inquiry when in fact the stories plaintiffs sought to tell were much broader).

24. Vance v. Ball State University, 570 U.S. 421 (2013).

25. Vance v. Ball State, no 1:06-CV-1452 (S.D. Ind. Sept. 10, 2008), 2008 WL 4247836 at *13. As mentioned in chapter 4, in finding that Kimes's behavior toward Vance was not because of Vance's race, the judge credited testimony by a coworker that she had "never heard or seen Bill Kimes or say something that indicates he is a racist, and I do not believe he is a racist."

26. Vance v. Ball State Univ., 646 F.3d 461, 471 (7th Cir. 2011).

27. Green, *Discrimination Laundering*.

28. Int'l Bthd. of Teamsters v. United States, 431 U.S. 321 (1977); Hazelwood Sch. Dist. v. United States, 433 U.S. 299 (1977).

29. Hazelwood v. United States.

30. For more on these and other measures, see Green, *Discrimination Laundering*.

31. Valerie Purdie Greenaway and Kate M. Turetsky, "Socioecological Diversity and Inclusion: A Framework for Advancing Diversity Science," *Current Opinion in Psychology* 32 (2020): 32, https://doi.org/10.1016/j.copsyc.2019.09.008 (emphasizing what they call socioecological diversity and socioecological inclusion, both of which turn in part on demographics of space).

32. Laurel Smith-Doerr, *Women's Work: Gender Equality v. Hierarchy in the Life Sciences* (Boulder, CO: Lynne Reiner, 2004).

33. Alexandra Kalev, "Cracking the Glass Cages?: Restructuring and Ascriptive Inequality at Work," *American Journal of Sociology* 114, no. 6 (2009): 1591–634, https://www-journals-uchicago-edu.eu1.proxy.openathens.net/doi/10.1086/597175.

34. Dobbin and Kalev, "Why Diversity Programs Fail."

35. Robin J. Ely and David A. Thomas, "Cultural Diversity at Work: The Effects of Diversity Perspectives on Work Group Processes and Outcomes," *Administrative Science Quarterly* 46, no. 2 (2001): 229–73, https://doi.org/10.2307/2667087; see also Stevens, Plaut, and Sanchez-Burks, "Unlocking the Benefits of Diversity."

36. Carol S. Dweck, *Mindset: The New Psychology of Success* (New York: Random House, 2006).

37. Steele, *Whistling Vivaldi*, 207. Along these same lines, another recent study found that whites were more likely to choose a Black conversation partner and engaged in fewer avoidance behaviors during the interaction when they were informed that anxiety in interracial interaction is common and that research suggests it is lessened in the long term the more contact one has. Jennifer R. Schultz, Sarah E. Gaither, Heather L. Urry, and Keith B. Maddox, "Reframing Anxiety to Encourage Interracial Interactions," *Transnational Issues in Psychological Science* 1, no. 4 (2015): 392–400, https://doi.org/10.1037/tps0000048. See also Pauker et al., "Believing That Prejudice Can Change."

38. Tristin K. Green, "Work Culture and Discrimination," *California Law Review* 93 (2005): 623.

39. Green, "'I'll See You at Work'" (advocating for including spatial features together with HR practices and work cultures as a category of organizational decision that affects relations and discrimination at work).

40. Compliance does not mean perfection, as in no discriminatory decisions; rather, compliance, too, needs to be understood as an ongoing, relational project.

See Ruthanne Huising and Susan S. Silbey, "Governing the Gap: Forging Safe Science through Relational Regulation," *Regulation and Governance* 5, no. 1 (2011): 18, doi:10.1111/j.1748-5991.2010.01100.x (talking about environmental standards and noting that "achieving compliance in an organization is a daily effort that requires the overseer to be alert, in tune, and adaptive with respect to not only other employees but also the material circumstances, patterns of interaction, and time pressures operating in the organization").

41. Green, "'I'll See You at Work.'"

42. Ben Waber et al., "Workspaces That Move People," *Harvard Business Review*, October 2014, https://hbr.org/2014/10/workspaces-that-move-people.

43. See Laszlo Bock, *Work Rules!: Insights from Inside Google That Will Transform How You Live and Lead* (New York: Hachette Book Group, 2015).

44. Illouz, *Saving the Modern Soul*, 85 ("Such definitions of power as self-possession are paradoxical: they tend to discourage the abusive displays of anger that we normally associate with the 'bullying boss,' but they also delegitimize the expression of workers' anger about other abuses of power that may be directed at them.").

45. White fragility, as Robin DiAngelo explains, "is a powerful means of white racial control and the protection of white advantage." DiAngelo, *White Fragility*, 2.

46. Illouz, *Saving the Modern Soul*, 10 ("Language defines categories of emotions, establishes what an 'emotional problem' is, provides causal frameworks and metaphors to make sense of these problems, and constrains the ways emotions are expressed, made sense of, and managed."); Ann Swidler, *Talk of Love: How Culture Matters* (Chicago: University of Chicago Press, 2001).

47. David Robson, "There Really Are 50 Words for 'Snow'," *Washington Post*, January 14, 2013.

48. Sociologist Arlie Hochschild has appendix on language, too. Hochschild, *Managed Heart*.

49. Barrett, *How Emotions Are Made*, 103–4.

50. Barrett, *How Emotions Are Made*, 141.

51. Barrett, *How Emotions Are Made*, 105.

52. Illouz, *Saving the Modern Soul*, 10. For more on language and power distribution, see John M. Conley, William M. O'Barr, and Robin Conley Riner, *Just Words: Law, Language, and Power* (Chicago: University of Chicago Press, 3rd ed., 2019).

53. Barrett, *How Emotions Are Made*, 182–83.

54. Janine Young Kim, "Racial Emotions and the Feeling of Equality," *University of Colorado Law Review* 87 (2016): 437, 498.

55. Carbado and Gulati, *Acting White?*.

56. Kenji Yoshino, *Covering: The Hidden Assault on Our Civil Rights* (New York: Random House, 2006).

57. Pierce, *Racing for Innocence.*

58. Cristina M. Rodríguez, "Language and Participation," *California Law Review* 94 (2006): 687.

59. Wendy Greene, "Splitting Hairs: The Eleventh Circuit's Take on Workplace Bans against Black Women's Natural Hair in *EEOC v. Catastrophe Management Solutions, Inc.*," *University of Miami Law Review* 71 (2017): 987.

60. Tamar Saguy et al., "The Irony of Harmony: Intergroup Contact Can Produce False Expectations for Equality," *Psychological Science* 20, no. 1 (2009): 114, https://doi.org/10.1111/j.1467-9280.2008.02261.x ("Whereas a sole emphasis on commonalities may deflect attention from issues of group disparities, encounters that emphasize both common connections and the problem of unjust group inequalities may promote intergroup understanding as well as recognition of the need for change."); Stephen Wright and Michael Lubensky, "The Struggle for Social Equality: Collective Action vs. Prejudice Reduction," in *Intergroup Misunderstandings: Impact of Divergent Social Realities*, ed. Stephanie Demoulin et al. (New York: Psychology Press, 2008), 291.

61. See Dobbin and Kalev, "Why Diversity Programs Fail"; Dobbin and Kalev, *Getting to Diversity.*

62. See Srivastava, "Tears, Fears and Careers."

63. For a short list of organizational-level reasons why "anti-bias training might fail," see Ifeoma Ajunwa, "10 Reasons Why Anti-Racism Training Is Not the Problem," *Forbes*, September 5, 2020, https://www.forbes.com/sites/ifeomaajunwa/2020/09/05/10-reasons-why-anti-racism-training-is-not-the-problem/.

64. Rhonda V. Magee, *The Inner Work of Racial Justice: Healing Ourselves and Transforming Our Communities through Mindfulness* (New York: Penguin Random House, 2019), 21 (providing mindfulness lessons aimed at supporting the ability "to sit compassionately with and talk about our own particular experiences with race, race-related injury, and alienation").

65. See Dolly Chugh, *The Person You Mean to Be: How Good People Fight Bias* (New York: HarperCollins, 2018) (arguing that being better should be the goal, not being a good person).

66. Hong, *Minor Feelings*, 88 ("Suddenly Americans feel self-conscious of their white identity and this self-consciousness misleads them into thinking their identity is under threat.").

67. This is true with respect to interpersonal relations and also structural sources of bias and discrimination. For specific suggestions for targets, allies, and bystanders at the micro, relational level, see Sue et al., *Microintervention Strategies*, and Derald Wing Sue, *Race Talk and the Conspiracy of Silence: Understanding and Facilitating Difficult Dialogues on Race* (New York: Wiley, 2015).

CONCLUSION

1. See Robert Livingston, "How to Promote Racial Equity in the Workplace," *Harvard Business Review*, September–October, 2020, https://hbr.org/2020/09/how-to-promote-racial-equity-in-the-workplace (introducing a five-step roadmap of which empathy is a part). While it seems to be currently rising in favor, the idea of empathy as crucial to more positive interracial interactions and ultimately to racial justice has been around for some time. Feagin and Vera, *White Racism* (noting that what sets white antiracists apart from the general white population is their ability to empathize with people of color); Richard Delgado, *The Coming Race War?: And Other Apocalyptic Tales of America after Affirmative Action and Welfare* (New York: NYU Press, 1996) (describing false empathy in whites, in which a person believes that they are identifying with a person of color, "but they are doing so only in a slight, superficial way" and noting that "false empathy is worse than indifference"); O'Brien, "The Political Is Personal," 253.

2. There are several helpful resources for working at this more microrelational level on our interactions at work and in other spaces. The field of mindfulness, for example, has proved generous on this front. See Magee, *Inner Work of Racial Justice*. Much of the important work being done to surface and explore individuals' emotions generally regarding race and racial power comes out of experiences and research in the field of education. Cheryl E. Matias, *Feeling White: Whiteness, Emotionality, and Education* (Boston: Sense, 2016); Megan Boler, *Feeling Power: Emotions and Education* (New York: Routledge, 1999); DiAngelo, *White Fragility*; Tatum, *Why Are All the Black Kids Sitting Together in the Cafeteria?*; Paula Ioanide, "Negotiating Privileged Students' Affective Resistances: Why a Pedagogy of Emotional Engagement Is Necessary," in *Seeing Race Again: Countering Colorblindness across the Disciplines*, ed. Kimberlé Williams Crenshaw et al. (Oakland: University of California Press, 2019); Zeus Leonardo and Michalinos Zembylas, "Whiteness as Technology of Affect: Implications for Educational Practice," *Equality and Excellence in Education* 46, no. 1 (2013): 150, https://doi.org/10.1080/10665684.2013.750539 ("It takes time and certainly much discomfort to discover how emotions can be engaged as critical and transformative forces in schools.").

3. For a recent article gathering social science research on what they call "racial anxiety" and framing institutional and individual solutions, some of which I have relied upon here, see Rachel D. Godsil and L. Song Richardson, "Racial Anxiety," *Iowa Law Review* 102 (2017): 2235 ("strategies to minimize racial anxiety," including "acknowledging anxiety," using "scripts," teaching about the "malleability of prejudice" and framing "learning" goals).

On the need to be working intraracially as well as interracially, see O'Brien, "The Political Is Personal," 253.

4. Srivastava, "Tears, Fears and Careers," 71. A similar point has been made in the context of divorce, where no-fault divorce is said to have disempowered women and facilitated dismissal of women's anger involving legitimate concerns. See Trina Grillo, "Process Dangers for Women," *Yale Law Journal* 100 (1991): 1545; Martha Albertson Fineman, *The Illusion of Equality: The Rhetoric and Reality of Divorce Reform* (Chicago: University of Chicago Press, 1991).

5. Craig and Richeson, "Majority No More?"

6. Paula Ioanide, *The Emotional Politics of Racism: How Feelings Trump Facts in an Era of Colorblindness* (Stanford: Stanford University Press, 2015); Bonilla-Silva, *Racism without Racists*; Anderson, *White Rage*; Haney Lopéz, Dog *Whistle Politics.*

7. Ahmed, "Affective Economies."

8. Heather McGhee, *The Sum of Us: What Racism Costs Everyone and How We Can Prosper Together* (New York: Random House, 2021).

Bibliography and Case List

BIBLIOGRAPHY

Abrams, Kathryn. *Open Hand, Closed Fist: Practices of Undocumented Organizing in a Hostile State*. Oakland: University of California Press, 2022.

Abrams, Kathryn, and Hila Keren. "Who's Afraid of Law and the Emotions?" *Minnesota Law Review* 94 (2010): 1997.

Achor, Shawn. *The Happiness Advantage: The Seven Principles of Positive Psychology That Fuel Success and Performance at Work*. New York: Random House, 2010.

Ahmed, Sara. "Affective Economies." *Social Text* 22, no. 2 (2004): 117–39. https://doi.org/10.1215/01642472-22-2_79-117.

Ahmed, Sara. *Complaint!* Durham, NC: Duke University Press, 2021.

Ahmed, Sara. *The Cultural Politics of Emotion*. Edinburgh: Edinburgh University Press, 2nd ed., 2014.

Ajunwa, Ifeoma. "10 Reasons Why Anti-Racism Training Is Not the Problem." *Forbes*, September 5, 2020. https://www.forbes.com/sites/ifeomaajunwa/2020/09/05/10-reasons-why-anti-racism-training-is-not-the-problem/.

Albiston, Catherine Ruth, and Tristin K. Green. "Social Closure Discrimination." *Berkeley Journal of Employment and Labor Law* 39 (2018): 1.

Allport, Gordon. *The Nature of Prejudice*. Cambridge, MA: Addison-Wesley, 1954.

Almeling, Rene. "Selling Genes, Selling Gender: Egg Agencies, Sperm Banks, and the Medical Market in Genetic Material." *American Sociological Review* 72, no. 3 (2007): 319–40. https://www.jstor.org/stable/25472466.

American Psychological Association. *Stress in America: The Impact of Discrimination*. Washington, DC: APA, 2016.

Anderson, Carol. *White Rage: The Unspoken Truth of Our Racial Divide*. New York: Bloomsbury, 2016.

Apfelbaum, Evan P., et al. "Learning (Not) to Talk about Race: When Older Children Underperform in Social Categorization." *Developmental Psychology* 44, no. 5 (2008): 1513–18. https://doi.org/10.1037/a0012835.

Apfelbaum, Evan P., and Samuel R. Sommers. "Seeing Race and Seeming Racist? Evaluating Strategic Colorblindness in Social Interaction." *Journal of Personality and Social Psychology* 95, no. 4 (2008): 918–32. https://doi.org/10.1037/a0011990.

Babbitt, Laura, Negin R. Toosi, and Samuel R. Sommers. "A Broad and Insidious Appeal: Unpacking the Reasons for Endorsing Racial Color Blindness." In *The Myth of Racial Colorblindness: Manifestations, Dynamics, and Impact*, edited by Helen A. Neville, Miguel E. Gallardo, and Derald Wing Sue, 53. Washington, DC: American Psychological Association, 2016.

Banaji, Mahzarin R., and Anthony G. Greenwald. *Blindspot: Hidden Biases of Good People*. New York: Random House, 2013.

Bandes, Susan A., ed. *The Passion of Law*. New York: New York University Press, 1999.

Bandes, Susan A., and Jeremy A. Blumenthal. "Emotion and the Law." *Annual Review of Law and Social Science* 8 (2012): 161.

Barbas, Samantha. "'I'll Take Chop Suey': Restaurants as Agents of Culinary and Cultural Change." *Journal of Popular Culture* 36, no. 4 (2003): 669–86. https://doi.org/10.1111/1540-5931.00040.

Bargetz, Birgitte. "The Distribution of Emotions: Affective Politics of Emancipation." *Hypatia* 30, no. 3 (2015): 580–96. https://www.jstor.org/stable/24542144.

Barrett, Lisa Feldman. *How Emotions Are Made: The Secret Life of the Brain*. New York: Houghton Mifflin, 2017.

Barrett, Lisa Feldman, and Eliza Bliss-Moreau. "She's Emotional. He's Having a Bad Day: Attributional Explanations for Emotion Stereotypes." *Emotion* 9, no. 5 (2009): 649–58. https://doi.org/10.1037/a0016821.

Barrett, Lisa Feldman, and Ajay B. Satpute. "Historical Pitfalls and New Directions in the Neuroscience of Emotion." *Neuroscience Letters* 693, no. 6 (2019): 9–18. https://doi.org/10.1016/j.neulet.2017.07.045.

Bass, Carla D-Nan. "Personality Tests Increasingly Popular among Employers." *Dallas Morning News*, December 13, 1999.

Bell, Sam Adler. "Behind the CRT Crackdown," *The Forum*, January 13, 2022. https://www.aapf.org/theforum-critical-race-theory-crackdown.

Belton, Robert. *The Crusade for Equality in the Workplace*. Lawrence: University Press of Kansas, 2014.

Bereni, Laure. Manuscript on file with author.

Bereni, Laure, and Camille Noûs. "La Valeur Professionnelle de L'Identité: Racialization, Genre, et Légitimité Managériale à New York et à Paris." *Sociétés Contemporaine* 117 (2020): 99.

Bergsieker, Hillary B., J. Nicole Shelton, and Jennifer A. Richeson. "To Be Liked Versus Respected: Divergent Goals in Interracial Interactions." *Journal of Personality and Social Psychology* 99, no. 2 (2010): 248–64. https://doi .org/10.1037/a0018474.

Berrey, Ellen. *The Enigma of Diversity: The Language of Race and the Limits of Racial Justice*. Chicago: University of Chicago Press, 2015.

Berrey, Ellen, Robert L. Nelson, and Laura Beth Nielsen. *Rights on Trial: How Workplace Discrimination Law Perpetuates Inequality*. Chicago: University of Chicago Press, 2017.

Bock, Laszlo. *Work Rules!: Insights from Inside Google That Will Transform How You Live and Lead*. New York: Hachette Book Group, 2015.

Boler, Megan. *Feeling Power: Emotions and Education*. New York: Routledge, 1999.

Bonilla-Silva, Eduardo. "Feeling Race: Theorizing the Racial Economy of Emotions." *American Sociological Review* 84, no. 1 (2019): 1–25. https:// www.jstor.org/stable/48588887.

Bonilla-Silva, Eduardo. *Racism without Racists: Color-Blind Racism and Racial Inequality in Contemporary America*. Lanham, MD: Rowman & Littlefield, 2010.

Branch, Enobong Hannah. *Opportunity Denied: Limiting Black Women to Devalued Work*. New Brunswick, NJ: Rutgers University Press, 2011.

Bridges, Khiara M. *Critical Race Theory: A Primer*. St. Paul, MN: West, 2019.

Brown, Christopher Leslie. "Foreword." In Winthrop D. Jordan, *White over Black: American Attitudes toward the Negro*. Chapel Hill: University of North Carolina Press, 2nd ed., 2012.

Buchanan, Kim Shayo, and Phillip Atiba Goff. "Racist Stereotype Threat in Civil Rights Law." *UCLA Law Review* 67 (2020): 316.

Butler, Judith. *Excitable Speech: The Politics of the Performative*. New York: Routledge, 2021.

Butz, David A., and E. Ashby Plant. "Perceiving Outgroup Members as Unresponsive: Implications for Approach-Related Emotions, Intentions, and Behavior." *Journal of Personality and Social Psychology* 91, no. 6 (2006): 1066–79. https://doi.org/10.1037/0022-3514.91.6.1066.

Cabanas, Edgar, and Eva Illouz. "The Making of a 'Happy Worker': Positive Psychology in Neoliberal Organizations." In *Beyond the Cubicle: Job Insecurity, Intimacy, and the Flexible Self*, edited by Allison J. Pugh, 22–50. New York: Oxford University Press, 2017.

Cabanas, Edgar, and Eva Illouz. *Manufacturing Happy Citizens: How the Science and Industry of Happiness Control Our Lives*. Cambridge: Polity Press, 2019.

Cabrera, Nolan. *White Guys on Campus: Racism, White Immunity, and the Myth of "Post-Racial" Higher Education (The American Campus)*. New Brunswick, NJ: Rutgers University Press, 2018.

Carbado, Devon W. "Critical What What?" *Connecticut Law Review* 43 (2011): 1593.

Carbado, Devon W., and Mitu Gulati. *Acting White?: Rethinking Race in "Post-Racial" America*. New York: Oxford University Press, 2013.

Carbado, Devon W., and Mitu Gulati. "The Fifth Black Woman." *Journal of Contemporary Legal Issues* 11 (2001): 701.

Cashin, Sheryll. *The Failures of Integration: How Race and Class Are Undermining the American Dream*. New York: Hachette Book Group, 2004.

Cashin, Sheryll. *White Space, Black Hood: Opportunity Hoarding and Segregation in the Age of Inequality*. New York: Random House, 2021.

Celeghin, Allessia, et al. "Basic Emotions in Human Neuroscience: Neuroimaging and Beyond." *Frontiers in Psychology* 8 (2017): 1432. https://doi.org/10.3389/fpsyg.2017.01432.

Cherry, Myisha. *The Case for Rage: Why Anger Is Essential to Anti-Racist Struggle*. New York: Oxford University Press, 2021.

Chin, Gabriel J., and John Ormonde. "The War against Chinese Restaurants." *Duke Law Journal* 67 (2018): 681–741.

Chugh, Dolly. *The Person You Mean to Be: How Good People Fight Bias*. New York: HarperCollins, 2018.

Clarke, Jessica A. "Explicit Bias." *Northwestern University Law Review* 113 (2018): 505.

Closson, Troy. "'Nobody Cares about Us Here': Anguish and Anger on Buffalo's East Side." *New York Times*, May 15, 2022. https://www.nytimes.com/2022/05/15/nyregion/east-side-buffalo-neighborhood.html.

Conley, John M., William M. O'Barr, and Robin Conley Riner. *Just Words: Law, Language, and Power*. Chicago: University of Chicago Press, 3rd ed., 2019.

Craft, William, and Ellen Craft. *Running a Thousand Miles to Freedom, Introduction by Barbara McCaskill*. Athens: University of Georgia Press, 1999.

Craig, Maureen A., and Jennifer A. Richeson. "Majority No More? The Influence of Neighborhood Racial Diversity and Salient National Population Changes on Whites' Perceptions of Racial Discrimination." *Russell Sage*

Foundation Journal of Social Science 4, no. 5 (2018): 141–57. https://doi.org /10.7758/RSF.2018.4.5.07.

Crocker, Jennifer, and Julia A. Garcia. "Downward and Upward Spirals in Intergroup Interactions: The Role of Egosystem and Ecosystem Goals." In *Handbook of Prejudice, Stereotyping and Discrimination*, edited by Todd D. Nelson, 229–46. New York: Psychology Press, 2009.

Dailey, Jane. *White Fright: The Sexual Panic at the Heart of America's Racist History*. New York: Basic Books, 2020.

Darum, Chad, and Karen Engle. "The Rise of the Personal Animosity Presumption in Title VII and the Return to 'No Cause' Employment." *Texas Law Review* 81 (2003): 1117.

Darwin, Charles. *The Expression of the Emotions in Man and Animals*. London: John Murray, 1872.

Deal, Terrence E., and Allen A. Kennedy. *Corporate Cultures: The Rites and Rituals of Corporate Life*. New York: Basic Books, 1982.

Delgado, Richard. *The Coming Race War?: And Other Apocalyptic Tales of America after Affirmative Action and Welfare*. New York: New York University Press, 1996.

Delgado, Richard, and Jean Stefancic. *Understanding Words That Wound*. New York: Routledge, 2004.

The Democracy and Government Reform Team. "Examining the Demographic Composition of U.S. and Circuit and District Courts." *Center for American Progress*, February 13, 2020. https://www.americanprogress.org/article /examining-demographic-compositions-u-s-circuit-district-courts/.

DiAngelo, Robin. *White Fragility: Why It's So Hard for White People to Talk about Racism*. Boston: Beacon Press, 2018.

Dobbin, Frank. *Inventing Equal Opportunity*. Princeton, NJ: Princeton University Press, 2009.

Dobbin, Frank, and Alexandra Kalev. *Getting to Diversity: What Works and What Doesn't*. Cambridge, MA: Harvard University Press, 2022.

Dobbin, Frank, and Alexandra Kalev. "Why Diversity Programs Fail. And What Works Better." *Harvard Business Review*, July–August 2016. https://hbr.org /2016/07/why-diversity-programs-fail.

Doerr, Celeste, E. Ashby Plant, Jonathan W. Kuntsman, and David Buck. "Interactions in Black and White: Racial Differences and Similarities in Response to Interracial Interactions." *Group Processes and Intergroup Relations* 14, no. 1 (2011): 31–43. https://:doi.org/10.1177/1368430210375250.

Dovidio, John F., and Samuel L. Gaertner. "Aversive Racism." In *Advances in Experimental Social Psychology* 36 (2004): 1–52. https://doi.org/10.1016 /S0065-2601(04)36001-6.

Dovidio, John F., Angelika Love, Fabian M. H. Schellhaas, and Miles Hewstone. "Reducing Intergroup Bias through Intergroup Contact: Twenty Years of

Progress and Future Directions." *Group Processes and Intergroup Relations* 20, no. 5 (2017): 606–20. https://doi.org/10.1177/1368430217712052.

Du Gay, Paul. *Consumption and Identity at Work*. London: SAGE, 1996.

Dukes, Daniel, et al. "Comment: The Rise of Affectivism." *Nature Human Behavior* 5 (2021): 816–20. https://doi.org/10.1038/s41562-021-01130-8.

Dweck, Carol S. *Mindset: The New Psychology of Success*. New York: Random House, 2006.

Dwyer, Erin Austin. *Mastering Emotions: Feelings, Power, and Slavery in the United States (America in the Nineteenth Century)*. Philadelphia: University of Pennsylvania Press, 2021.

Eberhardt, Jennifer L. *Biased: Uncovering the Hidden Prejudice That Shapes What We See, Think, and Do*. New York: Viking Press, 2019.

Edelman, Lauren B. *Working Law: Courts, Corporations, and Symbolic Civil Rights*. Chicago: University of Chicago Press, 2016.

Ehrenreich, Barbara. *Bright-Sided: How the Relentless Promotion of Positive Thinking Has Undermined America*. New York: Metropolitan Books, 2009.

Ekman, Paul, E. Richard Sorenson, and Wallace W. Friesen. "Pan-Cultural Elements in Facial Displays of Emotion." *Science* 164 (1969).

Ely, Robin J., and David A. Thomas. "Cultural Diversity at Work: The Effects of Diversity Perspectives on Work Group Processes and Outcomes." *Administrative Science Quarterly* 46, no. 2 (2001): 229–73. https://doi.org/10.2307/2667087.

Eyer, Katie. "That's Not Discrimination: American Beliefs and the Limits of Anti-Discrimination Law." *Minnesota Law Review* 96 (2012): 1275.

Faust, Drew Gilpin, ed. *The Ideology of Slavery: Post-Slavery Thought in the Antebellum South, 1830–1866*. New York: LSU Press, 1981.

Feagin, Joe R. *The White Racial Frame: Centuries of Racial Framing and Counter-Framing*. New York: Routledge, 3rd ed., 2020.

Feagin, Joe R., and Karyn D. McKinney. *The Many Costs of Racism*. New York: Rowman & Littlefield, 2005.

Feagin, Joe R., Hernán Vera, and Pinar Batur. *White Racism: The Basics*. New York: Routledge, 2nd ed., 2001.

Feingold, Jonathan P. "Reclaiming CRT: How Regressive Laws Can Advance Progressive Ends." *South Carolina Law Review* 73 (2022): 723.

Ferguson, John-Paul, and Rembrand Koning. "Firm Runover and the Return of Racial Establishment Segregation." *American Sociological Review* 83, no. 3 (2018): 445–74. https://www.jstor.org/stable/48588667.

Fineman, Martha Albertson. *The Illusion of Equality: The Rhetoric and Reality of Divorce Reform*. Chicago: University of Chicago Press, 1991.

Flagg, Barbara. "'Was Blind, but Now I See': White Race Consciousness and the Requirement of Discriminatory Intent." *Michigan Law Review* 91 (1993): 953.

Ford, Richard Thompson. "Bias in the Air: Rethinking Employment Discrimination Law." *Stanford Law Review* 66 (2014): 1381.

Ford, Richard Thompson. *The Race Card: How Bluffing about Bias Makes Race Relations Worse.* Stanford: Stanford University Press, 2008.

Fry, Richard, Jesse Bennett, and Amanda Barroso. "Racial and Ethnic Gaps in the U.S. Persist on Key Demographic Indicators." *Pew Research Center,* January 12, 2021. https://www.pewresearch.org/interactives/racial-and-ethnic-gaps-in-the-u-s-persist-on-key-demographic-indicators/.

Gallup. "Race Relations." Poll, 2021. https://news.gallup.com/poll/1687/Race-Relations.aspx.

Gladwell, Malcolm. *Blink: The Power of Thinking without Thinking.* New York: Little Brown, 2005.

Godsil, Rachel D., and L. Song Richardson. "Racial Anxiety." *Iowa Law Review* 102 (2017): 2235.

Goff, Phillip Atiba, Claude M. Steele, and Paul G. Davies. "The Space between Us: Stereotype Threat and Distance in Interracial Contexts." *Journal of Personality and Social Psychology* 94, no. 1 (2008): 91–107. https://doi.org/10.1037/0022-3514.94.1.91.

Goffman, Erving. *The Presentation of Self in Everyday Life.* New York: Doubleday, 1959 [1956].

Goleman, Daniel. *Working with Emotional Intelligence.* New York: Bantam Books, 1998.

Gómez, Laura E. "Off-White in an Age of White Supremacy: Mexican Elites and the Rights of Indians and Blacks in Nineteenth-Century New Mexico." *Chicano-Latina Law Review* 25 (2005): 9.

Green, Tristin K. *Discrimination Laundering: The Rise of Organizational Innocence and the Crisis of Equal Opportunity Law.* New York: Cambridge University Press, 2017.

Green, Tristin K. "'I'll See You at Work': Spatial Features and Discrimination." *UC Davis Law Review* 55 (2021): 141.

Green, Tristin K. "Rethinking Racial Entitlements: From Epithet to Theory." *University of Southern California Law Review* 93 (2020): 217.

Green, Tristin K. "Was Sexual Harassment a Mistake?: The Stories We Tell." *Yale Law Journal Forum* 128 (2018): 152.

Green, Tristin K. "Work Culture and Discrimination." *California Law Review* 93 (2005): 623.

Greenaway, Valerie Purdie, and Kate M. Turetsky. "Socioecological Diversity and Inclusion: A Framework for Advancing Diversity Science." *Current Opinion in Psychology* 32 (2020): 32–76. https://doi: 10.1016/j.copsyc.2019.09.008.

Greene, Wendy. "Splitting Hairs: The Eleventh Circuit's Take on Workplace Bans against Black Women's Natural Hair in *EEOC v. Catastrophe Management Solutions, Inc.*" *University of Miami Law Review* 71 (2017): 987.

Grillo, Trina. "Process Dangers for Women." *Yale Law Journal* 100 (1991): 1545.

Gross, Ariela. *What Blood Won't Tell: A History of Race on Trial in America.* Boston: Harvard University Press, 2008.

Gündemir, Suval, and Adam D. Galinsky. "Multicultural Blindfolds: How Organizational Multiculturalism Can Conceal Discrimination and Delegitimize Discrimination Claims." *Social Psychological and Personality Science* 9, no. 7 (2018): 825–34. https://doi.org/10.1177/1948550617726830.

Haney López, Ian. *Dog Whistle Politics: How Coded Racial Appeals Have Reinvented Racism and Wrecked the Middle Class.* New York: Oxford University Press, 2013.

Haney López, Ian. *White by Law: The Legal Construction of Race.* New York: New York University Press, 2nd ed., 2006.

Harpalani, Vinay. "Asian Americans, Racial Stereotypes, and Elite University Admissions." *Boston University Law Review* 102 (2021): 233.

Harris, Angela P. "Care and Danger: Feminism and Therapy Culture." *Studies in Law, Politics, and Society* 69 (2016): 113.

Harris, Kara, Angel D. Armenta, Christina Reyna, and Michale A. Zárate. "Latinx Stereotypes: Myths and Realities in the Twenty-First Century." In *Stereotypes: The Incidence and Impacts of Bias*, edited by Joel T. Nadler and Elora C. Voyles, 128–45. Santa Barbara: Praeger, 2020.

Hatch, Justin D. "Disassociating Power and Racism: Stokely Carmichael at Berkeley." *Advances in the History of Rhetoric* 22, no. 3 (2019): 303–25. https://doi.org/10.1080/15362426.2019.1671705.

Hayward, Lydia E., Linda R. Tropp, Matthew J. Hornsey, and Fiona Kate Barlow. "Toward a Comprehensive Understanding of Intergroup Contact: Descriptions and Mediators of Positive and Negative Contact among Majority and Minority Groups." *Personality and Social Psychology Bulletin* 43, no. 3 (2017): 347–64. https://doi.org/10.1177/0146167216685291.

Hickman, Craig R., and Michael A. Silva. *Creating Excellence: Managing Corporate Culture, Strategy, and Change in the New Age.* New York: Routledge, 1984.

Hochschild, Arlie Russell. *The Managed Heart: Commercialization of Human Feeling.* Berkeley: University of California Press, 2nd ed., 2003.

Hong, Cathy Park. *Minor Feelings: An Asian American Reckoning.* New York: One World, 2020.

Huising, Ruthanne, and Susan S. Silbey. "Governing the Gap: Forging Safe Science through Relational Regulation." *Regulation and Governance* 5, no. 1 (2011): 14–42. https://doi.org:10.1111/j.1748-5991.2010.01100.

Hutchinson, Darren Lenard. "Ignoring the Sexualization of Race: Heteronormativity, Critical Race Theory and Anti-Racist Politics." *Buffalo Law Review* 47 (1990): 83.

Ignatiev, Noel, and John Garvey, eds. *Race Traitor.* New York: Routledge, 1996.

Illouz, Eva. *Saving the Modern Soul: Therapy, Emotions, and the Culture of Self-Help*. Berkeley: University of California Press, 2008.

Ioanide, Paula. *The Emotional Politics of Racism: How Feelings Trump Facts in an Era of Colorblindness*. Stanford: Stanford University Press, 2015.

Ioanide, Paula. "Negotiating Privileged Students' Affective Resistances: Why a Pedagogy of Emotional Engagement Is Necessary." In *Seeing Race Again: Countering Colorblindness across the Disciplines*, edited by Kimberlé Williams Crenshaw et al., 327–51. Oakland: University of California Press, 2019.

James, Osamudia. "The 'Innocence' of Bias." *Michigan Law Review* 119 (2021): 1345.

James, Osamudia. "White Injury and Innocence: On the Legal Future of Antiracism Education." *Virginia Law Review* 108 (2022): 1689.

Jewell, K. Sue. *From Mammy to Miss America and Beyond: Cultural Images and the Shaping of US Social Policy*. New York: Routledge, 1993.

Jones, Jacqueline. *Labor of Love, Labor of Sorrow: Black Women, Work, and the Family, from Slavery to Present*. New York: Basic Books, 2009.

Jones, Trina, and Jessica Roberts. "Genetic Race? DNA Ancestry Tests, Racial Identity, and the Law." *Columbia Law Review* 120 (2020): 1929.

Jordan, Winthrop D. *White over Black: American Attitudes toward the Negro, 1550–1812*. Chapel Hill: University of North Carolina Press, 1968.

Kaestle, Carl. "Federalism and Inequality in Education: What Can History Tell Us?" In *The Dynamics of Opportunity in America: Evidence and Perspectives*, edited by Irwin Kirsch and Henry Braun, 35–96. Princeton, NJ: Educational Testing Service, 2016.

Kaiser, Cheryl R., et al. "Presumed Fair: Ironic Effects of Organizational Diversity Structures." *Journal of Personality and Social Psychology* 104, no. 3 (2013): 504–19. https://doi.org/10.1037/a0030838.

Kaiser, Cheryl R., and Brenda Major. "A Social Psychological Perspective on Perceiving and Reporting Discrimination." *Law and Social Inquiry* 31 (2003): 80.

Kaiser, Cheryl R., and Carol T. Miller. "Derogating the Victim: The Interpersonal Consequences of Blaming Events on Discrimination." *Group Processes and Intergroup Relations* 6, no. 3 (2003): 227–37. https://doi.org/10.1177/13684302030063001.

Kaiser, Cheryl R., and Carol T. Miller. "Stop Complaining! The Social Costs of Making Attributions to Discrimination." *Personality and Social Psychology Bulletin* 27, no. 6 (2001): 254–63. https://journals.sagepub.com/doi/pdf/10.1177/0146167201272010.

Kalev, Alexandra. "Cracking the Glass Cages?: Restructuring and Ascriptive Inequality at Work." *American Journal of Sociology* 114, no. 6 (2009): 1591–634. https://www-journals-uchicago-edu.eu1.proxy.openathens.net/doi/10.1086/597175.

Kanter, Rosabeth Moss. *Men and Women of the Corporation*. New York: Basic Books, 1977.

Keltner, Dacher, and Jennifer S. Learner. "Emotion." In *Handbook of Social Psychology, Vol. 1*, edited by Susan T. Fiske, Daniel T. Gilbert, and Gardner Lindzey, 317–52. Hoboken, NJ: John Wiley & Sons, 5th ed., 2010. https://doi.org/10.1002/9780470561119.socpsy001009.

Kendi, Ibram X. *How to Be an Antiracist*. New York: One World Press, 2019.

Kennedy, Randall. *Nigger: The Strange Career of a Troublesome Word*. New York: Random House, 2002.

Kim, Claire Jean. "The Racial Triangulation of Asian Americans." *Politics and Society* 27, no. 1 (1999): 105. https://doi.org/10.1177/0032329299027001.

Kim, Janine Young. "On Race and Persuasion." *CUNY Law Review* 20 (2017): 505.

Kim, Janine Young. "Racial Emotions and the Feeling of Equality." *University of Colorado Law Review* 87 (2016): 437–500.

King, Debra Walker. "The Not-So-Harmless Social Function of a Word That Wounds." In *Handbook of the Sociology of Racial and Ethnic Relations*, edited by Hernán Vera and Joe R. Feagin, 101–14. New York: Springer, 2007.

King, Eden B., et al. "Discrimination in the 21st Century: Are Science and the Law Aligned?" *Psychology Public Policy and the Law* 17, no. 1 (2010): 54–75. https://doi.org/10.1037/a0021673.

LaCosse, Jennifer, and E. Ashby Plant. "Internal Motivation to Respond without Prejudice Fosters Respectful Responses in Interracial Interactions." *Journal of Personality and Social Psychology* 119, no. 5 (2020), 1037–56. https://doi.org/10.1037/pspi0000219.

Lanctot, Catherine A. "Secrets and Lies: The Need for a Definitive Rule of Law in Pretext Cases." *Louisiana Law Review* 61 (2001): 539.

Larson, Jeff. "Introduction to the Special Section on Mixed Emotions." *Emotion Review* 9, no. 2 (2017): 97–98. https://doi.org/10.1177/1754073916672523.

Lawrence III, Charles. "The Id, the Ego, and Equal Protection: Reckoning with Unconscious Racism." *Stanford Law Review* 39 (1987): 317–88.

Lawrence III, Charles. "Unconscious Racism Revisited: Reflections on the Impact and Origins of the 'Id, the Ego, and Equal Protection.'" *Connecticut Law Review* 40 (2008): 931–78.

Leonardo, Zeus, and Michalinos Zembylas. "Whiteness as Technology of Affect: Implications for Educational Practice." *Equality and Excellence in Education* 46, no. 1 (2013): 150–65. https://doi.org/10.1080/10665684.2013.750539.

Leong, Nancy. *Identity Capitalists: The Powerful Insiders Who Exploit Diversity to Maintain Inequality*. Stanford: Stanford University Press, 2021.

Livingston, Robert. "How to Promote Racial Equity in the Workplace." *Harvard Business Review*, September–October, 2020. https://hbr.org/2020/09/how-to-promote-racial-equity-in-the-workplace.

Lorde, Audre. *Sister Outsider: Essays and Speeches*. New York: Random House, 1984.

Mackie, Diane M., Angela T. Maitner, and Eliot R. Smith. "Intergroup Emotions Theory." In *Handbook of Prejudice, Stereotyping, and Discrimination*, edited by Todd D. Nelson, 285–307. New York: Routledge, 2009.

Magee, Rhonda V. *The Inner Work of Racial Justice: Healing Ourselves and Transforming Our Communities through Mindfulness*. New York: Penguin Random House, 2019.

Magee, Rhonda V. "Legal Education and the Formation of Professional Identity: A Critical Spirituo-Humanistic—'Humanity Consciousness'—Perspective." *New York University Review of Law and Social Change* 31 (2007): 467.

Martin, Natasha. "Pretext in Peril." *Missouri Law Review* 75 (2010): 313.

Matias, Cheryl E. "'And Our Feelings Just Don't Feel It Anymore': Re-Feeling Whiteness, Resistance, and Emotionality." *Understanding and Dismantling Privilege* 42, no. 2 (2014): 135. https://www.wpcjournal.com/article/view/12176.

Matias, Cheryl E. *Feeling White: Whiteness, Emotionality, and Education*. Boston: Sense, 2016.

McGhee, Heather. *The Sum of Us: What Racism Costs Everyone and How We Can Prosper Together*. New York: Random House, 2021.

McWhorter, Ladelle. *Racism and Sexual Oppression in Anglo-America: A Genealogy*. Bloomington: Indiana University Press, 2009.

Migacheva, Katya, and Linda R. Tropp. "Learning Orientation as a Predictor of Positive Intergroup Contact." *Group Processes and Intergroup Relations* 16 (2012): 426–44.

Migacheva, Katya, Linda R. Tropp, and Jennifer Crocker. "Focusing beyond the Self: Goal Orientations in Intergroup Relations." In *Moving beyond Prejudice Reduction: Pathways to Positive Intergroup Relations*, edited by Linda L. Tropp and Robin K. Mallett, 99–115. Washington, DC: American Psychological Association, 2011.

Molina, Natalia, Daniel Martinez HoSang, and Ramón A. Gutiérrez. *Relational Formations of Race: Theory, Method, and Practice*. Berkeley: University of California Press, 2019.

Morning, Ann. *The Nature of Race: How Scientists Think and Teach about Human Difference*. Berkeley: University of California Press, 2011.

Morning, Ann, Hannah Brückner, and Alondra Nelson. "Socially Desirable Reporting and the Expression of Biological Concepts of Race." *Du Bois Review: Social Science Research on Race* 16, no. 2 (2019): 439–55. https://doi.org/10.1017/S1742058X19000195.

Murphy, Raymond. "The Structure of Closure: A Critique and Development of the Theories of Weber, Collins, and Parkin." *British Journal of Sociology* 35, no. 4 (1984): 547–67. https://doi.org/10.2307/590434.

Myers, Kristen. *Racetalk: Racism Hiding in Plain Sight*. Lanham, MD: Rowman & Littlefield, 2005.

Newkirk, Pamela. *Diversity Inc.: The Failed Promise of a Billion-Dollar Business*. New York: Bold Type Books, 2020.

Northup, Solomon. *Twelve Years a Slave: Narrative of Solomon Northup, A Citizen of New York, Kidnapped in Washington City in 1841, and Rescued in 1853, From a Cotton Plantation Near the Red River in Louisiana*. Edited by David Wilson. Minneapolis: Lerner, 2014.

Nussbaum, Martha C. *Hiding from Humanity: Disgust, Shame, and the Law*. Princeton, NJ: Princeton University Press, 2004.

Nussbaum, Martha. *Upheavals of Thought: The Intelligence of Emotions*. New York: Cambridge University Press, 2001.

O'Brien, Eileen. "The Political Is Personal: The Influence of White Supremacy on White Antiracists' Personal Relationships." In *White Out: The Continuing Significance of Racism*, edited by Ashley "Woody" Doane and Eduardo Bonilla-Silva, 252–66. New York: Routledge, 2003.

O'Hara, Erin Ann, and Sara Sun Beale. "Victims, 'Closure,' and the Sociology of Emotion." *Law and Contemporary Problems* 72 (2009): 1.

Omi, Michael, and Howard Winant. *Racial Formation in the United States: From the 1960s to the 1980s*. New York: Routledge, 2nd ed., 1994.

Onwuachi-Willig, Angela. "The Trauma of the Routine: Lessons on Cultural Trauma from the Emmett Till Verdict." *Sociological Theory* 34, no. 4 (2010): 335–57. https://doi.org:10.1177/0735275116679864.

Onwuachi-Willig, Angela. "What about #UsToo? The Invisibility of Race in the #MeToo Movement." *Yale Law Journal Forum* 128 (2018): 105.

Ouchi, William. *Theory Z: How American Business Can Meet the Japanese Challenge*. Reading, MA: Addison-Wesley, 1981.

Page-Gould, Elizabeth, Rodolfo Mendoza-Denton, and Linda R. Tropp. "With a Little Help from My Cross-Group Friend: Reducing Anxiety in Intergroup Contexts through Cross-Group Friendship." *Journal of Personality and Social Psychology* 95, no. 5 (2008): 1080–94. https://doi.org/10.1037/0022-3514.95.5.1080.

Parker, Martin. *Organizational Culture and Identity: Unity and Division at Work*. London: SAGE, 2000.

Pascoe, Elizabeth A., and Laura Smart Richman. "Perceived Discrimination and Health: A Meta-Analytic Review." *Psychological Bulletin* 135, no. 4 (2009): 531–54. https://doi.org/10.1037/a0016059.

Pauker, Kristen, Evan P. Apfelbaum, Carol S. Dweck, and Jennifer L. Eberhardt. "Believing That Prejudice Can Change Increases Children's Interest in Inter-racial Interactions." *Developmental Science* 25, no. 4 (2022): 1–14. https://doi.org/10.1111/desc.13233.

Peller, Gary. "History, Identity, and Alienation." *Connecticut Law Review* 43 (2011): 1479.

Peters, Thomas J., and Robert H. Waterman, Jr. *In Search of Excellence: Lessons from America's Best-Run Companies.* New York: Harper & Row, 1982.

Pettigrew, Thomas F., and Linda R. Tropp, "A Meta-Analytic Test of Intergroup Contact Theory." *Journal of Personality and Social Psychology* 90, no. 5 (2006): 751–83. https://doi.org/10.1037/0022-3514.90.5.751.

Picca, Leslie Houts, and Joe R. Feagin. *Two-Faced Racism: Whites in the Backstage and Frontstage.* New York: Routledge, 2007.

Pierce, Jennifer L. *Gender Trials: Emotional Lives in Contemporary Law Firms.* Berkeley: University of California Press, 1996.

Pierce, Jennifer L. *Racing for Innocence: Whiteness, Gender, and the Backlash against Affirmative Action.* Stanford: Stanford University Press, 2012.

Plamper, Jan. "The History of Emotions: An Interview with William Reddy, Barbara Rowenswein, and Peter Stearns." *History and Theory* 49, no. 2 (2010): 237–65. https://doi.org:10.1111/j.1468-2303.2010.00541.x.

Plamper, Jan. *The History of Emotions: An Introduction.* New York: Oxford University Press, 2015.

Plant, E. Ashby, and David A. Butz. "The Causes and Consequences of an Avoidance-Focus for Interracial Interactions." *Personality and Social Psychology Bulletin* 32, no. 6 (2006): 833–46. https://doi:10.1177/0146167206287182.

Plant, E. Ashby, and Patricia G. Devine. "The Antecedents and Implications of Interracial Anxiety." *Personality and Social Psychology Bulletin* 29, no. 6 (2003): 790–801. https://doi:10.1177/0146167203252880.

Plaut, Victoria C., Sapna Cheryan, and Flannery G. Stephens. "New Frontiers in Diversity Research: Conceptions of Diversity and Their Theoretical and Practical Implications." In *Handbook of Personality and Social Psychology: Attitudes and Social Cognition*, edited by Mario Mikulincer et al., 593–619. Washington, DC: American Psychological Association, 2015. https://doi.org/10.1037/14341-019.

Pritzker, Sonya E. "Language, Emotion, and the Politics of Vulnerability." *Annual Review of Anthropology* 49, no. 1 (2020): 241–56. https://www.annualreviews.org/doi/10.1146/annurev-anthro-010220-074429.

Quillian, Lincoln, John J. Lee, and Mariana Oliver. "Evidence from Field Experiments in Hiring Shows Substantial Additional Racial Discrimination after Callback." *Social Forces* 99, no. 2 (2020): 732–59. https://doi:10.1093/sf/soaa026.

Quillian, Lincoln, Devah Pager, Ole Hexel, and Arnfinn H. Midtboen. "Meta-Analysis of Field Experiments Shows No Change in Racial Discrimination in Hiring over Time." *Proceedings of the National Academy of Sciences of the United States of America*, 114, no. 41 (2017), 10870–75. https://doi.org/10.1073/pnas.1706255114.

Reskin, Barbara F. "Including Mechanisms in Our Models of Ascriptive Inequality: 2002 Presidential Address." *American Sociological Review* 68, no. 1 (2003): 1–21. https://doi.org/10.2307/3088900.

Rich, Camille Gear. "Contracting Our Way to Inequality: Race, Reproductive Freedom, and the Quest for the Perfect Child." *Minnesota Law Review* 104 (2020): 2375.

Rich, Camille Gear. "Elective Race: Recognizing Race Discrimination in the Era of Racial Self-Identification." *Georgetown Law Journal* 102 (2014): 1501.

Rich, Camille Gear. "Marginal Whiteness." *California Law Review* 98 (2010): 1497.

Risen, Clay. *The Bill of the Century: The Epic Battle for the Civil Rights Act*. New York: Bloomsbury Press, 2014.

Rivera, Lauren. "Go with Your Gut: Emotion and Evaluation in Job Interviews." *American Journal of Sociology* 120, no. 5 (2015): 1339–89. https://www-journals-uchicago-edu.eu1.proxy.openathens.net/doi/10.1086/681214.

Roberts, Dorothy E. *Fatal Invention: How Science, Politics, and Big Business Re-Create Race in the Twenty-First Century*. New York: New Press, 2012.

Robinson, Russell K. "Perceptual Segregation." *Columbia Law Review* 108 (2008): 1093.

Robson, David. "There Really Are 50 Words for 'Snow'." *Washington Post*, January 14, 2013. https://www.washingtonpost.com/national/health-science/there-really-are-50-eskimo-words-for-snow/2013/01/14/e0e3f4e0-59a0-11e2-beee-6e38f5215402_story.html.

Rodríguez, Cristina M. "Language and Participation." *California Law Review* 94 (2006): 687.

Rothstein, Richard. *The Color of Law: A Forgotten History of How Our Government Segregated America*. New York: Liveright, 2017.

Rugh, Jacob S., and Douglas S. Massey. "Segregation in Post–Civil Rights America: Stalled Integration or End of the Segregated Century?" *Du Bois Review: Social Science Research on Race* 11, no. 2 (2014): 205–32. https://doi:10.1017/S1742058X13000180.

Saguy, Tamar, et al. "The Irony of Harmony: Intergroup Contact Can Produce False Expectations for Equality." *Psychological Science* 20, no. 1 (2009): 114–21. https://doi.org/10.1111/j.1467-9280.2008.02261.x.

Saperstein, Aliya, and Andrew M. Penner. "Racial Fluidity and Inequality in the United States." *American Journal of Sociology* 118, no. 3 (2012): 676–727. https://doi.org/10.1086/667722.

Schultz, Jennifer R., Sarah E. Gaither, Heather L. Urry, and Keith B. Maddox. "Reframing Anxiety to Encourage Interracial Interactions." *Transnational Issues in Psychological Science* 1, no. 4 (2015): 392–400. https://doi.org/10.1037/tps0000048.

Seligman, Martin E.P., and Mihaly Csikszentmihalyi. "Positive Psychology, An Introduction." *American Psychologist* 35, no. 1 (2000): 13. https://doi.org/10.103710003-0665x.55.1.5.

Shelton, J. Nicole, and Jennifer A. Richeson. "Interacting across Racial Lines." In *Handbook of Personality and Social Psychology: Vol. 2*, 395–422. Washington, DC: American Psychological Association, 2015.

Shelton, J. Nicole, Jennifer A. Richeson, and Jessica Salvatore. "Expecting to Be the Target of Prejudice: Implications for Interethnic Interactions." *Personality and Social Psychology Bulletin* 31, no. 9 (2005): 1189–202. https://doi:10.1177/0146167205274894.

Shelton, J. Nicole, Jennifer A. Richeson, and Jacquie D. Vorauer. "Threatened Identities and Interethnic Interactions." *European Review of Social Psychology* 17, no. 1 (2006): 321–58. https://doi.org/10.1080/10463280601095240.

Smith, Terry. "Everyday Indignities." *Columbia Human Rights Law Review* 34 (2003): 529.

Smith-Doerr, Laurel. *Women's Work: Gender Equality v. Hierarchy in the Life Sciences*. Boulder, CO: Lynne Reiner, 2004.

Sperino, Sandra F., and Suja A. Thomas. *Unequal: How America's Courts Undermine Discrimination Law*. New York: Oxford University Press, 2017.

Srivastava, Sarita. "Tears, Fears and Careers: Racism and Emotion in Social Movement Organizations." *Canadian Journal of Sociology* 31, no. 1 (2006): 55–90. https://doi:10.2307/20058680.

Stainback, Kevin, and Donald Tomaskovic-Devey. *Documenting Desegregation: Racial and Gender Segregation in Private-Sector Employment since the Civil Rights Act*. New York: Russell Sage Foundation Press, 2012.

Stearns, Peter N. *American Cool: Constructing a Twentieth-Century Emotional Style*. New York: New York University Press, 1994.

Steele, Claude M. *Whistling Vivaldi: How Stereotypes Affect Us and What We Can Do*. New York: W. W. Norton, 2010.

Steiner, Claude. *Achieving Emotional Literacy: A Personal Program to Improve Your Emotional Intelligence*. New York: William Morrow, 1997.

Steinhorn, Leonard, and Barbara Diggs-Brown. *By the Color of Our Skin: The Illusion of Integration and the Reality of Race*. New York: Penguin Group, 1999.

Stephan, Walter G., and Cookie White Stephan. "Intergroup Threats." In *The Cambridge Handbook of the Psychology of Prejudice*, edited by Chris G. Sibley and Fiona Kate Barlow, 131–48. Cambridge: Cambridge University Press, 2016.

Stephan, Walter G., Oscar Ybarra, and Kimberly Rios Morrison. "Intergroup Threat Theory." In *Handbook of Prejudice, Stereotyping, and Discrimination*, edited by Todd D. Nelson, 43–59. New York: Psychology Press, 2009.

Stevens, Flannery G., Victoria C. Plaut, and Jeffrey Sanchez-Burks. "Unlocking the Benefits of Diversity: All-Inclusive Multiculturalism and Positive Organizational Change." *Applied Behavioral Science* 44, no. 1 (2008): 116–34. https://doi.org/10.1177/0021886308314460.

Stone, Katherine V. W., *From Widgets to Digits: Employment Regulation for the Changing Workplace*. New York: Cambridge University Press, 2004.

Stone, Kerri Lynn. "Taking in Strays: A Critique of the Stray Comment Doctrine in Employment Discrimination Law." *Missouri Law Review* 77 (2012): 149.

Sue, Derald Wing. *Race Talk and the Conspiracy of Silence: Understanding and Facilitating Difficult Dialogues on Race*. New York: Wiley, 2015.

Sue, Derald Wing, Cassandra Z. Calle, Narolyn Mendez, Sarah Asaidi, and Elisabeth Glaeser. *Microintervention Strategies: What You Can Do to Disarm and Dismantle Individual and Systemic Racism and Bias*. New York: Wiley, 2021.

Sue, Derald Wing, et al. "Disarming Racial Microaggressions: Microintervention Strategies for Targets, White Allies, and Bystanders." *American Psychologist* 74, no. 1 (2019): 128–42. https://doi.org/10.1037/amp0000296.

Sue, Derald Wing, et al. "Racial Microaggressions in Everyday Life: Implications for Clinical Practice." *American Psychology* 62, no. 4 (2007): 271–86. https://doi.org/10.1037/0003-066X.62.4.271

Suk, Julie. "Race without Cards?" *Stanford Journal of Civil Rights and Civil Liberties* 5 (2009): 111.

Sullivan, Jessica, Leigh Wilton, and Evan P. Apfelbaum. "Adults Delay Conversations about Race Because They Underestimate Children's Processing of Race." *Journal of Experimental Psychology: General* 150, no. 2 (2021): 395–400. DOI: 10.1037/xge0000851.

Swidler, Ann. *Talk of Love: How Culture Matters*. Chicago: University of Chicago Press, 2001.

Takaki, Ronald. *Strangers from a Different Shore: A History of Asian Americans*. Boston: Little, Brown, 1989.

Tatum, Beverly Daniel. *Why Are All the Black Kids Sitting Together in the Cafeteria?* New York: Hachette Book Group, 2017.

Thomas, Jr., R. Roosevelt. "From Affirmative Action to Affirming Diversity." *Harvard Business Review*, March–April 1990. https://hbr.org/1990/03/from-affirmative-action-to-affirming-diversity.

Toosi, Negin R., Laura G. Babbit, Nalini Ambady, and Samuel R. Sommers. "Dyadic Interracial Interactions: A Meta-Analysis." *Psychological Bulletin* 138, no. 1 (2012): 1–27. https://doi.org/10.1037/a0025767.

Tropp, Linda R., and Thomas F. Pettigrew. "Differential Relationships between Intergroup Contact and Affective and Cognitive Dimensions of Prejudice." *Personality and Social Psychology Bulletin* 31, no. 8 (2005): 1145–58. https://doi.org/10.1177/0146167205274854.

Waber, Ben, et al. "Workspaces That Move People." *Harvard Business Review*, October 2014. https://hbr.org/2014/10/workspaces-that-move-people.

Walen, Charles, and Barbara Walen. *The Longest Debate: A Legislative History of the 1964 Civil Rights Act*. Cabin John, MD: Seven Locks Press, 1985.

Wang, Joan S. "Race, Gender, and Laundry Work: The Roles of Chinese Laundrymen and American Women in the United States, 1850–1950." *Journal of American Ethnic History* 58, no. 1 (2004): 58–99. https://www .jstor.org/stable/2750153.

Wang, Lu-In, and Zachary Brewster. "Dignity Transacted: Emotional Labor and the Racialized Workplace." *University of Michigan Journal of Legal Reform* 53 (2020): 531.

Want, Jerry. "Corporate Culture: Illuminating a Black Hole." *Journal of Business Strategy* 24, no. 4 (2003): 14–21. https://doi.org/10.1108 /02756660310698542.

Warner, Judith. "Psychiatry Confronts Its Racist Past, and Tries to Make Amends." *New York Times*, May 1, 2021. https://www.nytimes.com/2021/04/30/health /psychiatry-racism-black-americans.html.

Waterson, Jim. "Were Trump's Racist Tweets Racist? Some News Outlets Won't Say." *The Guardian*, July 16, 2019. https://www.theguardian.com/media /2019/jul/16/were-trumps-racist-tweets-racist-some-news-outlets-wont-say.

Waytz, Adam. "Spotlight on the Emotional Organization: The Limits of Empathy." *Harvard Business Review*, February 2016. https://hbr.org/2016/01/the-limits-of-empathy.

Weber, Max. "Bureaucracy." In *From Max Weber: Essays in Sociology*, edited and translated by H. H. Gerth and C. Wright Mills, 215. New York: Routledge, 1991.

Wessel, Harry. "Attracting the Best: Can Standardized Tests Really Predict How Well You'll Do on the Job?" *Chicago Tribune*, February 5, 2003. https:// www.chicagotribune.com/news/ct-xpm-2003-02-05-0302080309-story .html.

Williams, Patricia, J. "The Elusive Variability of Race." In *Race and the Genetic Revolution: Science, Myth, and Culture*, edited by Sheldon Krimsky and Kathleen Sloan, 241–54. New York: Columbia University Press, 2011.

Wilton, Leigh S., Evan P. Apfelbaum, and Jessica J. Good. "Valuing Differences and Reinforcing Them: Multiculturalism Increases Race Essentialism." *Social Psychological and Personality Science* 10, no. 5 (2019), 681–89. https://doi.org/10.1177/1948550618780728.

Wingfield, Adia Harvey. "Are Some Emotions Marked 'Whites Only'? Racialized Feeling Rules in Professional Workplaces." *Social Problems* 57, no. 2 (2010): 251–68. https://doi.org/10.1525/sp.2010.57.2.251.

Wingfield, Adia Harvey. *Flatlining: Race, Work, and Health Care in the New Economy*. Berkeley: University of California Press, 2019.

Witt, John Fabien. *The Accidental Republic: Crippled Workingmen, Destitute Women, and the Remaking of American Law*. Cambridge, MA: Harvard University Press, 2004.

Wright, Stephen, and Michael Lubensky. "The Struggle for Social Equality: Collective Action vs. Prejudice Reduction." In *Intergroup Misunderstandings: Impact of Divergent Social Realities*, edited by Stephanie Demoulin, Jacques-Philippe Leyens, and John F. Dividio, 291. New York: Psychology Press, 2008.

Yoshino, Kenji. *Covering: The Hidden Assault on Our Civil Rights*. New York: Random House, 2006.

CASE LIST

Abdel-Ghani v. Target Corp., 686 F. App'x 377 (8th Cir. 2017).

Alexander v. Opelika City Sch., No. 3:06-CV-0498, 2008 WL 401353 (M.D. Ala. 2008).

Alexander v. Opelika City Sch., 352 F. App'x 390 (11th Cir. 2009).

Arroyo v. West LB Admin, Inc., 54 F. Supp. 2d 224 (S.D. N.Y. 1999).

Ash v. Tyson Foods Inc., No. 96-RA-3257, 2004 WL 5138005 (N.D. Ala. 2004).

Ash v. Tyson Foods, Inc., 129 F. App'x 529 (11th Cir. 2005).

Ash v. Tyson Foods, Inc., 129 F. App'x 924 (11th Cir. 2006).

Ash v. Tyson Foods Inc., 392 F. App'x 817 (11th Cir. 2010).

Ash v. Tyson Foods, Inc., 546 U.S. 454 (2006) (per curiam).

Ash v. Tyson Foods, Inc., 664 F.3d 883 (11th Cir. 2011).

Barrow v. Georgia Pacific Corp., 144 F. App'x 54 (11th Cir. 2005).

Blue v. City of Hartford, No. 3:18-CV-974, 2019 WL 7882565 (D. Conn. 2019).

Bolden v. PRC Inc., 43 F.3d 545 (10th Cir. 1994).

Bostock v. Clayton Cnty., 140 S. Ct. 1731 (2020).

Cain v. Elgin, Joliet E. Ry. Co., No. 04-CV-0347, 2006 U.S. Dist. LEXIS 4373 (N.D. Ind. 2006).

Ceus v. City of Tampa, 803 F. App'x 235 (11th Cir. 2020).

City of Richmond v. J.A. Croson Co., 488 U.S. 469 (1989).

Clack v. Rock-Tenn Co., 304 F. App'x 399 (6th Cir. 2008).

Colenburg v. Starcon Int'l, Inc., 619 F.3d 986 (8th Cir. 2010).

Collier v. Dallas Cnty. Hosp. Dist., 827 F. App'x 373 (5th Cir. 2020).

Costa v. Desert Palace, Inc., 299 F.3d 838 (9th Cir. 2002).

Dailey v. Shintech, Inc., 629 F. App'x 638 (5th Cir. 2015).

Desert Palace, Inc. v. Costa, 539 U.S. 90 (2003).

Dred Scott v. Sanford, 60 U.S. 393 (1857).

Edwards v. Foucar, Ray & Simon, Inc., No. C-79-0313-SC, 1980 U.S. Dist. LEXIS 13748 (N.D. Cal. 1980).

EEOC v. A. Sam & Sons Produce Co., 872 F. Supp. 29 (W.D. N.Y. 1994).

EEOC v. RJB Properties, Inc., 857 F. Supp. 2d 727 (N.D. Ill. 2012).

EEOC v. Rotary Corp., 297 F. Supp. 2d 643 (N.D. N.Y. 2003).

Frazier v. Sabine River Auth., 509 F. App'x 370 (5th Cir. 2013).

Felder-Ward v. Flexible Staffing Services Inc., No. 14-C-9246, 2018 WL 1235013 (N.D. Ill. 2018).

Furnco Constr. Corp. v. Waters, 438 U.S. 567 (1978).

Gress v. Temple Univ. Health Sys., 784 F. App'x 100 (3rd Cir. 2019).

Griggs v. Duke Power, 401 U.S. 424 (1971).

Harris v. Forklift Syst., Inc., 510 U.S. 17 (1993).

Hazelwood Sch. Dist. v. United States, 433 U.S. 299 (1977).

Henao v. Wyndham Vacation Resorts, Inc., 927 F. Supp. 978 (D. Ha. 2013).

Int'l Bthd. of Teamsters v. United States, 431 U.S. 324 (1977).

Jansen v. Packaging Corp. of America, 123 F.3d 490 (7th Cir. 1997).

Laughlin v. Metropolitan Washington Airports Authority, 149 F.3d 253 (4th Cir. 1998).

Lawrence v. Chemprene, Inc., No. 18-CV-2537, 2019 WL 5449844 (S.D. N.Y. 2019).

Los Angeles Dept. of Water & Power v. Manhart, 435 U.S. 702 (1978).

Lounds v. Lincare, Inc., 812 F.3d 1208 (10th Cir. 2015).

McCann v. Tillman, 526 F.3d 1370 (11th Cir. 2008).

McNeal v. Montgomery Cnty., 307 F. App'x 766 (4th Cir. 2009) (Mem.) (No. 07-1323).

Meredith v. Jefferson Cnty. Bd. of Educ., 548 U.S. 938 (2006).

Meritor Savings Bank v. Vinson, 477 U.S. 57 (1986).

Nat'l RR Passenger Co. v. Morgan, 526 U.S. 101 (2002).

Nichols v. Mich. City Plant Planning Dep't, 755 F.3d 594 (7th Cir. 2014).

Niswander v. Cincinnati Ins. Co., 529 F.3d 714 (6th Cir. 2008).

Pratt v. Austal, USA, No. 08-00155, 2011 WL 3203740 (S.D. Ala. 2011).

Price Waterhouse v. Hopkins, 490 U.S. 228 (1989).

Reeves v. Sanderson Plumbing Products, Inc., 530 U.S. 133 (2000).

Regents of Univ. of California Davis v. Bakke, 438 U.S. 265 (1976).

Ricci v. DeStefano, 557 U.S. 557 (2005).

Roberts v. Potter, 378 F. App'x 913 (11th Cir. 2010).

Rogers v. EEOC, 454 F.2d 234 (5th Cir. 1971).

Slack v. Havens, 552 F. 2d 1091 (9th Cir. 1975).

St. Mary's Honor Ctr. v. Hicks, 509 U.S. 502 (1993).

Sweezer v. Mich. Dep't of Corr., 229 F.3d 1154 (table), 2000 WL 1175644 (5th Cir. 2000).

Tademy v. Union Pacific Corp., 614 F.3d 1132 (10th Cir. 2011).

Taylor v. Potter, No. 99-CV-4841, 2004 WL 1811423, aff'd Taylor v. Potter, 148 F. App'x 33 (2nd Cir. 2005).

U.S. Postal Service v. Aikens, 460 U.S. 711 (1983).

Vance v. Ball State Univ., No. 1:06-CV-1452, 2008 WL 4247836 (S.D. Ind. 2008).

Vance v. Ball State Univ., 646 F.3d 461 (7th Cir. 2011).

Vance v. Ball State Univ., 570 U.S. 421 (2013).

Vaughn v. Pool Offshore Co., 683 F.2d 922 (5th Cir. 1982).

Washington v. Cnt'y of Onandaga, No. 04-CV-0997, 2009 WL 3171787 (N.D. N.Y. 2009).

Watson v. Fort Worth Bank and Trust, 798 F.2d 791 (5th Cir. 1986).

Watson v. Fort Worth Bank & Trust, 487 U.S. 977 (1988).

White v. Gov't Emps. Ins., 457 F. App'x 374 (5th Cir. 2012) (Mem.).

Wilcoxon v. Ramsey Action Programs, Inc., No. 04-92, 2005 WL 2216289 (D. Minn. 2005).

Yelling v. St. Vincent's Health Syst., No. 2:17-CV-01607, 2020 WL 7059450 (N.D. Ala. 2020).

Index

Founded in 1893,
UNIVERSITY OF CALIFORNIA PRESS
publishes bold, progressive books and journals
on topics in the arts, humanities, social sciences,
and natural sciences—with a focus on social
justice issues—that inspire thought and action
among readers worldwide.

The UC PRESS FOUNDATION
raises funds to uphold the press's vital role
as an independent, nonprofit publisher, and
receives philanthropic support from a wide
range of individuals and institutions—and from
committed readers like you. To learn more, visit
ucpress.edu/supportus.